ENCODING RACE, ENCODING CLASS

ENCODING RACE, ENCODING CLASS

INDIAN IT WORKERS IN BERLIN

SAREETA AMRUTE

DUKE UNIVERSITY PRESS
DURHAM AND LONDON   2016

Library of Congress Cataloging-in-Publication Data
Names: Amrute, Sareeta Bipin, author.
Title: Encoding race, encoding class : Indian IT workers in Berlin /
Sareeta Amrute.
Description: Durham : Duke University Press, 2016. | Includes
bibliographical references and index.
Identifiers: LCCN 2016004523 (print) | LCCN 2016006128 (ebook)
ISBN 9780822361176 (hardcover : alk. paper)
ISBN 9780822361350 (pbk. : alk. paper)
ISBN 9780822374275 (e-book)
Subjects: LCSH: East Indians—Germany—Berlin. | Foreign workers,
East Indian—Germany—Berlin. | Information technology—
Germany—Berlin—Employees. | Computer programmers—
Germany—Berlin. | Computer programmers—India.
Classification: LCC DD78.E28 A47 2016 (print) | LCC DD78.E28 (ebook) |
DDC 331.6/254043155—dc23
LC record available at http://lccn.loc.gov/2016004523

Cover design by Natalie F. Smith

Cover art: © Sean Pavone / Alamy Stock Photo. Friedrichstrasse Shopping
Street in Berlin, September 16, 2013.

Until the wise are satisfied, I cannot feel that skill is shown,
The best-trained mind requires support, and does not trust itself alone.
—Kālidāsa, *Shakuntala*

The whole cannot be put together by adding the separated halves, but in both there appear, however distantly, the changes of the whole, which only moves in contradiction.
—Theodor W. Adorno, "On the Festish Character in **Music and the Regression of Listening"**

CONTENTS

ACKNOWLEDGMENTS

An idea, Ursula Le Guin tells us, "is like grass—it craves light, likes crowds, thrives on crossbreeding, grows better for being stepped on." Though this book may have a single writer, its authors are those who nourished its flourishing ideas. The institutional givers of light were the Committee for Southern Asian Studies at the University of Chicago, the Fulbright Foundation, the Social Science Research Council Berlin Program, the Center for Cultural Analysis at Rutgers University Postdoctoral Fellowship, the Society of Fellows of the Simpson Center for the Humanities at the University of Washington, the American Institute for Indian Studies Dissertation-to-Book Workshop, and the Wenner-Gren Hunt Postdoctoral Fellowship. Gentle stomps came from my mentors Elizabeth Povinelli, Jean Comaroff, Susan Gal, and John Kelly. Invaluable treading in the form of questions came at key moments from Dipesh Chakrabarty, Amita Baviskar, Michael Warner, Brent Edwards, Susan Wadley, William Mazzarella, Kavita Philip, A. Aneesh, and Arjun Appadurai. Kathleen Woodward and Judith Howard's support was like much-needed sunshine on an otherwise rainy Seattle day.

My friends and colleagues at the University of Washington—Gina Neff, Philip Howard, Sonal Kullar, Sasha Welland, Danny Hoffman, Sunila Kale, Christian Novetzke, Alys Weinbaum, Habiba Ibrahim, Chandan Reddy, Jennifer Dubrow, and Jameel Ahmed—who read countless drafts of these chapters, seemed always to know when to jump around and when to let the ideas run a little wild. Rucha Ambikar, Praseeda Gopinath, Mihir Pandya, Sonali Shah, Vicki Brennan, Kenneth McGill, Gretchen Bakke, Andrea Muehlebach, Meg Stalcup, and Sharif Youssef contributed critical crossbreeding in regular intervals, and I look forward to many more years of fruitful labor together. Timely steps across the lawn came from my editors Elizabeth Ault and Ken Wissoker. Sheela Amrute and Sundeep Amrute read my work and fertilized even my most unusual thought-varietals. Nishant Amrute and Monish Amrute ferried me around Mumbai, Pawai, and everywhere in between, happily showing me their worlds and following my whims. Vishwas and Jaya Gogte gave me a home away from home in Pune. My patient interlocutors and their families in Berlin always put up with my funny questions and did their best to ask me some of their own. Marika Grethe-Gulicova and Manjula Schöppler helped me grow during particularly difficult times.

The line quoted in the epigraph by Theodor W. Adorno is from his essay "On the Fetish Character in Music and Regression in Listening," from *The Essential Frankfurt School Reader*, edited by Andrew Arato and Eike Gephardt, 1978, used by kind permission of the Bloomsbury Continuum, an imprint of Bloomsbury Publishing. A version of chapter 3 was previously published in *Social Anthropology*.

Rohan, Anika, and David Tobey returned me, refreshed, to tend the grass anew at the beginning of each day. Even when this book seemed to be mostly weeds, their careful tending always brought it back to life, greener and more luxuriant than ever.

Cognitive Work, Cognitive Bodies

In 2003, twenty-five-year-old Meenakshi P. worked in Berlin for a well-known software and business services firm. She was on a short-term visa for computer programmers called the German green card. At the end of each long day, she came home to the flat she shared with her friend Rajeshwari talking excitedly about her work. Most nights, she shared dinner and sometimes tea with other Indian programmers and students who gathered at their house. In the mornings, she brushed her short bob into submission, donned work slacks, a button-down shirt, and sensible shoes with a low heel, and bounded out the door. About an hour later, when sure her flatmate Rajeshwari was gone, Meenakshi circled back to the apartment. Or, she went to Bipin and Madhu's home one U-Bahn stop away, to which she had a key and where there was a desktop computer and a landline. From there she scanned job ads, made cold calls, and replied to e-mails, searching for positions in IT (information technology) management, software engineering, and business process development in Berlin and elsewhere in Germany.

Meenakshi had lost her previous job after the project she was working on was completed and her work contract expired. For three months she pretended to go to work every day but instead spent hours alone in her room or walking the streets of her neighborhood, wondering if any of the résumés she sent out would come through with an offer in time. After three more months of searching with no luck, she received a letter from the Foreigners' Office threatening her with forced expulsion. Her right of residence had expired—IT workers on the German green card were given six months after their last day of employment to find another job. Meenakshi had used up all of her time. The same evening she received the letter, Meenakshi finally confided in Rajeshwari, and one week later, under cover of darkness and telling none of her other friends or colleagues, she slipped off to the airport, back to India and the anonymity of home.

Encoding Race, Encoding Class is about how knowledge work realigns and reimagines race and class and how these in turn give rise to alternatives within the neoliberal colonization of life by work. Meenakshi's secret story confounds the notion that Indian programmers are merely elite subjects of capitalism. Indian programmers are nonwhite migrant workers whose labor is cheapened through short-term employment *and* upwardly mobile, middle-class subjects. Meenakshi enjoyed her job and looked forward to going to the office every day; she relished her ability to fit in with her work team and was confident she would be successful in the IT industry, eventually moving up to a managerial position. Yet, she also was beholden to migration regimes that discounted the importance of that labor. While Meenakshi was very close to her group of friends, sharing apartment keys, meals, and workplace strategies, she was too worried about her reputation as an upwardly mobile programmer to confide in them about her precarious situation.

This book examines the alignments, realignments, and misalignments of race and class in transnational coding economies. Most often, scholars of capitalism treat the work that is done in global software and service offices as examples of *knowledge work, cognitive labor, immaterial labor,* or, more simply, *post-Fordist, postfactory production.*[1] These terms focus our attention on two factors: first, that intangible goods—including social relations and methods of communication—are the primary products of these economies and, second, that the personality, individual quirks, and mental capacities of workers are resources critical to producing such "immaterial" goods.

Although each of these terms—knowledge work, cognitive labor, and immaterial labor—has a specific valence, they are plagued by the same problem. They all—sometimes despite an explicit interest in embodiment—imagine the cognitive worker as a universal, unmarked subject. This theoretical foreshortening obscures the embodied realities of work, where much cognitive labor is performed by Indian and other migrant coders on short-term contracts.[2] Comprehending how the contradiction between being a racialized migrant and a middle-class subject plays out in their lives necessitates shifting the analytic to consider how race and class constitute a global terrain for cognitive work, rather than imagining that corporate economies can unproblematically create workers according to their own needs.[3]

Meenakshi's experience as an Indian IT worker in Germany reveals the two antinomies that are at the heart of this book. First, as an Indian programmer in Germany, she was subject to tightly restricted migration policies and workplace hierarchies that impeded her movement through the firm at the same time that they created a specific kind of temporary coding labor for the transnational IT industry. The chapters in part I of this book, "Encoding Race," track Meenakshi's and other Indian IT workers' emplotment both within German migration debates and within IT offices. I demonstrate that the Indian IT worker is a figure through which relations between race, labor, and European and German identity are managed. Second, as an Indian diasporic programmer, Meenakshi is also part of an Indian middle class that relies on success abroad to shore up reputations and economic strategies at home. The chapters in part II of this book, "Encoding Class," address how Indian programmers abroad think of, remake, and respond to their positioning as vanguards in a "new Indian middle class." Meenakshi's attachment to the vision of success laid out in class terms is ultimately incompatible with the realities of the racialization of short-term knowledge work that I outline in part I. Her continued pursuance of this vision raises the important question of exactly how race and class operate across a terrain of transnational labor that values expertise yet differentially recognizes and rewards that expertise—in other words, the case of the Indian IT worker in Germany requires us to "put the whole together," as Adorno might write, in its moving contradictions.[4]

In the global IT economy, Indian programmers are racialized—ascribed characteristics as workers that are laminated onto outward, embodied signs such as skin color, odor, dress, accent, and habit—in multiple ways.[5] As under industrial capitalism, they are bulked together as a group of workers who are able because of their cultural capacities to do long stints of repetitive coding labor. Within the German politics of migration, Indian programmers provide a constitutive "outside" to German identity, a foreign presence on German soil that can be both a comforting sign of

German cosmopolitanism and a worrying portent of the precarity of the welfare state's ability to care for its citizens. Yet, as a representative post-Fordist industry, global software and services also mobilize race in another way—as a container for future profitability.[6] Indian programmers are valued in this last way for their ability to provide new ideas for the expansion of business services, even while they are called on to provide explanations for evaluating future returns.

The Indian programmers who are my interlocutors here are themselves working through and reinventing ways of inhabiting a changed landscape of work and value, thus making them representatives of those patterns of work for other (European and American) populations.[7] *Encoding Race, Encoding Class* shares the concerns of earlier scholarship on Indian IT workers with the use of ethnicity and culture to hierarchically organize Indian and American workers in the Indian IT industry.[8] Yet, the argument in this book moves past a discussion of mimicry on the part of Indian workers of American and European culture to understand how racializations intersect with class aspiration. Crucially, my approach treats race as a concept that is itself in flux, since racialization as I use it does not imply an ultimate truth about race.

The Indian middle class fashions itself in part by carefully calibrating the demands of global tech industries with the narrative of Indian national success. Smitha Radhakrishnan, for instance, demonstrates how call center workers in India—especially women—negotiate the dual demands of being global and Indian at the same time.[9] Yet, while I share Radhakrishnan's concern with commensuration between worlds, the language of "appropriateness" can obscure more dynamic aspects of being middle class. I describe how middle-class authority is created and maintained through diasporic connections that both demand an authoritative position on cognitive work and allow middle classes to reinvent practices of leisure and consumption outside the tight imbrication of Indian exceptionalism and IT labor.

These theoretical insights emerge from some unexpected fieldwork findings. Intending to study the way that Indian IT workers unsettled existing tropes of German identity, conversations with Germans working in the IT industry suggested that the racialization of Indian IT workers was not only used to exclude nonwhite, non-German others from national identity. I found that race was also used as a tool to come to terms with ways of working that had become unmoored from traditional industry, trade union control, and the German welfare state. Intending to track how Indian programmers inhabit their niche in global software work, I spent time with Indian programmers outside of work. I soon realized that these archetypes of corporate professionalism had an ambivalent, even agonistic relationship to their careers and devoted considerable time and energy to developing alternative ways of living explicitly pitched against the expansion of work into all areas of life. I began to think of how Indian programmers were both attached to work that disenchanted their life—what Lauren Berlant calls "cruel optimism"—and developed paths away from this attachment— what Kathi Weeks calls "imagining critical utopias."[10]

Of course, workers of various kinds—from Asian women who were said to have "nimble fingers" working in electronics assembly to Irish dockworkers who were considered to be passionate and suited to hard labor—have been racialized to fit the demands of industrial capitalism and its divisions of labor. Equally, workers have always found the critical capacities outside of work to produce alternatives to these modes of labor organization.[11] Yet, the literature on both Indian IT workers and cognitive labor has largely ignored such findings.[12] *Encoding Race, Encoding Class* argues that cognitive labor both opposes manual labor and is embodied. Concomitantly, Indian programmers are elite, privileged workers in cognitive economies *and* racialized workers troubling such economies.

My argument both uses and extends autonomist Marxist analyses of neoliberal capitalism. Autonomist Marxism understands the cognitive worker as someone who devotes herself fully to the office. Her creative capacities, developed outside the office in leisure and free time, are a vital resource to be tapped (at any time) by a cognitive economy that relies on the circulation of ideas and symbols to produce value. At the same time, this creative capacity can sow seeds of solidarity among different sorts of workers who may recognize the shared inhumanity of their labor and the shared potential of creative activity undertaken in common and for the common good. This is the potential of slowing down time and refusing the expansion of work into life that Bifo Berardi, revisiting Herbert Marcuse's work, terms *eros*.[13] According to Berardi's analysis, we are incited to share and be open to multiple kinds of impulses; yet, these impulses are directed toward a particular idea of happiness rooted in accumulation. I find Berardi's sense of eros useful for the way it opens up a discussion of other modes of happiness and life within cognitive economies.[14]

While Berardi locates eros outside realms of what he calls "info-work," I found eros in the everyday activities of Indian coders. At work, they try to bend regimes of labor to their own needs, and after work, they spend time resisting making their emotional and cognitive capacities available for insertion into capitalist economies. When Indian programmers pursue eros, they are not just refusing work, as autonomist Marxist thinkers acknowledge. They are refusing their position in coding economies as limited grunt workers and their slot in European fantasies of migration that compare them with other black and brown bodies.[15]

Eros equally attaches to a politics of Indian middle-class pleasure that is contested and redefined in part in contrast to regimes of work. When pursuing pleasure directed against how their labor is organized in coding economies, Indian programmers are also redefining a relationship between work and pleasure that they can claim as elements of a good (middle-class) life. Crucially, traces of alternative ways of life are found not only outside but also within the domains of cognitive work. They are made visible by attending to the everyday practices of work and especially when following the fractures of work produced by and through racialized discourses. In other words, because *Encoding Race, Encoding Class* begins by positing a differentiated rather than unmarked cognitive worker, the "info-office" itself emerges as a fractured and contradictory space. Equally important, alternatives to the way immaterial economies organize labor do not exist only in radical, vanguardist environments outside corporate offices, as is often presumed in discussions of "free" and open source software.[16] They are instead present in what has been theorized from the outside as the paradigm of new economy work—corporate software—and for what has been often taken as a model of the new economy worker—the Indian software engineer. In these spaces, refusing the organization of work is also a practice of building a different relationship between pleasure and work. Resisting the demands that work makes on life also redirects cognitive work into the channels of Indian middle-class identity.[17] As such, eros describes both a politics of refusal and of deflection.

Kinder statt Inder: The German Green Card Debates
Germany presents a particularly sharp and visible version of the global dynamics of race in software economies that at once engage with Indian programmers as unwanted job-takers and as wanted harbingers of tech-

nological modernity. Meenakshi's journey to Germany was made possible by a visa program begun by the German government in 2000. A five-year visa for IT professionals, the German green card program was announced by then chancellor Gerhard Schröder on February 23, 2000, at an annual communications and IT technology expo called CeBIT.[18] The German green card—officially called the Regulation on Work Permits for Highly Qualified Foreign Laborers in Information and Communication Technology (IT/ArGV)—was issued for up to three years and did not lead to permanent residency. The entire program could be stopped at any time if economic conditions changed and a large IT workforce was no longer needed.[19] Thus, while the former East Germany (the German Democratic Republic) progressively lost its young people to the West, factories shuttered their doors, and unemployment across Europe remained at a level 7.7 percent through the first half of the new decade, information technology industry associations such as Bitcom argued successfully that there was not enough engineering talent in Germany to fill immediate needs.

Despite the severe limitations on residency and duration, the announcement of the green card program set off a storm of protest, bringing to the surface long-simmering tensions about the outcome of the *Gastarbeiter* [guest worker] program, the declining German birthrate, and the legacy of German strength in science and engineering. As in the United States and Australia, in Europe the figure of the Indian software engineer became a specter haunting the stability of white-collar careers in Europe, threatening the loss of technical skill and engineering know-how to the "third world."[20]

The most infamous and succinct expression of the anti–green card sentiment in Germany was the election slogan *Kinder statt Inder* (Children instead of Indians). Jürgen Rüttgers, candidate for the right-centrist party the Christian Democratic Union (CDU), used the slogan as an anti-immigration rallying cry, calling for Germans to have more children instead of allowing Indians into the country. Although he was ultimately unsuccessful in his bid for a seat in parliament, the slogan captured a way of seeing the Indian programmer as an immigrant threat to German job security.

The green card renewed fears of unwanted migration in a Germany that claims to *have* migrants but not be a country *of* migrants. In public debates, the green card was tied closely to the question of the integration of Turkish immigrants who entered Germany as guest workers (*Gastarbeiter*) from the 1950s to the 1970s and subsequently took up permanent residency, now accounting for about 1.7 million of Germany's 81.9 million people.[21]

Of the 14,876 programmers who came to Germany on the visa, one quarter—the largest share—were from India. In the end, less than half of the allowable number of green card visas were issued. Experts remain undecided about the low number of visa takers: some attribute it to Germany's anti-immigrant reputation, others to its inability to compete with the United States and England, and still others to the ill-timed nature of the initiative. The need for IT workers, according to those partial to this last analysis, plummeted just as the green card program was launched, since the program was initiated as the market for IT services began to slump, first in Silicon Valley, then everywhere else.[22] Thus, although the green card allowed for 20,000 visas, there were not enough jobs in IT and related services to match these needs.

Despite the low number of visa takers, the German green card was hotly debated and everywhere accompanied by discussions of the IT *Inder* (IT Indians). Even though the visa program was not targeted at India, it quickly became laminated onto these debates as if they had always been a part of them. In Germany, a postwar politics of guest working that makes distinctions rooted in law and national identity between Germans and "foreigners" jostles against the country's—and especially Berlin's—reputation as a forward-looking, new economy metropole. The Indian IT worker is singled out, often in contrast to other migrants, to represent that economy.

The German green card was a compromise with native worker protectionist sentiments because it limited the number and duration of such IT visas. It solidified India's association with global technology labor even while it underlined divides between European and migrant workers. The unintended effects produced by the German green card program suggest that neoliberalism is best understood as a compromise with preexisting modes of governance tasked with caring for populations.[23] In particular, I use the lens of race and class to understand how German and Indian coders, managers, and other business professionals take up, remake, and materialize paradigms of difference in work and working bodies, both inside the office and beyond its glass façades and open floor plans.

Limited Entrée to the Office, Loads of Life after Work

Participant observation allows a researcher to move analytically between what subjects do and what they say. Sometimes, though, when fieldwork is "written up," the peculiarities of access across a field site disappear. In fieldwork with these Indian IT workers, I was included in free time activities more completely, while the office was available to observation from time to time. Often, my access in corporate spaces was limited to a single interview, a single day shadowing a manager, or a few weeks of team observation.[24] Following this uneven access revealed to me the specific contours of the corporate office, where time should not be wasted, workers should not be distracted, and knowledge is a potentially valuable commodity. It also revealed the rich and complex life that coders have outside the office.

I conducted fieldwork over eighteen months between 2002 and 2004, with a three-month follow-up visit to Berlin in 2006. I shadowed Indian IT workers in their office setting while also interviewing their German (and occasionally British, Australian, and American) managers and colleagues. Most Indian programmers I met in Berlin were upper caste and Hindu. Of the fifty-plus programmers I eventually interviewed, four were Muslim. Approximately two-thirds of these programmers were from the South Indian state of Andhra Pradesh; the rest were from North and West India. Twenty-two were women. In addition to these Indian programmers, I interviewed thirty-two German, American, Australian, and Indian managers and programmers I met in offices, through mutual contacts, and at trade fairs.

The arguments in this book emerge from following a core group of about twenty programmers before, after, and during work. I shadowed six of this group in the firms where they passed their days, evenings, and occasionally nights. The rest of this core group I interacted with in their free time. These programmers are distinctive for the short-term nature of their work (one to two years) and for the fact that they took jobs in Germany, which most saw as a stepping-stone to either a permanent position in the country or a better position in the United States, Canada, or India. They were thus faced with a particularly sharp version of the paradox of contingent software work: demonstrating the skill set necessary to the job at hand yet proving while working their capacity to move into management.

Over the course of fieldwork, I came to understand the ways in which work did and did not govern their lives. My focus shifted, as I noticed the richness found in the contrast between work spaces—characterized by an ethic of time-driven work projects—and those of nonwork spaces, with their conviviality, alternative ethics of pleasure and enjoyment, and practiced de-emphasis on managing time efficiently.[25] By following a co-hort, I was able to understand their processes of forging a middle-class Indian identity even while working through the antimonies of their work contracts.

Of the five firms I observed over extended periods, two produced soft-ware for other businesses to help these firms manage their data and pro-cesses; another made and maintained original pieces of software that were specializations to existing software packages made by large firms; the fourth was a start-up trying to market new products directly to consum-ers; and the fifth was a vendor that ran a small part of a client-oriented business for another firm, which was a mobile phone company. These of-fices were chosen for variety of size and industry focus, while at the same time I was restricted to those firms where I could gain access. My fieldwork in offices ranged from periodic office visits to monthlong observation and interviews with follow-up visits. Access to firms was mostly facilitated through networks of management professionals I cultivated in early days of fieldwork by attending regional and national technology fairs and conferences. Sometimes, Indian short-term programmers I met were able to introduce me to their managers; much more often, however, they wor-ried that bringing me into the office might jeopardize their reputation with their bosses. I therefore worked within the time limits of observation with which my interlocutors felt comfortable, which varied according to per-sonal disposition and evaluation of job security.

Indian programmers on short-term visas often were reluctant to bring a "participant-observer" into the workroom. Many expressed anxiety that the management would not like someone watching how work was executed. Others were worried that their reputations would be compromised if a potentially critical monitor went with them to work. One programmer quipped, "Our jobs are only as long as the project, then we have to get hired onto another one," to support his sense of vulnerability. Many pro-grammers believed that managers would think they were wasting time talking to someone about work rather than doing it, a fear that particularly attached to low-level coding and testing work outside the conversation-dependent "creative" jobs such as project development. These reasons point to the ways racialization worked to thicken the association between Indian programmers and long work hours as part of their jobs and as part of their (assumed) cultural makeup, an association to which Indian migrant coders were particularly susceptible because of the job insecurity of project-based work contracts.

Then, there was the issue of workplace secrets. In certain meetings, managers were concerned that an anthropologist would have access to software applications that were still in development and were considered trade secrets. At the same time, some managers were interested in finding out more about how to better manage an "intercultural team," as work teams with programmers from Germany, Australia, India, and, to a lesser extent, Russia, Brazil, and China were called. These managers would often want to talk to me in private, outside the workplace when possible, to probe how their teams were doing. I opted to allow the demands of programmers and their bosses to act as bars to total access, from which I learned that while transparency and expertise is overtly valued, all forms of knowledge may be used to decide on the future direction of a project or firm, making knowledge a potentially valuable and well-guarded commodity.

In this milieu, no participant, including this anthropologist, is a privileged observer. This method makes explicit that ethnography does not represent a neutral reality but instead follows the realities of the life of its protagonists.[26] What is more, part of the realities this ethnography represents is made up of closed doors, indirectly accessible estimations, and calculations about the future strategy. In the few cases where I spoke with both programmers and their managers separately, I chose to keep confidential what workers told me outside the office about their managers. Workers rarely asked me about my conversations with managers, preferring to form their own opinions through shared anecdotes and daily observations. They were their own careful ethnographers of the office, trying to discern an office culture, adapt to it, and evaluate it collectively.

While I believe ethnographers should work to gain entrée to the "hidden abode of production" behind the sign reading "no admittance except on business,"[27] should learn programming languages, and especially should foreground their attempts to do so as part of an anthropological engagement with the conditions of knowledge production, restricting the ethnography of coding cultures to office life and the study of coding practices tells only a partial story. A worldly anthropology should also be attuned to techné that draw on and yet unsettle standard narratives and modes of representation more widely.[28] I devoted considerable time to life outside work, where, in trying to make different expertise line up, Indian programmers innovated ways of being in the world that are often antithetical to the demands of neoliberal labor. Junaid Rana writes, "Transnational labor migration is fraught with all sorts of possibilities, desires, and unexpected outcomes that transcend reductive structural explanations."[29] One unexpected outcome revealed by following corporate coders after work is that Indian programmers were often critical of and actively resisted the way time was managed in the office, insisting that personal and community time should not always be sacrificed to work time.[30]

Because the programmers from whom I learned worked in corporate offices rather than as volunteers, in universities, or in not-for-profit settings, the nature of my research is quite different from earlier ethnographic projects with free software developers, open source coders, and hackers, such as Chris Kelty's *Two Bits*, Yuri Takhteyev's *Coding Places*, and Gabriella Coleman's *Coding Freedom*. My research is more concerned with what happens at the boundary between the office and the world outside the office—with moments of encounter and translation that define the particular standpoint of the Indian middle-class coder. Among my interlocutors, the main concern was finding a way to understand their experiences in the office within a larger field of engagement that variously defined them as Indian elites, global experts, and representatives of their families, sometimes their religion, their regional groups, and the Indian nation.[31]

The names given to some of the principal actors in this book—Mihir and Meenakshi, Rajeshwari, Madhu and Bipin, Srinu, Mayur, Adi and Maya—are first names in keeping with both the informality of office culture and the closeness of friendship. The names bleed across the boundaries of work and afterwork and indicate how the channels through which technocapital flows are hewn from the hard rock of the workplace and tilled in the rich fields of play. Over the course of eighteen months, I interviewed, shadowed, ate and drank with, and generally hung around this group of friends and colleagues, all programmers on the German green card, all recent arrivals in Berlin. They met one another through work, at the Indian embassy, and through contacts in India. In many ways, they understood me to be in a similar position as they were, having come to Germany for a short but necessary interval in the making of a scientifically oriented career.

I first met some of them on a U-Bahn platform at Gesundbrunnen Station, a medium-size subway station in the north-central part of the city. The rest of the cohort I met over months as they visited one another's houses and went on outings throughout the city, with me tagging along. Relating this encounter on the subway platform as I do below demonstrates the shape of this fieldwork, where work and leisure time took on equal significance for me, as I tried to understand how programmers knit together the divergent visions of the "how" of life that circulated in these worlds.

On a hot August day, my interlocutors and I would discover that we were all practically neighbors, living in the working-class neighborhood of Wedding. I was on my way to the Indian eambassy for an Independence Day celebration, where I hoped to meet with local officials and business professionals. Mihir, Rajeshwari, Adi, and Maya were on their way there too—embassy events were an occasion for them to meet up with other programmers in the city. Sometimes, the embassy televised cricket matches that were always extremely well attended. This day's activities would include saluting the flag and singing *Jana Gana Mana*, the Indian national anthem, outside the newly built embassy, then heading inside for a recitation of President Kalam's speech, covering the history of the independence movement and its freedom fighters, the problems of Jammu and Kashmir, and outlining a vision of a developed India. His speech was preceded by remarks by the current ambassador and followed by sweets and snacks.

As I waited on the U-Bahn platform, this group of four hailed me. They had mistaken me at this distance for Meenakshi, who would join us a few minutes later. I soon fell in with them as we realized we were all going to the same place, and talking with Mihir on the way to the embassy, we began comparing notes on the quality of life for Indian migrants in the United States, Germany, and Canada. A "baptismal" act in the course of fieldwork, this moment of misrecognition on the train platform named me as both one of them and a curiosity—an Indian American who sometimes dressed in a sari, who was studying and striving like they were, but who was also studying them.[32] In retrospect, this moment and others like it made me particularly attuned to both the dilemmas of massing and the realities of separation; to the commonalities of life stage, background, and even racialization that joined us together; and to the differences in visa restriction, ability to move at will, and life course that held us apart. Indeed, as a graduate student in the social sciences from the United States studying with newly minted computer programmers from India, my chances for economic security in the future were both more and less precarious than theirs. The relationships I formed with my interlocutors arose in this crucible where the lines between class and other backgrounds are never clearly drawn.

Neither Cybercoolie nor Cyberstar, but Still Racialized

Speichern—sicher zu erahnen—
Tastendruck nur auf "BRAHMANEN."
Gibt's Probleme—"MANTRA" wählen.
Und dann das Problem erzählen.
Unverzüglich kommt hervor
"BUDDHA aus dem MONITOR."

Save—easy to guess—
Simply press "BRAHMIN."
Are there problems?—choose "MANTRA."
And then relate the problem.
Instantaneously there appears,
"BUDDHA on the MONITOR."
—Jürgen Frühling, "Inder Nett"[33]

Some may critique this project for speaking of race when other terms such as *ethnicity* or *culture* might do. While ethnicity and culture can capture the way capitalism exacerbates and sediments differences among groups, thinking through race centers the multiple ways capital is embodied by drawing attention to how individual workers' inner characteristics are interpreted through their skin color, dress, language, smell, accent, hairstyle, way of walking, facial expressions, and behavior.[34] I argue that in coding economies racialization happens when the question is raised: is being good at programming fixed in certain kinds of bodies? I use the terms *race* and *racialization* here to describe how work ethics, the capacity to labor in particular ways, and cultural knowledge are "epidermalized," as Fanon writes—mapped onto the skin, clothing, smell, and mannerisms of living bodies.[35] With this starting definition of race and racialization, I follow rather than predefine how race operates across transnational terrains. In this book, race moves across several fields of expression. Race helps divide native and "foreign" populations, old and new styles of working, and stable identities and flexible ones. In Germany, the long history of interest in India meets the comparatively shallow history of the guest worker program. These histories help establish a hierarchy of wanted and unwanted working brown bodies that set Indian migrants apart from Turkish migrants. Thinking through race in the current moment also draws immigrant bodies into a postracial, postgenomic uncertainty about the fixity of race itself. The idea, supported by the genomic sciences, that racial characteristics are to be understood as tendencies makes race seem both unimportant and newly interesting as a source of knowledge about different populations.[36] I investigate how racialization opens up a variety of ways of imagining the relationship of work and worker subjectivity. Rather than simply adding an analysis of race to the story of corporate coding, I seek to investigate how race itself is a multivalent sign that works in three main ways. First, it helps write convincing scripts for reforming the work habits of European populations by holding up the tech-savvy foreign worker for comparison. Second, it justifies unequal conditions of labor for European and migrant workers. And, third, race enhances the potential productivity of firms that hire Indian workers by promising that such workers will generate monetizable ideas.

Like elsewhere in postgenomic, postracial deployments of race, in the discourses that circulate around Indian IT workers in Germany, racism is posited as having been overcome at the same time that race as a marker of probable characteristics is validated. Following the multiple meanings of race as related to worker quality, as I do in this book, demands thinking of race in its specifically postgenomic guise, where race is no longer considered a fixed trait but instead describes population traits in flux. This new racial imaginary, according to analysts of genomic sciences, creates new markets around these genetically coded population traits.[37] What I explore in this book is how a postgenomic understanding of race that is uncertain about whether or not racial traits are fixed in populations is used to comment on and understand flexible economies and flexible workers.[38] I am interested in how the race of the Indian IT worker is used to generalize about emerging economies by providing a frame through which to speculate on the kinds of traits that make a good cognitive worker and to further imagine what populations might possess such traits. Likewise, I track how the idea that racial traits are probabilities rather than certainties allows the figure of the Indian IT worker to be held up as a mirror through which European populations can be reformed; that is, it taught through example how to be good cognitive workers.[39]

The argument presented in the 2010 book *Deutschland schafft sich ab* illustrates how a "folk genomics" moves into the domain of assessing migrant groups in Germany. The author of this best-selling hardcover nonfiction text, Thilo Sarrazin, is a prominent German politician, who was previously on the board of *die Deutsche Bundesbank* (the German Federal Bank). In its pages, he argues that Muslims in Germany will not assimilate and that they are not as intelligent as other (including Jewish) populations. Throughout the book, he uses examples from human genetics to ground his arguments about the cultural differences of Turkish and Arab people. In addition to claiming that all Jews share a gene, the author also claims that the intelligence of the general population of Germany is diminishing because of the immigration of people from Africa and the Middle East. Sarrazin's mixing of gene theory (of a folk kind) with an assessment of the effects of migration, education, and religion is an example of one way that the genomic sciences are taken up within political discourse. Sarrazin's was an extreme—though very popular when judged in terms of book sales—admixture of race and culture. In everyday interactions inside and outside the workplace, such mixing of genomics and cultural traits can move in many different directions, from shoring up ideas of workplace hierarchy to critiquing the failings of European working classes.[40]

Often, within this general use of folk genomics to prove cultural arguments, Indian programmers were subject to a particular kind of scrutiny. Rather than being judged in terms of their assimilative potential (as were Turks and Muslims), they were understood as embodying corporate technical skills, such as the ability to work hard for extended periods, knowledge of math and science, and an innate understanding of how computer technologies work. One question I ask is what happens when the Indian IT worker as a figure who embodies neoliberalism is sutured to anxieties about where Euro-American populations will land in an economy that values these particular skills?

Neoliberal Ways of Working

My interpretation of contemporary shifts in capitalism is informed by the work of Bifo Berardi, Gilles Deleuze, Paolo Virno, and others who investigate a kind of capitalism that extracts surplus value from the circulation of signs (rather than from the production of wares). Each of these authors describes a recent shift in capitalism that incorporates the human potential for communication into the labor process. Value comes from developing and then placing bets on this human ability to innovate. This economy, often glossed as "late capitalist," is driven by probabilities, wagers on uncertainty, and speculation without end as a supplement to the circulation of tangible wares.[41] According to these theorists, this shift from Fordist to post-Fordist production transformed the labor demanded of workers, from primarily producing commodity-objects to also performing continuously their potential for future productivity. In the end, "activity without end . . . becomes the prototype of all wage labor."[42]

Importantly, human subjectivity remains the central creative element of a late capitalist economy of signs because of the generative capacity of the subject to produce fresh ideas and new forms of communication. Berardi writes of knowledge workers, whom he calls the "cognitariat": "They prepare their nervous system as an active receiving terminal for as much time as possible. The entire lived day becomes subject to a semiotic activation which becomes directly productive only when necessary."[43] Though the language is abstruse, Berardi points out how cognitariats are constantly producing ideas and impulses that may be called on later for further elaboration by capital. "In this way," he writes, "workers offer their entire day to capital and are paid only for the moments when their time is made cellular." As cognitive laborers, Indian IT workers are Berardi's cognitariat. They are a class of workers who offer up their creative, analytic, and communicative labor power to capital. Yet, they are also affected by an economy that uses and remakes race such that being *Indian* programmers becomes synonymous with accepting precarious work contracts and visas, extending the working day, and performing cultural knowledge as a part of work. Berardi underlines the corporeal aspects of communicative work by describing the cognitariat as "the social corporeality of cognitive labor."[44] I read this as an invitation to think about knowledge work as embedded in the desires and dreams, thoughts and tremblings of working bodies.[45] The cognitive worker also has a body that, to paraphrase Berardi, is affected, effects, and has needs.

In this book, therefore, I extend the autonomist analysis of capitalism put forward by such theorists as Virno and Berardi to encompass race and class. It is not that they ignore how embodiments of race and class imbricate with creative and communicative work. Virno is quick to point out that there are manual workers (those who produce on factory assembly lines), although the nature and direction of their work has changed. But the question of race and class is approached indirectly in their theorization of cognitive labor because they begin from the position of an unmarked knowledge worker and then take the characteristics of this worker as the norm. This leaves the worker's body as a remainder and an aberration.[46] In Berardi's telling, mental labor makes physical demands on the body, but one cognitive worker is very much like the next. Instead, I provide a fine-grained analysis of how the lived experience of the body both works against and supports the formation of the cognitariat in the way Berardi describes.

To understand how neoliberal regimes of work—that is, those that in corporate offices emphasize worker flexibility, the investment of the personality of the worker in the workplace, and the production value through the exchange of ideas and structures of communication—compromise with other arrangements of life and work, I argue for bringing materiality and the body back into an analysis of knowledge work. But, it is not enough to bring these in from the outside, when almost all is said and done, like a god from the machine. Rather, I show how race and class are integral both to producing differently valued bodies at work and to producing the communicative content of so-called immaterial goods.

As I argue in this book, the ambivalence around Indian IT workers in Germany is attributable to their double location, as both an unwanted migrant and a model of neoliberal work practice that requires a worker to be always at the ready, always able to respond to quickly changing demands. At the same time, Indian tech diasporas continue the project of Indian national development through technocratic expertise that began in the Nehruvian era. The disjuncture between Indian class politics and the politics of race in knowledge work globally is not between race and class as opposing categories of belonging but between racialization as a means of dividing up workers and also a sign of value and the establishment of the Indian IT worker as authoritative voice within the Indian middle classes.

Making the Indian Middle Class Abroad

In Europe and the United States, the Indian programmer is a source of cheap labor; in India, the very same figure is a member of a burgeoning middle class increasingly able to flex its consumption-based muscle. This contradiction makes Indian programmers at once laboring migrants and desiring citizen-consumers, both spectral figures threatening European and American jobs and emblems of India's global success.

Scholars of India's "new" middle class investigate the increasing authority and assertiveness that now accrue to these classes in India.[47] In previous decades, the middle class was an influential but limited group of government officials, small businessmen, professionals such as doctors and lawyers, and medium-scale farmers. This class was able to take advantage of economic opportunities that developed in the private sphere as the economy liberalized. Soon, the sons and daughters of doctors and civil servants turned their attention to private economies and especially the software industry as the focus of their education and careers. Such jobs garnered higher paychecks than earlier avenues of employment. Coupled with these privatized careers was the arrival on the Indian scene of more material goods after the end of import substitution (domestic market protection through restrictions on imports) in 1991.

The new Indian middle class increasingly defines itself through consumption. Leela Fernandes, among the first to study the new Indian middle class, defines the newness of the contemporary middle classes as a "cultural characteristic" associated with "lifestyles and consumption practices" realized through "commodities made available in India's liberalizing economy."[48] The primacy given to the middle class in India today, according to Fernandes, is rooted in its ability to symbolize a powerful and globalizing India through conspicuous consumption. Fernandes usefully locates the symbolic power of India's middle class in its ability to produce through consumption a modern Indian citizen subject that is prosperous, of the world, and also belongs to the nation. Yet, such an analysis may assume too quickly the homogeneity (and thus hegemony) of this class.[50] In this work, I investigate how middle-class authority is built—and contested—from within diasporic spaces.

I focus on how Indian programmers both form and contest their inclusion in an authoritative Indian middle class. This approach, which treats class as a process rather than a thing, shows how programmers both assert a collective class identity and an individual expert identity. I explore the process of establishing middle-class authority in chapter 5, where I argue that middle-class authority emerges through the comparison of work and leisure rather than through an unabashed celebration of work as a means to consumption, as generalized theories of Indian middle-class culture would suggest. Instead, Indian programmers debate the boundaries and limits of the extension of work into free time. Their authority stems from their ability to question what a proper relationship between work and leisure should be; that is, they set parameters that reinsert work and the purchasing power of their jobs into a moral and ethical framework of family, friendship, and enjoyment, or eros.

Diaspora is not a category of belonging that comes ready-made. It must be stitched together across geography through what Brent Edwards calls *décalage*, the removing of an artificial prop that reestablishes "a changing core of difference."[49] This basic fact required of producing diaspora entails that it includes conflict and contradiction. For the Indian programmers in this story, the "artificial prop" of identity through consumption is revisited time and again to produce a more nuanced understanding of their relationship to work, the demands of capital, and an Indian national imaginary of the consumer-citizen, a dynamic I unpack in chapter 6. I likewise explore the dialectic between collective class identity and individual identity in the conclusion, where Meenakshi's story (which opened this introduction) plays out for her peers as evidence of personal failing rather than of a failed strategy.

I trace in this book how Indian programmers reframe the incommensurabilities between the way they are positioned as raced cognitive workers and as members of the new Indian middle class. While the demands of working hard, in short-term labor contracts, and in often-repetitive work clearly support economically middle-class aspirations, Indian programmers also think of themselves as refusing neoliberalism's most stringent demands. This self-conception arises precisely from the different and not always commensurable ways they are positioned as both cheap labor and as a rising elite.

Coding can be a site for working through the contradiction between labor and a middle-class imaginary of a good life. In the sections of volume 1 of *Capital* that concern machines, Marx emphasized technology's dual nature in a way that remains convincing today. "Machinery," he writes, "is misused," transforming the worker into a cog in a machine instead of freeing the worker from the exigencies of labor.[51] "The most powerful instrument for rescuing labor-time suffers a dialectical inversion and becomes the most unfailing means for turning the whole lifetime of the worker and his family into labor-time at capital's disposal for its own valorization."[52] The logic of capital, pace Marx, had commanded the machines' abilities just as it had hijacked labor power and thwarted the "many-sided play of muscles" (including the minds) of workers.

Indian programmers voiced a similar critique when they pointed out what code, in their opinion, ought to do: to solve common problems and erase political boundaries, especially the ones that restrict their own abilities to migrate. They often were frustrated by what corporate coding culture as it is currently organized has made it do, in their opinion: answer client demands, however unreasonable. When Indian IT workers talk about code, they talk about it in ways that echo how Marx talked about the machine, as a technology that ought to free them to pursue their many-sidedness but has instead been harnessed to a business strategy that sees them mostly as expendable, cheap labor.

Coding can be a tool to extend and think through human possibilities.[53] As I trace out in chapter 3, the critique of working life that programmers elaborate through their understanding of code yields strategies of bending the code, their time in the office, and their free time toward the full development of themselves. I use the idea of "proprietary freedom" to suggest that their main strategy is one based on a relation of carving out spaces and times in the office to pursue their own coding projects that allow them temporary ownership over their work. In this way, they innovate ways of being a part-time knowledge worker who is less than entirely enthralled by the discourse of hard work as an end in itself.

It is not just the Indian IT worker who sees a gap between what is and what ought to be when it comes to working life, personal freedom, and the freedom of code. Increasingly, many scholars and activists see the capabilities of code to lay down pathways of access as being corralled and blocked. Activist groups such as the Electronic Frontier Foundation have tried to unblock these impulses by organizing around issues such as net neutrality and the right to privacy. Such organizations argue for continued access to and use of digital media technologies as a nonhierarchical means of address and organization. The ideological suppositions of these movements generally pit free access against corporate and government control. But freedom is a historically and contextually situated rather than an unqualified and universal good. The impulse to unblock information and to foster free movement does not a priori lead to freedom. It can also render an intensification of entrepreneurial individualism and a renewal of, as Jason Smith writes in the introduction to Berardi's *The Soul at Work*, "the entry of the soul into the production process."[54] I begin instead with Indian programmers' practices of carving out limited freedoms that concomitantly are part of and resist the logic of the free traffic in commodities and ideas that is a cornerstone of corporate philosophy. Freedom, in this approach, emerges in a historically mediated context where it can become the focus of social practice precisely because of the way it is defined—as freedom from constraint—in neoliberal worlds. Indian programmers take up this idea of freedom and turn it toward a critique of the office, on the one hand, and toward an elaboration of what it might mean for middle-class Indians to live a good and fulfilling life, on the other.

The Chapters

By now there is a significant literature tracking the Indian programming phenomenon in the Silicon Valley and in Bangalore, in Australia and in Europe. Indian programming illustrates well two of the tenets of globalization theory: technological spread and the spread of migration. Accordingly, studies of Indian programming—such as A. Aneesh's *Virtual Migration*, Xiang Biao's *Global Bodyshopping*, Reena Patel's *Working the Night Shift*, Shezad Nadeem's *Dead Ringers*, and Smitha Radhakrishnan's *Appropriately Indian*—thus far have sketched out the topography of technology and culture to show how IT worlds connect across transnational space, how call center cultures are reshaping gender, and how such technologies as providing software and support services and maintaining, creating, and testing code create capital flows that consolidate wealth around the Indian middle class.[55]

In this book, I offer a more uncertain and fragile view of things in comparison with the well-established worlds of Silicon Valley and Bangalore. This transnational, tenuous world is more in keeping with what most cognitive workers experience today. That is, for most programmers in India and abroad, conditions of work are uncertain. It is only the select few who reach levels of success that could make them "cyberstars." Yet, the image of a technosavvy Indian programmer continues to resonate in an extraeconomic sense. In tracking both these realities—the day-to-day conditions of work and the figurative meanings of the Indian programmer—I show how the idea of the Indian programmer is just as much a part of the reality of cognitive labor as is Indian programmers' contract-based employment.

Encoding Race, Encoding Class is divided into two parts. Part I, "Encoding Race," is made up of three chapters. Chapter 1, "Imagining the Indian IT Body," uses political cartoons and ethnographic interviews to document racialized depictions of Indian IT workers. I use these images to show the multifaceted nature of the discussion of race in public. I situate Indian programmers as ambivalent subjects between Turkish guest workers and Afro-German migrants in German national debate around immigration and assimilation. Comparing these images and their narratives with the production of difference in the office, I show how office culture uses liberal, tolerant notions of race even while it sediments office hierarchies through folk theories of cultural difference. I use this chapter to argue that postgenomic uncertainty over whether race is a fixed or malleable property of human populations makes race "good to think with" about the equally uncertain futures that neoliberal capitalism promises.

Chapter 2, "The Postracial Office," uses ethnographic observation in corporate offices and interviews with programmers and managers from India, Germany, Australia, and the United States to show how race is refracted and reimagined through evaluations of worker quality. I explore the ways that race is deployed around cognitive work, arguing that it is a means of dividing office work into skilled "front room" and grunt "back room" coding. Firms pay attention to race as a source of information on foreign populations of potential customers and also as a rubric to evaluate the desired traits of cognitive workers. In a postracial office, race is denied as a salient factor in decision making through an emphasis on worker quality, even while worker quality is attributed to race. This chapter explores the multiple ways that race is made meaningful in such an environment.

Chapter 3, "Proprietary Freedoms in an IT Office," discusses the strategies Indian programmers use to be successful in short-term work contracts, including framing the work as a necessary, temporary step on the way to elite status and thinking of programming skills as a kind of wealth they control. They develop two sets of complementary practices: first, they criticize existing migration law that treats them as second-class citizens even while the code they write is so highly valued. Second, they try to extend their work projects beyond the length of their visas. I read this second practice as a claim for a kind of proprietary freedom, one that puts forth a temporary ownership over work against the general ethic of workplace sharing and its corollary—mobile and replaceable labor. I use this idea of freedom-in-ownership to upend the usual way freedom in software is understood, highlighting that it is often the company and not its employees that is invested in the free exchange of information.

Part II, "Encoding Class," investigates the relationship between the politics of work and the making of an Indian middle class. In chapter 4, "The Stroke of Midnight and the Spirit of Entrepreneurship: A History of the Computer in India," I demonstrate that the long tradition linking technology, elite subjects, and nation building in India is currently reimagined through the lionization of private individual achievement. Indian coders are heirs to a technocratic discourse that puts them at the vanguard of national development. Viewed within this framing, short-term work contracts are stepping-stones to both individual and national self-determination. As such, the critique of migration regimes by diasporic Indian programmers is muted by the discourse of technoelite success through individual achievement to which they also subscribe.

In chapter 5, "Computers Are Very Stupid Cooks: Reinventing Leisure as a Politics of Pleasure," I take readers into the homes of Indian programmers. The home is where their experiences on the street and in the office are parsed. I use the variety of activities they engage in at home—eating, gossip sessions, wide-ranging discussions that go deep into the night—to revisit scholarly understandings of the relationship between work and leisure under neoliberalism. By and large, Indian programmers do not allow work demands to intrude on leisure time; in fact, they actively resist doing so. I argue that leisure time is so preserved because it allows programmers to develop a politics of pleasure in the everyday (that I call eros), which helps define being middle class. I argue that alternatives to the colonization of leisure by work exist even within neoliberal regimes of work. These alternatives to immaterial labor flourish in the interstices between work as organized by firms and a middle-class imaginary of a good life.

In chapter 6, "The Traveling Diaper Bag: Gifts and Jokes as Materializing Immaterial Labor," I analyze two ways that Indian programmers materialize cognitive work: telling jokes and giving gifts. Though much anthropological attention has focused recently on the gift as a site to think through contemporary capitalism and its alternatives, jokes have been given less attention. I put jokes and gifts together to suggest another reading of the gift—not as an alternative to capitalist exchange but as a material instantiation of the problem of commensuration. Both jokes and gifts help commensurate the dictates of work and the demands of middle-class identity. I argue that jokes told about work, about Indian software engineers, and about outsourcing help ease the racial division of labor that Indian IT workers experience in the office by doing affective unwork. That is, they help loosen the investment in work. Gifts, on the other hand, do the affective work of reinforcing cognitive economies by extending care across distance through sentimental objects (such as diaper bags and clothing for children). I analyze these gifts as a mode of commensuration that makes the experience of coding as labor into a resource for securing a good life.

In the conclusion, "A Speculative Conclusion: Secrets and Lives," I revisit Meenakshi's experience to illustrate the nuance in these stories of Indian migrant programmers. I use the story of how she loses her job, hides this from her friends, and has to return to India as an opportunity to discuss the multiple trajectories that Indian programmers may take as they move through cognitive economies. I argue that Meenakshi's story should be understood in its complexity rather than being reduced to evidence for the inherent risks involved in transnational labor. In particular, I consider her story as both an example demonstrating the "cruel optimism" of jobs that promise an entrée into the upper echelons of global software work, which they rarely deliver, and as an example of the "critical utopias" that allow Meenakshi to exit the scene of this labor, perhaps on her own terms. Finally, I argue that such nuanced readings of her story can only emerge by reconceptualizing cognitive work as a kind of labor that plays out both materially and symbolically across a terrain of race and difference.

Encoding Race, Encoding Class stitches together unlikely places and moves across social institutions in an acknowledgment of the ways that leisure and family, work and friendship are conjoined. As many scholars and popular commentators have noted, digital media has made much of this dispersion possible; the smartphone makes work portable and inserts work in sites formerly reserved for leisure. But technology is about more than making new worlds or disenchanting already existing ones. Because technological things extend the capacities of the human, they also initiate reflection on the human condition. I emphasize throughout the book the double-sided nature of technology, to make and to be a medium for reflection, to entail behaviors it seems only to describe and in equal measure to be braided into the narrative of what should, could, and ought to be in life.

In 1997, technology theorist Langdon Winner worried about what the computer revolution had brought to the late twentieth century. "Will people beyond our immediate family, professional colleagues and circle of on-line friends," he wondered, "be seen as connected to us in important, potentially fulfilling ways? Or will they be seen as mere annoyances, as unwanted human surplus that needs to be walled off, controlled, and ignored?"[56] Winner raised the question of difference, afraid for those who, excluded through technology, would be treated as "bare life."[57] He had in mind the way that communications technology could set up divides between those with shared interests and assumptions and an undifferentiated mass of others.

Today, we need a more graduated conception of technological connection and disconnection. Much exists between the extremes of technology democratizing social relations, on the one hand, and solidifying power, on the other. There are proliferations of forms of life that exceed walling in and walling out. The stories of cognitive workers are important moments in the elaboration of technology and the self, work and difference.

The study of Indian programmers—so often lost in a cul-de-sac of economic debates about outsourcing—reveals a significant political-economic picture of the refashioning of work and subjectivity today. The story told here, of striving to make a life on the terrain of fluid capitalism, is at once specific to the class of Indian technoelites with whom I worked and generalizable as a fundamental condition of life in times of uncertainty. The precarity that is fundamental to their story is not only restrictive but generative of multiple kinds of ways of imagining and living in the world. These narratives will no doubt be taken up by ever new actors in hitherto unimagined ways.

1 • ENCODING RACE

In the pages of the journal *American Anthropologist*, Laura Ahearn laments the lack of studies of race in anthropology. Using a keyword search of articles published over two decades, she concludes, "Perhaps scholars should hesitate before claiming that the discipline focuses equally on race, class, and gender," since authors name gender and then class more often than they list race.[1] Following on Ahearn's suggestion, I foreground race in this first section as an underanalyzed aspect of programming economies. Until now, knowledge workers have largely been conceptualized as generalized individuals, an unmarked category of educated, middle-class knowledge experts without race and gender. An anthropology of programming economies can offer an analysis of how the ideal of the knowledge worker who transcends the body intersects with the lived realities of embodied differences.[2]

By turning to the study of Indian programmers in Germany, I develop both an analysis of race in Germany and an analysis of Indian programming. The former is often reduced to the study of Turkish guest workers, while the latter is often reduced to studies of Indian programmers in the United States or India. But a *globalized* understanding of race needs to come to terms with how race is produced in localities and how these different racializations come together, however unevenly. This book concomitantly situates race in Germany within local imaginaries of person and place and presents the circulation of temporary knowledge workers from

India as emerging from a particular transnational niche in programming economies.

All globalized knowledge work takes place within particular national and regional contexts; race is a conceptual tool—one among many—that allows actors in such settings to determine how these contexts may or may not fit together. Unlike culture or ethnicity, race is a border concept that allows me to explore "the permeability of walls [and] the reconstitution of boundaries" that both make use of and set into motion existing dualisms.[3] In Germany, the contemporary circulation of race runs through the long history of Nazi blood-purity ideology and its overturning through liberal German multiculturalism. It also intersects with the racialization of Turkish guest workers starting in the 1950s; the history of Afrodeutsch in Germany, the sons and daughters of African immigrants and Germans, along with African American soldiers stationed in Germany after World War II; and the history of German Orientalism's search for spiritualized asceticism and abundance in classical Sanskritic texts. In these complicated histories, race overlaps with religion, nation, and culture. My job as ethnographer, in following these overlaps and tracing other emerging ones that play out in particular around the relationship between the stability and instability of work, is to see where formulations of race as social process lead, rather than determining a fixed meaning for race in advance. These meanings themselves can be contradictory. For example, while Indian programmers can be positioned in the office as good migrants as opposed to problematic ones, such as Turkish guest workers, they can also represent a neoliberal economy that endangers German jobs and ways of life by ushering in an era of speed, global labor arbitrage, and financial risk.

Treating race in this way, I believe, also necessitates assessing the larger milieu in which race as a folk concept now operates.[4] While in the nineteenth century race was conceptualized as an unchangeable biological entity residing in the blood, in a postgenomic age, it is now conceptualized as clustered probabilities among populations. As I show in the following chapters, the simultaneous fixity of race as a "true" concept and its reconceptualization as probabilistic makes it (once again) an apt concept for actors to think through the relationship between local populations and global work practices.

ONE

IMAGINING THE INDIAN IT BODY

Sitting in a café one early autumn afternoon in the trendy East Berlin neighborhood of Prenzlauer Berg, Marika and I drank lattes in the last warm rays of the setting sun. Marika had her feet propped up on the chair opposite her. An older woman with a flower-print scarf tied neatly under her chin walked by, stopped and stared at Marika's feet, and, with a look of horror on her face, strode on. "Their city just doesn't make sense to them any more. Their world is evaporating before their eyes." Marika gestured toward the woman's receding back. In the old Berlin, chairs were for sitting on, and Marika's feet were a sign of bad manners. Out of place on her own street corner, the older resident of the city simply said nothing and moved on. Much like the way Walter Benjamin moved through the city looking for dialectical images that crystallized a portentous moment of change, Berliners new and old could look to such scenes for a message of the world to come.[1]

Marika's commentary on the scene suggested a kinetic image culture in the city. "I feel sorry for her," Marika said, herself from the Eastern European city Riga, "these old East Berliners." In the Berlin of the new millennium, images were highly politicized objects, their portrait functions always imbued with political proxies, and at the same time, even the most political images could always function as spectator commodities— consumed through viewing practices as signs of the future. The circulating images of Indian IT workers were part of this complex new world, and the viewers of these images were engaged in a street-level semiosis that would try to situate the migrant coder and the new German subject in an emerging economy of signs. The appearance of Indian workers on Berlin streets could be interrogated as an indicator of economic change. A discussion of the circulating image of the Indian IT body lays the groundwork for understanding the racialization of Indian coders both inside and outside the office. Like Marika's feet for the older East German woman, the Indian IT worker was a potent sign of seemingly inexorable transformation.

The archive of images assembled here traces out a subterranean story that ran beneath formal debates on visas for high-tech workers. I collected political cartoons, digital memes, and article illustrations over the course of fieldwork from Internet sites, local magazines, and national newspapers. Some appeared as large, full-color photographs in multipage articles about Indian IT workers in Germany. I noticed others, mostly small cartoons, inserted into the blank space at the bottom of a page of movie listings. Still more surfaced in the humor section of a website dedicated to Indians in Germany, which pulled these images from other sources online (www .theinder.net), the original provenance of which I am unable to trace.[2] Collectively, they demonstrate how Indian programmers were mobilized in statements about a highly unstable future. They emerge out of a particular image culture and reiterate the tight bind between the Indian body, the computer as machine, and exotic cultural practices.[3]

The work that goes on in IT offices, called "business process" or "information technology" and related services, is notoriously abstract. Theories of cognitive labor that developed in part through the example of software work tend to emphasize the abstract or "virtual" nature of this work. Cognitive work, as described by autonomist Marxists, emerges out of the replacement of work by machines, which had the effect of further pushing human labor toward abstract, cognitive tasks, including the manipulation of symbols and the evaluation and refinement of emotions and information. Yet, cognitive work is also concrete. In software work, the materialization of the digital is inaugurated by, for example, graphic interfaces that allow users to interact with the underlying structures of programming, the many artists and hackers who tweak existing software to reveal and take advantage of underlying quirks in the machine, or the many metaphors that software engineers use to describe what they do, such as architecture, triage, slave (to describe the process that receives commands from another), or virus.[4]

This chapter looks at the corollary to such machinic materialization for labor. Outside (and sometimes inside) the world of software work, perhaps no other figure best embodies cognitive labor than the Indian IT worker. Software work is made tangible through imagining Indian IT workers as naturally and culturally endowed with particular characteristics that make them good—often machinelike—new economy workers. Racialized images of the Indian coder also incorporate and produce the contradictory possibilities opened up by a cognitive economy. The images that follow—a handful of the many that circulated in Berlin's newspapers, online, and in magazines—are arranged thematically to unpack how Indian IT workers were imagined, how those figurations helped sketch out the meaning of digital technologies for an uneasy German populace, and what a cognitive economy might mean for the future of work in Europe.

Berlin, Electronic Capital of the Twenty-First Century

In Kreuzberg, the halls of the newly constructed Jewish Museum by Daniel Libeskind stood empty for years—no one could decide what to put in them. The political function of the museum was being fought out behind its façade. The museum opened empty for visitors to see the dark spaces, themselves a monument to architectural greatness and historical tragedy. Elsewhere, communist infrastructures were subjected to a similar treatment. The old parliament building was opened as a party and tourist site in the months before it was torn down; there was too much asbestos, according to popular rumors, to keep it hanging around or preserve it. But that did not stop promoters from selling tickets to see its gutted insides one last time. The Reichstag (parliament) building received a new glass cupola, while across the field the Bundeskanzleramt (Chancellery) was erected. The reunited government inhabited these new and rebuilt state structures under the aegis—symbolized by the Reichstag cupola—of transparency.[5] The city presented a layer of images past and future, images of possible utopias long gone and being torn down, images of a city with a new purpose and a new public image as a cosmopolitan European capital.

Berlin is a highly textual city, inhabited by a highly literate public and producing an informed urban citizen through the plaques, memorials, and informational kiosks that erupt from the topography of its streets.[6] Yet, beyond these official markers of state discourse, Berlin's streets are also graffitied and dirty, murals are tucked into the vaulted archways of building entrances, and layers of posters for political parties and dance parties hang on open wall space. These unofficial visual signs are a complement to official, governmental Berlin. It is in these images, found in the margins of sanctioned discourse, that a volatile discussion of the race of the Indian tech workers could be found. If in the nineteenth and twentieth centuries race was a marker of a stable antecedent; now it was also an unstable sign of future possibilities.

In Katherine Ewing's study of Muslim men in Berlin, she suggests that the stigmatization of Turkish Muslims is tied to the production of values that are taken to be universal but are actually culturally coded. In her striking discussion of headscarves and public nudity, she shows how moral purity in the German context is marked by the absence of coverings, while in the Muslim context it is marked by modest dress. In Germany, bareness signifies purity and justice, whereas covering up (especially in a headscarf) is associated with Muslim male patriarchy. In this milieu, Turkish Muslim men are stigmatized as unjust traditionalists, while German citizens emerge as ethical universalists.[7] Damani Partridge's work on Afro-German culture demonstrates how black bodies are figured as local forms of escape at the same time as, when they are part of debates on migration or asylum, they become unwanted threats to economy and society.[8]

As Ewing's and Partridge's work points out, migrant bodies are crucial to national imaginaries that define liberal German subjects in opposition to the assumed intolerance of male Muslim others and hypersexualized African bodies, respectively.[9] Here, I put the question of racializing migrants in Germany into a productive (and I believe necessary) conversation with the question of changing patterns of work and labor. In doing so, I reveal the way that race is used as a way to figure, and figure out, what a new knowledge-based economy has in store for German working subjects. Unlike the Turkish Muslim man, the Indian programmer sometimes figures as a welcome and comforting "other" who can uphold notions of tolerance and universalism. But the Indian IT worker also threatens German job security by being a machinelike presence that is ultimately unknowable.

In early twenty-first-century Germany, images functioned as guideposts to historical reconstructions; the task of Berlin's residents was to find their place and mark themselves out as valid citizens of the changed city. A new bourgeoisie crowded around the former centers of the East, flaunting baby carriages and asymmetrical haircuts; in the West, the old guard wondered what would happen to their liberal enclaves once the government was installed again. Already they could see the radical squats being sanitized. Among these new ways of life, images could be both a fetish and a symptom—both something spectacularly commoditized and something that might, if read correctly, hold the key to underlying dynamics of change.

This manner of treating images can be described as a culture of abduction, a process of understanding meanings that link consequences to both what came before and what might come to pass, to both hypothetical antecedents and future possible worlds.[10] The culture of visual abduction in Germany and especially in Berlin suggested to residents that images have a particular kind of power as signs of possible futurity. In a city that seemed to be always in motion, the practice of viewing images crystallized a particular moment in history and invested in these circulating images a portent of things to come.[11]

By reading off images the significance of the Indian IT worker for this future, German citizens make judgments about their own. In these abductions, the race of the IT worker is key precisely because race had become ambiguous in its own right, signaling both biological givens and extremely malleable proclivities. As befits practices of abduction, images racialize Indian IT workers by drawing on a repository of past images of India and then yoking these notions together to hazard guesses about the future.

The first image, "What the Indian computer specialists have over us!" (figure 1.1), demonstrates the multiple cuts made across the body of the Indian IT worker. The image shows a young couple with a gas station attendant. The man is wearing a turban, shirt, and tie; his wife is dressed in a cream-colored sari with green blouse. Behind them is a gas station; the attendant, dressed in a smart uniform with bow tie and cap, points out something on the paper the couple is reading, which is possibly a road map. This picture has been copied, manipulated, and redeployed, though without attribution. The uniforms, gas station architecture, hairstyles, and color saturation suggest it would date to the 1960s. The image tries to explain what would otherwise remain a mystery: How could India, stuck in the past even by the terms of the 1960s ambiance created by this picture, outpace Germany? Over the map that these three are studying, the maker of the new image has inserted a close-up box of the wife's forehead. Her *bindi* is the focus of this inset; over its red circle the word "reset" appears

Was indische Computer-Spezialisten uns voraus haben!

RESET

Figure 1.1. What Indian computer specialists have over us.

in large capital letters. The computer has merged completely with the Indian woman's body. The Indian programmer can "cheat," fixing a computer problem by resetting his wife, the machine.

The placement of the reset box obscures the original images; the gas station attendant begins to look like a son, the group pictured a family of three. The programmer's very family, his conjugal life, is the repository of "the dark arts" of computing. At the same time that the image satirizes the debates on letting Indian IT workers into Germany by wondering aloud what special skill they have, it also conjures frightening images of the brown migrant family in all its recognizable difference. Even while it mocks the impossibility that Indian computer specialists could really have a shortcut to technological greatness, it isolates difference—condensed in the bindi as target practice—and makes of the Indian programmer a body on which to concentrate anxiety, ambivalence, and opposition.

The image that asks, "What the Indian computer specialists have over us!" suggests a three-part relationship between an Indian programmer as model and threat and a European subject who must respond.[12] Either the Indian programmer models ways of laboring that European workers can emulate, or the Indian programmer threatens European ways of life through secret shortcuts that put Indians ahead in the globalization game. In the context of a newly energized Berlin, these images pointed toward uncertainty about and resistance to the future.

Good and Bad German Workers: Indian Programmers within the Matrix of German Migration Debates

The India that circulates in Germany today first emerged in the nineteenth century. In Germany, Hindu-Buddhist philosophy was incorporated into the tenets of German Romanticism, which posited both an underlying unity of mankind and nature and a unique place for German culture in Europe. Beginning perhaps with Karl Wilhelm Friedrich Schlegel and Johann Gottfried Herder, German philosophers, philologists, litterateurs, and theologians placed India on the side of spirituality, sexuality, decadence, escape, indolence, and excess and Western Europe on the side of capital, materialism, rationality, and order. Schlegel turned to India as part of an effort to define Germany within a larger European context and especially against what he understood as French materialism. His writings, along with those of the philologist Max Müller, consolidated a philosophical tradition that placed Sanskrit and Indian Vedic religion at a spiritual, original center to humanity and German language and culture close to it. Schlegel's contemporaries, such as Herder, similarly thought of India as the motherland of humankind.[13]

Later in the nineteenth century, India stood for spirituality even while its valuation varied. While Georg Wilhelm Friedrich Hegel, for instance, ranked India in the middle of a civilizational order that placed Europe on top and Africa on the bottom, Johann Wolfgang von Goethe both used Kālidāsa's *Shakuntala* (first German translation 1791) as a model for his own play *Faust* (1808) and described the East in his *West-östlicher Diwan* (1819) as a place to which one could "flee [from] current events" and enter "a timeless present."[14] Later philosophers such as Arthur Schopenhauer continued this line of thought by attempting to synthesize Christian, Hindu, and Buddhist philosophies in *The World as Will and Representation* (1844).[15]

India was also subject of the speculative politics of empire in Germany where, in the nineteenth century, leaders such as Otto von Bismarck pursued a "German Raj" to answer to and compete with Britain's claim to colonial supremacy.[16] In popular newspaper accounts about, for instance, the Indian Mutiny of 1857, German papers simultaneously denounced British rule in India and upheld the importance of colonial rule on the subcontinent, thereby imagining a better, German colonial relationship.[17] In the late nineteenth century, Karl Marx and Max Weber took up India as examples of anticapitalist places that would be brought into modern industrial capitalism through the colonial project (whether for good or for bad). For Marx, colonialism, despite causing, by his own admission, the death and starvation of thousands of cotton weavers, would nevertheless catapult India into modern industrial capitalist relations as a precursor to overthrowing both colonialism and capitalism.[18] In Weber's analyses, India was a foil for Weber's thesis on the origins of capitalism—as Hindu asceticism looked inward, according to Weber, Protestant asceticism looked toward the world, allowing it to foster capital-creating accumulation.[19] Finally, in the tracts of Nazi philosophers, the "Aryans" of India were mythologized as a superior race of Europeans who conquered Asia, only to be corrupted by its putative "native" populations; thus India served to caution against the corrupting powers of Oriental decadence.[20]

In these varied writings across the late nineteenth and twentieth centuries, India stood for an escape from the industrialized present into a nonmodern past. By the latter half of the twentieth century, the image of India that existed in Germany was of a country spiritually rich and economically poor, needing technoscientific development and offering release from the psychic burdens of urban, Western, and secular life.[21]

The spiritual India and material Germany dyad met a serious test of its validity in the German green card program. An India that trained expert software engineers who could take jobs in Germany cut against this earlier logic. The proper direction of give-and-take was reversed, and the Orient began to provide technical expertise to the Occident.

An uncertainty about what India was and Germany's relationship to India now unfolded in local, everyday contexts. One well-populated meeting I attended in 2003 of the *Deutsche-Indische Gesellschaft* (German-Indian Society), a local Berlin group dedicated to Indian culture and German-Indian relations, featured a speaker from Humboldt University lecturing on the recent disciplinary change from Indology to South Asian studies. The speaker explained that the new name included all countries in South Asia, not just India. The talk was followed by a healthy discussion in which one member welcomed these new scientific developments, whereas another lamented the loss of focus on what she thought at bottom remained the same across the countries of South Asia—Indian culture. She thought that the regional name "brought in politics unnecessarily." This debate was one of the ways in which the legacy of German Orientalism precipitated out in everyday life in the early twenty-first century. It seemed to some participants, perhaps, that the very thing that was interesting about India—its unchanging otherworldliness—was coming undone.

Germany joined the United States in creating a temporary visa for IT workers that was aimed at India and other sources of engineering talent, such as China, Brazil, and Russia. The history of Indian engineering talent is told in greater detail in chapter 5. Here it is important to note that while the Indian IT professional seems in popular press accounts to have emerged suddenly on the world stage, it is more accurate to say that deep reservoirs of engineering talent were cultivated in India beginning in the 1950s and that engineers and other professionals had been emigrating from India to Europe and the United States for at least as long. The real innovation in Indian IT services emerged when these transnational engineers were able to create the material infrastructures that would link programming operations in India to businesses in the United States. These infrastructures included satellite and other mass communications devices that allow lines between India and Europe and the United States to be set up with minimal interference and at cost. And they also included networks of Indian experts who could link business needs in the United States and Europe to pools of engineering graduates in India.[22] In contrast to this historically nuanced story, the persuasive affect of suddenness could mobilize the reform and self-management of nonmigrant European and American populations.

The German green card as temporary work visa has its roots in the guest worker (*Gastarbeiter*) programs of the postwar West German economy. The West German *Gastarbeiter* program began in 1955 as an element of the booming postwar economy called the *Wirtschaftswunder* (economic miracle). Through a series of agreements between West Germany and Turkey, Yugoslavia, Italy, Portugal, and Greece, immigrants were allowed to take jobs on temporary work visas. Most of the jobs available were on construction sites and in factories, and most of the guest workers came from Turkey. The guest worker program was designed for laborers to enter Germany for a number of years and then return to their country of origin, but the program gained notoriety as there were no provisions in the law to provide language training or a path to citizenship for migrants or their families. The guest worker program was stopped in 1973 as a result of its mounting unpopularity for allowing "too many" immigrants into the country.[23] Turkish immigrants, statistically making up about 9 percent of the country's population, were seen as a social and economic problem in most large German cities, often criticized for failing to assimilate, on the one hand, and for failing to return home, on the other.

The guest worker program was inaugurated in a postwar Germany with strict divides between citizens and outsiders. German citizenship law lacks provisions for birthright citizenship (jus soli) and was instead based on the principle of citizenship by shared blood (jus sanguinis).[24] Recent changes to the immigration law created an opportunity for those born in Germany after 2000 to choose German citizenship at majority, providing a narrow path toward citizenship by birthplace. As a result, Germany remains relatively closed to outsiders, providing few legal or social incentives for migrants either to formally become citizens or to see themselves as part of the German nation. *Ausländer* (foreigners) are tolerated within the *Bundesrepublik* but not assimilated; the theoretical possibility always exists that they may be returned home.[25]

The image of the Indian programmer is played out in many ways against the history of the Turkish guest worker. While Turkish guest workers are conceived of as Muslim threats within Europe, the Indian workers, according to these pictures, appear as Sikh or Hindu. Like the guest worker program, the German green card offered no pathway to permanent residency or citizenship. Stopped in 2006, it functioned as a temporary measure to fill a labor shortage. Again according to popular perception, while Turkish workers are uneducated and blue collar, the Indian worker is technologically educated and white collar, and while the Turkish immigrant threatens the stability of German society, the Indian worker brings desirable clothing, food, and entertainments. And yet, the history of the temporary-permanent Turkish guest worker haunts the idea of a temporary, nonthreatening Indian worker.[26] The Indian programmer, as "new guest worker" in Germany, cannot be easily accommodated within an existing discourse of German nationalism that aligns whiteness, Germanness, and mental labor, on one side, and non-whiteness, foreignness, and manual labor, on the other. This foreign body appears to be ushering in a new era in which economic advantage no longer aligns with European identity and in which the borders of Europe are necessarily porous to global capital and the migrants who come with it. Against these shifting figurations of migration, foreignness, and race, the image of the Indian programmer serves as both a promise of global cosmopolitanism and a warning sign of new, less prosperous European worlds that may be in the offing.

The dominant frame for the integration of Indian migrants into everyday life was rather different in East Germany, where agreements between Soviet-aligned and nonaligned countries meant that students from the third world came to the German Democratic Republic to study and apprentice at trade. They were housed in separate dormitories, and like the West German *Gastarbeiter*, they were expected to return home when they finished their education. According to this model, the stronger and more economically developed socialist states would educate and uplift those that lagged behind. These students were to transmit East German technical and scientific knowledge to institutions at home. Students were enthusiastically welcomed into the country in the 1950s, and their arrivals were highly publicized as evidence of cooperation among noncapitalist countries. East German citizens had for the most part little contact with foreign students, who, after the collapse of the East German government in 1998, they were expected to depart for home. After the fall of the Berlin Wall, these students were seen as symbols of the old Soviet bureaucracy and the special privileges afforded the select few.

Before the fall of the Berlin Wall, most Indians who came to both East and West Germany were students earning technical degrees or doctorates in fields such as engineering or math. They sometimes settled permanently in Germany and took German spouses, and they were almost always men.[27] Following a trend evident in the United States, the USSR, and England, experts from Germany traveled to India to advise local scientists and guide development projects. Among other things, the West German government took an active role in developing the Indian Institute of Technology (IIT) Madras, helping to design coursework and placing a greater emphasis on combining theoretical and practical training than at other technology learning centers.[28]

During the 1990s, a spate of neo-Nazi violence against foreigners in the former East Germany revealed the problems of German reunification. After reunification in 1990, the German government decided to equally distribute asylum seekers in dormitories across the country. Many asylum seekers waiting to have their cases heard were sent to small East German towns where they were a visible and unwanted presence. According to the rules of asylum, they were not allowed to hold jobs or move into dwellings of their own. They became targets of vicious attacks; in one case, an asylum seeker's dormitory was burned down while local police did nothing to intervene.[29]

Right-wing violence in East Germany was often attributed to the lack of exposure to foreigners under communism and to East German totalitarianism, which did not work to "de-Nazify" its citizens. This argument suggested that once communist rule was lifted, long-simmering racial hatred reemerged. As East Germany continued to lag behind West Germany economically even decades after reunification, foreigners were seen as an unfair economic burden for the Eastern states and as an obvious sign of the collapse of an unwanted but familiar order. This primordialist argument on racism in Eastern Europe does not adequately capture historical change or the unfolding story of race, migration, and economy told here. Instead, while East German framings of India through the idiom of shared socialist-developmental work practices is largely erased from the scene of migration politics in Germany today, East Germans are often judged—and found wanting—in terms of their inability to adapt to a logic of flexible global capital.

Within this framing, the Indian programmer circulates not only as a way of discerning between proper German and non-German subjects but also as a means to understand and question the legitimate class positions of German workers. Figures 1.2 and 1.3 contrast manual and white-collar

Figure 1.2. Of course it looks strange, but he has the Green Card.

workers in terms of the way they might respond to an Indian coder. In figure 1.2, an Internet image that I found in the humor section of an Indian-
German website (www.theinder.net), two office managers, identifiable by
their suits and glasses, their authoritative stances and white skin, stand
over a programmer figured as an ascetic yogi. Naked from the waist up,
thin, and turbaned, the Indian yogi-worker sits on a bed of nails. The yogi
does not need to touch a keyboard but rather charms the mouse, which
levitates for him. He is in such deep concentration that he does not appear to be aware of the men in suits observing him. They are astounded
by his magic. He is like a snake charmer of computers, a fakir. Indeed, the
two reactions of his bosses, one perhaps angry, the other perhaps cynical,
play on the dual meaning of yogi and fakir, a highly refined practitioner
and a trickster. Is he a more highly evolved form of abstract thinker? Can
the German managers simply guide his work without having to concern
themselves with how he is doing it? Can they manage his innate talents
rather than control and discipline them? Or, is it possible that he is a faker

Figure 1.3. You look forward to the experts from India, I'll look forward to the widow burnings.

(fakir), conning through some trick they have yet to discern? The Indian programmer has received government sanction through his green card; his presence is a sign of legitimate enterprise. At the same time, a mystified and mysterious work practice accompanies and undermines this legitimacy, signaled by the ascetic and exotic appearance of the Indian worker.

Figure 1.3 is from the *Frankfurter Allgemeine Zeitung* (FAZ), a daily national newspaper that leans conservative-centrist. The cartoonists, Achim Greser and Heribert Lenz, are well-known political satirists who draw regularly for FAZ, the satirical magazine *Titanic*, and the news magazine *Stern*.[30] This cartoon sits on page 2 next to an editorial about the green card legislation that estimates that Germany needs around 12,000 IT workers to meet current demand and then describes how politicians from Bavaria, Berlin, and elsewhere have reacted to the proposal. A businessman stands with his arms folded as the basement of his house fills up with water. A plumber dressed in a plaid shirt and overalls stands wrench in hand while he gives his own political commentary. Adding a working-class voice to the arguments of politicians and businessmen, the plumber contrasts the image of Indians as computer experts with Indians as committers of sati, or widow-burners. The businessman's reaction is anger, but why? Because the plumber is a truth teller who can do what the businessman is no longer capable of, from fixing his own leaks to recognizing his own mistakes? Or because the plumber as a member of the working class is intractable, sticking to old economy ways and old ways of thinking, refusing to embrace a new Germany where Indian professionals are a sign of the coming prosperity? The racialization of the Indian workers by means of reference to widow-burning plays out German national ambivalence around a future that will be increasingly dominated by cognitive labor and transnational corporate classes.[31]

As theorists of semiocapital note, the turn to cognitive labor implies the incorporation of communicative potential into the production of surplus value, making all traits and characteristics, including "the heritable characteristics of the lineage," potentially valuable.[32] The images betray foreboding about the way knowledge economies threaten to further draw apart middle-class managers from European working classes. The Indian workers might split open the very idea of national unity without being able to resolve for certain who, the plumber or the businessman, will end up on the right side of history.

Malleability at the Heart of Race

The Indian IT worker's body incorporates multiple possibilities of future subjectivity and, in doing so, becomes a body through which a self-conducting European subject can be inaugurated.[33] When taken as legible sign of embodied traits, race sits at the intersection of the cultivation of qualities and their inheritance. The deployment of race as a way to understand digital economies and race's refashioning of genomics both rely on and deny the salience of race as a fixed biological category.

New racial formations have emerged over the last three decades at the intersection of biotechnologies and contemporary capitalisms. Race is no longer conceived of, if it ever was, as any one thing. It has moved from marking normal and abnormal genetic populations to describing the genetic risks inhering in individuals, who normatively should be responsible for managing such risks.[34] Similarly, cultural products and practices can now be marketed as inseparable from bodies—as a kind of speculative monopoly capitalism that is both heritable and changeable.[35] To consider one's genetic composition and its attendant risks and benefits

Gewalt gegen die Rechner — so etwas ist dem indischen Fachkraft fremd. Der abgestürzte Computer wird im Hungerstreik bezwungen.

Figure 1.4. Violence against the machine—such things are unknown to the Indian workforce.

is to act with the knowledge of probable outcomes.[36] Perhaps, the politics of colonial difference that Frantz Fanon emphasized have now been folded into a discourse of manageable probabilities where race "is simultaneously present and absent . . . rendered obsolete by the new forms of genetic knowledge, and . . . simultaneously reinvigorated" by practices that tie together social reproduction with recognizable and marked biological characteristics.[37]

In figure 1.4, the programmer is Gandhi, and he sits on the floor and wills the machine into submission with a hunger strike. The German uses violence against the machine; the Indian, passive resistance. The German is ham-fisted and fleshy, the Indian emaciated and bespectacled. Perhaps the German is again the figure of a working-class man who has failed to adapt to the demands of cognitive labor. He is angry and uses violence against an old and bulky computer, whereas the Indian is at one with his new and efficient flat screen. For the German, the computer is difficult, unmanageable; it needs to be charmed. For the Indian programmer, the computer is commanded through nonviolent means.

Such images begin to shift the frame in which race is deployed. As the computer is a mysterious object not easily understood, so the computer's operator is similarly mysterious. While these figures call into question the true identity of Indian programmers, they also call into question the capabilities of the normative body of white German male workers. In figuring the debates on work and migration in these terms, the images invest in the Indian IT body the most fundamental changes in the constitution of European political economies—restructuring the welfare state, shifting risk onto individual subjects, and reimagining capital accumulation as taking place through transnational transactions facilitated by the nation-state. Deployed in this way, race does not divide embodied from disembodied subjects, third from first worlds, or traditional from immaterial labor.[38] While characteristics desired in new economies may inhere in particular bodies, it is not clear that those characteristics cannot be acquired. Can the ham-fisted German become more like the Gandhi-Indian? Would he want to?

The Difference That Seduces

The question of new migrant labor turns in the next set of images toward a vision of managing foreignness through commodity discipline. According to the way figures 1.5, 1.6, and 1.7 frame Indian IT workers, the programmer can also be an enhancer of middle-class pleasure.[39] The programmer is a site of libidinal fantasy. The programmer is known by the commodities for which he stands, and the threat of the Indian programmer to German ways of life is neutralized through the development of desire. He might fit, according to this model, into a commodification of race that makes the dark body a source of self-development for white subjects through proximate desire.[40] In these pictures, Germany is represented as a young blonde woman, ready to taste the delights India has to offer. The race of Germany as white is clear, and the possibility that there may be dark-skinned Germans utterly occluded. At the same time, the German man or woman can undergo a "conversion experience" where Indian bodies simultaneously offer up absolution from a racist Nazi past and relief both from the racial inequality of modern-day Germany and from the purported one-sided materialism of contemporary white German culture.[41]

In these images, the Indian body is not only commoditized but also extended through commodities. Perhaps, the pictures intimate, German bodies can become more like Indian bodies through consuming their products: lassi, a smooth Indian yogurt drink that rides with transgressive sexual pleasure on the upper lip of the drinking German woman; saris, which "seduce with one piece of fabric"; talcum powder, which "is better

Leben
DIE ZEIT No. 15 6.April 2000

Trinkt Lassi!

Liebt euren Computer! Habt guten Sex! Schiebt eine ruhige Kugel!
sowie zehn weitere Dinge, die wir von den Indern lernen können
Seite 6

Figure 1.5. Drinking Lassi!

than any perfumed deodorant stick that comes from a factory"; or meditation balls that demonstrate "how through doing nothing one can achieve
everything."

These associations need to be read in a lineage of Oriental scholarship
in German-speaking countries, which I outlined briefly above—India as
spiritual and historical crucible of human thought, to which Germany bears
resemblance over and against the materialist West; sensual and decadent

Figure 1.6. Drive the men crazy with a piece of cloth.

India as a cautionary tale of civilizational decline; India in need of paternalistic guidance but not from the incompetent British; India as producing initial universal truths that will come to fruition in a modern, Christian nation-state.[42] In the current moment, the injunction to become Indian through consuming like an Indian points toward the way exotic India circulates as a positive trope of experience and desire. Indian programmers offer up to German subjects realms of desire outside the working day. This India promises the German subject that in exchange for letting in a few more immigrants and letting them have good jobs, they will be given (carnal) knowledge of the secrets of the East. This narrative inaugurates a politics of cultural mimicry, whereby Germans can learn from Indians how to be successful in a changed marketplace. More may be demanded of the German subject than just to enjoy "the difference that seduces."[43] The German subject may also be called on to transform herself in emulation of the Indian programmer.

Figure 1.7. Learn programming and ten other things we can learn from the Indians.

Becoming Indian

The penultimate image accompanies an article on education for the future (figure 1.8). The image shows a person changing from white to brown. The title of the article asks, "Wie werde ich Inder?" (How do I become Indian?). "Further education in information technology can evidently further help," reads the byline. It goes on to assure the reader that it is not about being Indian or not Indian but about having software know-how or no software know-how. The author admits that "since the Green Card Debate and Jürgen Rüttgers idiocy, 'children instead of Indians,' India has become a synonym for a kind of Silicon Valley." The article details how a person can get an education in information technology and multimedia and suggests skipping the canon and pursuing education according to "flexible and individualized concepts." All these tips and more that the article cannot cover,

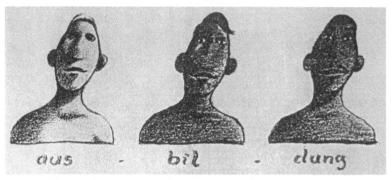

aus - bil - dung

Figure 1.8. "Ed-u-ca-tion"

writes the author, provide further education in Berlin to being an Indian (*bildet in Berlin zum Inder weiter*).

The image in figure 1.8 and the article frame race as a nonissue at the same time as they leave completely unquestioned the tie between Indians and "computer know-how." Naturalizing the link between India and coding expertise at the same time suggests that know-how can be learned. A racial imaginary becomes subject to management. The key passage, it seems to me, is the rhetorical shift from capacity as embedded in race to capacity as trainable, but only if subjects will move from standard disciplines to flexible and individualized reeducation. In the picture accompanying the article, the figure literally turns from white to brown as a result of this training. Race-based arguments become the frame and the lever to shift bodies toward taking charge of and managing their own reeducation. The article follows such a body who abandoned the traditional disciplines of literature and a career in journalism to become a programmer. The author, expecting to hear a critique from the former journalist, finds she has become a convert. Computing is her new love.

The final image (figure 1.9) seems to undercut this cheery message of getting the training right. A man in the background is on the phone to his boss. He has been put in charge of the next generation of new economy techno-Germans. He is dressed in a smock like the foreman of a factory might be, and he has tried everything. The next-generation baby is already working a monitor and keyboard from his pram, his toys have screens in their bellies, and sometimes the toy's entire head has been replaced by a computer screen. His high chair has a screen attached. The toys and

Figure 1.9. We're doing everything. Nevertheless, we need the Indians, boss!

the boy look sad, bug-eyed, and already overworked. Despite doing everything, says the manager, "we need the Indians!" Comparing the beleaguered German baby to the beatific Indian programmer as yogi or to the commodity-objects that signal an Indian's calm and composure in the face of overwork, this final image reinforces the idea that the work that techno-economies demand is something that is more suited to Indian bodies than to European ones. The costs of this type of thinking for migrant high-tech workers come to rest on the ground of racializing arguments that are continually reiterated throughout this archive.

Attending to Race as a Means of Correct Training

We were walking up the stairs to the apartment Rajeshwari and Meenakshi share. We pushed the solid, round black plastic button at the bottom of the stairs to turn on the hallway lights that would stay on just long enough for us to reach the third floor. As we passed the landing to the first-floor apartments, sounds of loud, drunken laughter and of music came through the door on the right-hand side. Rajeshwari and I exchanged glances, the noise unusual in the otherwise still hallway. "Turkey-people," she said, holding her nose, "they smell." I was shocked at her assessment; I had never heard her say anything like this before. "Did somebody tell you that?" I asked. Rajeshwari responded, "But they are easygoing. They do not mind when we have parties, even if they go on 'til late."

Racialized images consolidate types of people with habits, attitudes, proclivities, essences that are given and ascribed as if from nature. The irreality of satirical images helps deny their work of racialization behind their overt mimicry. The work they do is in part made possible by the deniability of the power of the image itself. In the images discussed here, the programmer is the object of both carnal desire and paranoia.[44] In the first story of this chapter, Marika pointed out the inability of older residents of the city to understand the new Berlin. She explained their visual overload when faced with a new order that no longer fits with the order they knew. I suggest that in this new Berlin, images, especially those of transitory migrants such as Indian IT workers, were also signs of a destabilized relationship between labor and race, where racial traits were signs of something as yet undetermined and unfolding. My conversation with Rajeshwari confirms that racialized discourses in such a milieu are not fixed. They move outside the ambit of the office and the newspaper and inform a reading of ethnic proclivity that can "slot" groups in terms of their desirable and undesirable characteristics. As Rajeshwari's statement makes clear, these uses of race draw on existing stereotypes (about meat-eating Muslims; Rajeshwari is a strict vegetarian), even as they make room for reassessments that spin the content of a racial imaginary in new directions.

As the images discussed here try to emplot the Indian body in a politics of multicultural enjoyment, the particular fantasy of acceptable and unacceptable others always seems to be undercut. Working, professional high-tech bodies offer up a plotline that decenters a German national allegory precisely because it is linked in an ancillary fashion to emerging modes of cognitive labor—and to class differences. These "new economies" threaten to undo national imaginaries because they point out differences between a middle-class politics of enjoyment of the other and a working-class politics of resistance to being modeled on the other.

The fantasy of the Indian programmer is not backward looking, although it sweeps a collection of Orientalist stereotypes before it. The goal of this fantasy is to figure out, in the mode of abduction, what the future holds. In this new age of commodity-image, ethnicity itself takes on the properties of race reconceived as biologically inherited and malleable, usable and acquirable. When put into conversation with the politics of migration and global capitalism, this idea of traits as fixed and transferable feeds into the fantasy of control of unwanted individuals (keeping them in their place), the fear of the spread of those unwanted into the positions previously held by the West, and the commodification of ethnicity as a kind of capital with specific qualities that can be acquired through contact with an ethnic other. The images incline toward a fantasy of managing difference and race by binding them clearly to limited sites of work and to particular technologies.

Caricatures and cartoon images leave undecided—and therefore open for further reflection and elaboration—the ultimate significance of such "cyborg" bodies as the Indian programmer for the European working subject.[45] Studying mass-mediated cartoon images ethnographically—that is, by treating them as condensed signs of anxiety and expectation—uncovers a changing and debated sense of race in context and illuminates how the racial imaginary of the office becomes a site through which to approach the problem of neoliberal work.[46] The capacity of images to borrow the visual grammar of that which they claim to represent can mask their indexical power, their ability to make connections by pointing to other kinds of signs themselves laden with meaning.[47] In this sense, not only referential but also temporally and socially expansive associations and meanings attach to the image of the Indian IT worker.

The figure of the Indian IT worker is sutured to two possible futures for the German nation, one in which German workers acquire the characteristics of programmers and ensure the financial security of the nation, and the other in which these characteristics are not acquirable and the Indian worker becomes the future that the German worker cannot grasp. This fantasy of the Indian programmer is at once determining and constructed, race as embodied in working bodies is both a sign of future possibility and future horror for European populations caught between old ways of working and the demands of flexible work. For Indian programmers who take jobs as contingent workers in IT economies, bearing up within this fantasy will mean navigating between being a model and a pariah and evaluating their chances, not only economically but also politically and culturally, in the countries in which they work.

Emerging meanings of race, though often contradictory, point toward a future "portend[ing] a metaphysics of race in which race and technology are linked not to settle human limits but instead to explore human thresholds."[48] Even as race is used to consolidate the flexible subject, it can also be deployed in a way that differentiates between working-class and white-collar bodies, bodies that manage and those that are managed, and bodies with value in the new economy and those, like the Turkish guest workers who preceded the Indian programmers, whose history of race and labor has been transformed into a story of unwanted populations and uncivilized practices. Visibly raced bodies, such as those of Indian IT workers, become a screen on which to project and adjudicate a world in which all bodies might be reconceived as malleable.

TWO

THE POSTRACIAL OFFICE

On a Wednesday morning in June 2002, I was scheduled to meet Jan, a project manager at Globus. I entered the lobby of the glass and steel tower flanking Potsdamer Platz that housed Globus's offices together with two Hyderabadi programmers I knew. The programmers flashed their ID cards while I signed in and showed my passport to the security desk. We took the stairs up to the fourth floor, they hurried to their workstations, and I waited to meet Jan on a low, curved bench upholstered in cranberry-colored velvet. A svelte fortyish secretary in a checkered suit sat behind a blond wood desk, whose organic curves mimicked the shape of the bench. She busily answered the first phone calls of the morning; behind her the company logo—a globe orbited by a shooting star—was painted on the wall in its signature cranberry and gray. As I waited in the lobby, a spot of powder blue caught my eye high up on the wall. In the top left corner above the secretary's desk was a stick-on decal of the head and shoulders of Venkateshwar, the Hindu god easily recognizable by his golden crown and the shield he wears before his eyes to prevent us from being blinded by the power of his gaze. As I pondered how Venkateshwar could have gotten way up there, Jan came forward to greet me. Jan is in his midfifties with a thick shock of black hair, graying at the temples and combed neatly to the side, and a generous paunch spilling over his belted dress pants. I have been introduced to Jan by Adi, who worked on his team before trying to start his own company. Adi had gotten a master of science degree in computer science at Berlin's Technical University and had coded for Jan for over four years before branching out on his own. He had described Jan to me as a generous and friendly person, and I found Jan easygoing and gregarious. As I stood to greet him, I gestured toward the figure of Venkateshwar on the wall above. He looked briefly up and shrugged, but the secretary, watching closely, nervously bustled out from behind her desk to tell him that she has no idea who put it there, suggesting she was not responsible for it. Jan barely seemed to hear her and just smiled, ushering us toward the hallway to his office.

Jan was not bothered by Venkateshwar hovering in the entranceway yet the deity gave the administrative assistant pause. She was eager to distance herself from this potential matter-out-of-place in front of her superior. Taken together, the administrator's and the manager's reactions encapsulate two different attitudes toward Indians in German offices. The administrator is the face of the company to clients and visitors. She sits in the most designed part of the office, beneath the official logo. Although I did not have a chance to interview her (a sign, I think, of how I was slotted into the office as a researcher meant to interact with other middle-class cognitive workers), the administrator's concern may be read in terms of her position in the office. Though well compensated, her nontech, administrative role and her position at the front desk clearly indicate her comparatively unsophisticated educational background and working-class status.[1] She is unsure of whether she will be made responsible for a potentially unofficial, and perhaps damaging, representation of Globus to clients. Such moments point to class hierarchies in the office. Jan appears to have a more cavalier attitude toward such displays. As I explore below, he thinks of Indians in the office as personally interesting and potentially profitable. Like the cartoon of the plumber and the businessman discussed in chapter 1 (fig. 1.3), this interaction plays out between the two dominant ways that race will figure in the office—as potential threat and as possible resource.

The lobby scene juxtaposes Globus's corporate logo, a globe with a shooting star navigating its equator, with the decal of Venkateshwar, whose gaze is so powerful that if he looked directly at the world, he would scorch it. Globus is a 16,000-person software services company that supports the travel and tourism industry. Globus's tagline, "Solutions That Move You," evokes a world of seamless transitions from one locality to the next. The software that it provides, like the star that travels around the globe, will link the transnational parts of a business with speed and acumen. Venkateshwar's purview is larger still. Venkateshwar's four hands hold a conch and a golden discus, and he then extends his hands downward in a gesture of protection and surrender. He is the main deity of Tirupati, a vast and wealthy temple in South India estimated to receive 30–40 million visitors per year. How do these two emblems come together within a corporate idea of work and of personhood? What ways of figuring the Indian IT worker emerge and are elaborated on in the space between Venkateshwar above and Globus in the middle atmosphere, above the earth but below the divine? While both Venkateshwar and Globus symbolize success and prosperity, inconsistencies in the way race moves through global spaces emerge when they are brought together in the office lobby.

Analyzing IT economies from outside and as an example of an overall direction in the changing nature of work, theorists of cognitive labor posit a universal, unmarked subject of new economy work—a cognitariat who manipulates signs and symbols through a computer screen. I show in this book that this view fails to capture how such work is embodied. The point is not simply to fill a gap in scholarship by adding in race after the fact but to follow the multiple ways that cognitive work is made real through its embodiment. As Wendy Chun suggests, information "is always embodied, whether in a machine or an animal. To make information appear disembodied requires a lot of work."[2] As the argument of this book continues in this chapter, we will see how racializations are used to create divisions of labor in the office that seem natural—as if emerging from characteristics of the workers themselves. That is, the racialization of IT work is one way that information is made to seem naturally produced without the interference, or messiness, of disciplining bodies. At the same time, and as I argue in later chapters, this materialization of work can free Indian programmers both to pursue middle-class success marked by access to consumer goods, satisfying work, and leisure time and to resist the colonization of life by work.

Race in the Cognitive Economy

In the carpeted hallways of coding economies, discussions of life outside work are as important to managers as technical discussions of process; at the end of the day, cognitive workers often bring work home from the office, and the personality of the worker is parsed by a worker herself and by managers for meaningful and monetizable ideas.[3] Boundaries between work and leisure are blurred, as a supervisor might come to work in jeans and the office Christmas party takes place at a local bar. At Globus, the rooms are named for prominent German inventors—the Diesel Room, the Zuse Room (after Konrad Zuse, an early computer pioneer), and so on; the transparent walls between conference rooms invite communication. How might the knowledge that circulates around the difference of Indian workers fit into this model of work that fosters communication as a source of immaterial commodities? How might such knowledge also be used to organize workers hierarchically in terms of perceived racial characteristics?

At its core, cognitive labor describes a shift in the locus of production from the production of things to the circulation of ideas and symbols. According to this argument, surplus value is now produced through symbolic systems—such as financial derivatives—that sit atop other financial products. The exchange of these, and other similar abstract (or immaterial) goods, such as Internet page views, online services, and new software platforms, drives global revenue.[4] Following this description of a new economy, it stands to reason that the relationship of the worker to what she produces has also changed. The new economy worker produces ideas, concepts, and abstract products rather than tangible things.[5] For theorists of cognitive labor, the importance of this shift is that even while flexible economies promise an end to alienation, alienation has intensified. That is, since the product of work is no longer made concrete in an object that is separate from the person producing it, the worker is no longer alienated (in the Hegelian and Marxian sense) from the product of work. But, rather than implying a more fulfilling relationship to labor, as one reading of Marx's theory of alienation would predict, cognitive labor entails turning the cognitive capacities of the worker into commodities: "The mobility of the product was made possible by the assembly-line workers who had to remain motionless in space and time. Info-workers, instead, constantly move all along the length, breadth and depth of cyberspace. They move to find signs, to elaborate experience, or simply to follow the paths of their existence. *But at every moment and place they are reachable and can be called back to perform a productive function that will be reinserted into the global cycle of production* [italics mine]."[6]

In other words, cognitive labor at once promises uniting what was once torn asunder—the qualities of the worker and the work itself—and betrays that promise by instead treating the worker's qualities as themselves alienable commodities. Cognitive labor demands a worker who is always plugged into a network, ready to produce packets of communicated meaning that can be taken up and circulated further in the production of value. In this milieu, knowledge should proliferate by virtue of its links to future earnings potential. Similarly, for management, knowing the internal dispositions of workers is important, not to mold workers into interchangeable factory bodies but to harness their characteristics within a horizon of futurity. As I will argue below, many managers consider the outward habits and appearance of cognitive workers as signs telegraphing their dispositions. As part of what Junaid Rana calls a transnational "migration industry,"[7] race in a cognitive economy becomes a condensed sign of potentials, both acknowledged and disavowed.

Many managers I worked with in Germany expressed surprise and even disappointment that programmers from India did not meet their expectations. Indian workers were unyielding, suggested one in passing; "their mind-set was hierarchical." Another said over lunch that it was necessary for Indian workers to "pay respect to those above them while Westerners were used to working in an open environment where ideas were expressed freely." "I hear," said one Australian programmer in a recorded interview, "that India produces more engineers per year than the rest of the world," and then he went on to be amazed that their quality was so poor. In defense of migrant programmers, another manager of a firm reminded me, "It is only when workers cannot be found for these jobs that we try to find Indian programmers."

These snippets of ongoing conversations about Indian programmers suggest that race functions on multiple registers: as a means of bringing the world outside the office inside its walls as an expression of the personalities of the workers (what we might call "workplace humanism"); as a means of dividing labor in the office according to the perceived abilities of foreign and European or American workers (what we might call a "racialized division of IT labor"); and as a way to allow new impulses into the office that might generate new leads and new creative avenues for producing surpluses (what we might call "racialization as creative content"). Repeated moments of interaction where the strangeness of Indian workers is elicited and commented on begin to make these discourses seem like industry common sense. They devalue Indian coding as "reproductive" rather than productive labor.[8]

In a cognitive economy, race as a sign of human particularity is valued as a repository of human potential even while its salience as a factor in evaluating work and dividing labor is denied, making the office a postra-cial work environment. In the following sections I explore the varieties of racialization that cohere around the Indian IT worker. I use the term *race* to indicate when a particular kind of question is raised: namely, is being good at programming (or other skills, such as managing people) fixed in certain kinds of bodies? I follow the different ways that this question is answered, which in their particularities frequently evoke explanations of culture and education. These terms are often ways of talking about how difference adheres in bodies, through training and socialization, in post-racial environments.

Postracial discourses construe race as constructed and no longer important—a relic of past eras of slavery, segregation, and legal discrim-ination.[9] They position the current period as a time after race, at the same time as they allow race to continue to determine conditions of ac-cess and inclusion to public goods by valuing "unmarked" success. While most studies of the postrace phenomenon place its emergence squarely after the election of Barack Obama and in the United States,[10] its genealogy in Germany is longer and passes through the history of liberal citizenship after the end of the Third Reich. In Germany today, there are at least three vectors through which German identity passes: the negation of the Nazi past, a rejection of East German history as a history of totalitarianism or the rejection of West German history as a history of capitalist class soci-ety, and the use of "the non-German Other to construct notions of the Self."[11] German postracial discourses place racism squarely "in the Nazi anti-Semitic past and in the violent neo-Nazi present, but not [in] racism's institutionalized everyday persistence," as Damani Partridge argues.[12] Pos-tracial thinking in Germany is informed by the use of race in the creation of European identities that attributes both actually existing racisms to non-liberal (often East German) publics and essential otherness to nonwhite immigrant populations.[13]

In IT workplaces, Indian "cultural differences"—a coded language through which to talk of race in postracial offices—is often used as an analytic to evaluate worker skill and as a humanistic sentiment indicating a *weltoffen* liberalism (a liberalism open to the world) as a type of expert knowledge that contributes to workplace creativity. The multiple ways that race signi-fies in the office are made by the official, postracial suppression of race's continued salience. Culture talk can proliferate freely because it becomes an indicator of the importance of communication to office work. By writing of offices in Germany as postracial, I intend to broaden this category to include an expansive sense of what race might mean. Rather than describe postracial discourses as a mask that hides the truth of racism, I explore the proliferation of race—the meanings and associations between people, their backgrounds, and the work they do that are mediated by race. These multiple senses of what race means suggests that in the office, the race of Indian coders is used to reflect on knowledge work more generally, as each idea of the Indian IT worker comes with a different set of associations, from "machinelike" to "mystical."

The question "Do work skills inhere in bodies?" is often answered by means of linking racialized bodies to nonhuman things, such as machines.[14] Pointing out interactions between humans and machines has been useful in moving beyond both a human-centered idea of agency and technological determinism. Here, I build on this approach pioneered by Donna Haraway, Bruno Latour, and others to tease out how racializations occur when programmers and programming technologies meet.[15] Following the movement of race across multiple actors, opinions, and demands reveals how racializing Indian IT workers also serves to evaluate the opportunities, difficulties, and demands placed on working subjects in global cognitive economies. Tracing the links between Indian coders and computers is a way to understand human-nonhuman interactions as social processes that draw out potential ways of forming matter and social relationships simultaneously. Various couplings of Indian bodies and computers happen at boundaries and thresholds, where the possible relationship between coding technologies and worker subjectivity is constituted.[16] In the following sections, I first describe how Indian workers create a *weltoffen* workplace. Then, I show how they are racialized in office divisions of labor through comparison with other migrants and with machines. Finally, I turn to how the office mines Indian programmers for the creative content they might provide in the workplace, even while Indian programmers try to discern how to treat these requests for spiritual knowledge in ways that will increase their job security.

Workplace Humanism: The Indian Programmer as Valuable Resource

"I appreciate the cultural things that Indian programmers can introduce me to," said Jan. "They are a valuable resource." We were having a lunch of falafel, hummus, and stuffed grape leaves at a Lebanese restaurant around the corner from the office. I had spent the morning shadowing him as he sat in meetings and had an all-hands session with his team. Project management at Globus was Jan's second career. He had been a successful real estate agent and made a significant amount of money in speculating on the neighborhoods of East Berlin that became trendy after the fall of the Wall. He used his money to fund a small business services start-up, which closed after a heady year. He was then able to leverage his experience to be hired into Globus. Globus specialized in integrating software platforms for the travel and transportation industries, though its products were also used to manage international conventions and to coordinate complicated international shipping operations. The company had smaller satellite offices in New York, Singapore, and Bangalore. Jan had hired two engineers from India for his team and also sent his colleagues to India to meet with people there. He hoped to increase his outsourcing presence in India. Jan felt that he knew quite a bit about India from employees. He pointed out that Indian engineers can talk to the people in India in their own language and make everything work faster. They also provided valuable information on the Indian mind-set and the Indian market, which he glossed as the *etwas anderes* (something different) that he really enjoyed talking to them about. Jan was glad he hired programmers from India, not just because of their coding skills but also because they brought exposure to a different way of life.

According to programmers who coded on his team, Jan was fond of popping into their work area, asking such things as, "Why do Indians worship monkeys?" "What is the significance of 'red' in Indian culture?" and "What does the red dot on the forehead of Indian women mean?" The queries were confusing to these programmers because they could not puzzle out the relationship between these questions and his job, which is to evaluate and guide their work. Jan thought of his interest in India as enhancing workplace culture, as an expression of his desire to be open with his workforce and take an interest in their lives outside of work.

Andrea Muehlebach writes of morality as part of the structural transformations of neoliberalism, inserting selflessness into the heart of capitalism.[17] The "something different" that Jan said made Globus a cutting-edge place to work also comprises a moral project making him a tolerant and world-open German citizen and creating a global office where differences are happily accepted. Jan's questions demonstrated that he was a liberal German subject. Such liberal tolerance of non-German others is one way that German citizens can show distance from the race hatred of the Nazi past, the East German totalitarian past, and the West German class society.[18]

Outside the office, programmers discussed how to respond to Jan's questions about India. It turns out that many other programmers have heard similar questions, if not from managers, then from curious coworkers. One programmer told me that "it is embarrassing that they seem to know so much about India," especially when these are things that Indians themselves do not know as well. Another said that it is "baffling as the questions come out of nowhere and it is hard to respond," so he just agrees with whatever the person who is asking thinks. A third recommended trying to give a simple answer, with which the questioner is mostly satisfied.

One thing that most managers and programmers explicitly agree on is that background (nationality, gender, race, and so on) should not matter. All that should matter is that a person has the skills to get the job done. Yet, talk about religion, symbolic meanings, attitudes, and predilections swirls all around the workplace, and especially around Indian programmers. It is unclear to most programmers why this continues to be so. Some see the curiosity about India as evidence of world openness, as Jan does. Some see the questions as evidence of the superior knowledge of their European colleagues, who seem to know so much already about India. Some put it down to simple curiosity, while others think that the questions are a test to see how well they can adapt to a Western work environment, coded as transparent and nonhierarchical. These instances of cultural curiosity and the intense strategy sessions among programmers that they spark speak also to the way a picture of Indian difference builds up over time, through a series of individual interactions, and then condenses into a sign of the likely proclivities of the Indian workforce.

Racialization as a Division of Labor: Indian Coders as Uncreative

Michael was in his midthirties and had moved to Berlin five years earlier when I met him in 2003. He had close-cropped hair and square, black-framed glasses. He wore high-end leather tennis shoes and expensive jeans with button-down shirts. He loved obscure 1970s psychedelia, and when he was not in the office, he would take me to record stores in Kreuzberg, on Savignyplatz, and in Prenzlauer Berg looking for rare pressings. Michael worked for a small start-up that made translation software for government publications. The company was hoping to pitch its product to the EU administrative units in Brussels. While combing the record bins in a tiny, dusty shop in Pestalozzistrasse, Michael broke down for me the organizational divisions in his small office in the trendy neighborhood of Prenzlauer Berg. First, he outlined the difference between those who answer how-to questions about software packages over the phone (tech support) and those who write the source code of a project (software developers). Tech support commands neither the same salary nor the same knowledge as developers. He characterized this as a general divide between degrees of skilled labor. Another type of divide—between soft and hard skills—complicated this picture. Pulling out a copy of an early Pink Floyd album called *A Saucerful of Secrets* with a boyish grin, he continued, "Most offices are divided between front-facing areas for interfacing with clients and back-facing areas where problems are solved. These are called front-end and back-end functions." Front-office people, he went on to tell me, were said to have good communications skills that back-office people lacked and therefore commanded higher salaries and comparatively greater job security. Finally, there was the issue of an employee's potential—what the programmer may bring to the company in terms of possible future earnings. In Michael's firm, the Indian programmers hired to do software testing were often included in meetings where, in Michael's opinion, their expertise was not really applicable. Michael suggested that his boss was hoping they might chime in with what he called "cultural knowledge" (*kulturelles Wissen*) that might help him the next time he needed to hire a short-term Indian programmer. Michael did not fear that one day his job would be done by a migrant programmer or that it would be outsourced, for he knew his place in the division of labor outlined above. He was a "creative," a project designer who did upper-level, front-facing work, for which he was uniquely skilled by virtue of his schooling, which stressed creative problem solving, and his "interpersonal communications" skills (his term), which ensured he would interface with clients.

The inclusion of Indian programmers in meetings, which could be read as a sign that they were being groomed for management, had another function according to Michael. They were there as reservoirs of cultural knowledge that might be tapped in future management operations. I was surprised at how often Indian programmers were included in management meetings and often asked about it. Sometimes, this was part of training for management, but often, firm managers had other purposes in mind.

In an interview with one project manager at the annual technology conference in Hannover, Germany, in 2006, I asked about the inclusion of his Indian developers in these team meetings, called "scrums" in many firms. He answered by revealing that his firm was hoping to build another satellite office in India, and to do so, he needed to train Indians "to be Indian but to dream in German." He unwittingly (most likely) rehearsed thereby an earlier moment of elite Indian class formation, when British colonial policy inclined toward producing a cadre of Indian civil servants who were "a subject of difference that is almost the same, but not quite."[19] As Thomas Babington Macaulay, writer of *Minute on Indian Education*, could not help but imagine in 1835, "A class of interpreters between us and the millions whom we govern—a class of persons Indian in blood and color, but English in tastes, in opinions, in morals and in intellect."[20] Though, in this case, the taste, opinions, morals, and intellect would be German.

For some, culture talk makes a workplace global. For others, culture talk—when carefully parsed as talk about education or family values, not biological essentialism—is about learning to better manage a culturally diverse workforce. The patterning of ideas about Indian programmers cohered around the limited ability of Indian programmers to intuitively grasp Euro-American standards of bodily comportment and office etiquette. It justified their relegation to short-term jobs and repetitive coding. Importantly, these opinions were shared by Indian cognitariats who had reached the upper echelons of management. The following conversation is representative of conversations I have had about Indian knowledge workers with regularity over the past five years, in Seattle, Mumbai, and Berlin and even in airplanes hurtling through the skies somewhere above and between these places.

"The IT industry is ruining India," exclaimed Rahul, the ice in his whiskey and soda clinking thickly as he gesticulated. "The salary for IT work is so high," he told me, "most comp sci [computer science] students do not go on past their undergraduate degrees. India is not emerging as an R&D center the way it could be." I was on a plane bound for New York, sitting next to this Indian Institute of Technology (IIT)–trained computer scientist who lived in the United States and worked in the computer science department at a large state university. I took notes on our conversation as he talked, telling him I was writing a book on upward mobility in the IT industry and soliciting his opinion. Rahul traveled frequently between the United States, Germany, and India on research and recruiting tips. He was frustrated with the majority of Indian technology workers. While he understood the allure of a good paycheck and told the undergraduates he met in India they were right to pursue these jobs, he felt stymied by the lack of innovation on the part of Indian engineers. In the end, he complained, echoing other managers I meet, the Indian computer programmer is diligent but not creative. "I use the analogy of the architect and the stonemason," he said. "The Indian engineers are very competent stonemasons but do not become architects." Rahul blamed the education system. A government stipend for graduate education is paltry compared with what a corporate job would yield. I asked him why Indian companies do not try to fund education, he thought a moment and answered, "I don't know. They are making so much money doing what they are doing, they don't see the need to make architects."

In a famous passage in *Capital*, Marx compares architects to bees: "What distinguishes the worst architect from the best of bees is that the architect builds the cell in his mind before he constructs it in wax."[21] Rahul, when comparing architects and stonemasons, echoes this sentiment, calling out the Indian education system for being content to train engineers not to think but simply to reproduce pre-given forms. Marx points to a distinction between plan and instinct. When man labors through plans, he "develops his slumbering powers and compels them to act in obedience to his sway," writes Marx, in an exposition of how humans not only affect their environment but also can purposely affect human life, or species-being, itself.[22] Rahul instead reasserts a division within cognitive labor between those who are assimilated to planners and those manual laborers who are merely executors. He folds Marx's call for denaturalizing the conditions of life into a Smithian naturalized division of labor.[23]

A French Canadian director of sales for a French company in a thirty-person office in Berlin, with primarily German and Eastern European clients, whom I meet at a regional trade fair, had an even lower opinion of the Indian engineer. His company makes a piece of software that, as he described it, "sits on top of another software application," making it customizable for the needs of various companies. He was regularly asked to support their product when companies cannot resolve issues themselves.

In this capacity, he often dealt with outsourcing operations in India that provide technical support to these companies. The technical support teams simply forwarded queries about the software to him, without first finding out if they could solve the problem on their own. "Indian IT people need a lot of hand-holding," was how he puts it to me when I interviewed him one day in the offices of his firm. In his opinion Indian programmers were not very good. In his experience they did not try to solve anything themselves; they simply passed it on to someone else and waited for the answer. I asked him what he thought the outcome of the German green card program would be, given his low opinion of Indian programmers. Perhaps bringing them over here for training and then sending them back to India, he answered, would be better because they would learn how to think and do on their own. He used an analogy, telling me that software development and maintenance were like designing a car and being a car mechanic. The designer was the one who makes the new Ford, whereas the mechanic keeps it running and repairs it. "Most Indian developers are more like car mechanics," he concluded, "than like designers." Indian programmers figure as problem workers who lack creativity and initiative—as lower-class workers who are car mechanics, not designers.

Analogies like the architect and the stonemason and the designer and the car mechanic downgrade Indian expertise. In a meditation on how the question of intelligent labor played out in relationship to technology, Simon Schaffer notes that the question of human and other kinds of intelligences was long used as a means of marking nonwhite, non-European populations: "In many western myths of mechanical intelligence, with Chinese or Japanese, Turks or Nazis as their protagonists, aliens are automata, mindless subjects of tyranny; they build automata, because they possess fiendish cunning. . . . There is, perhaps, a long-term political and aesthetic relationship between intelligent automata, orientalism and the covert."[24]

Mechanics, stonemasons, and bees all possess a craft but not a plan. They may be cunning but are not creative. As metaphors for Indian workers, they provide an example of the way unofficial discourses of race circulate in a postracial office, where racialization naturalizes division of cognitive labor, embodying certain forms of work in particular, nationally branded kinds of workers. These figurations of the IT worker help create them as essentially different, because their intelligence is outside the ambit of the human intelligence of the architect or car designer and represents instead the instinctual, otherworldly intelligence of the bee or the untrustworthy intelligence of the car mechanic. Indian programmers who have a mechanical intelligence may be incorporated into the corporate office, but forever in a subordinate position.

Exposure to an Indian workforce is highly prized by many managers. Being able to demonstrate effectively that they are culturally confident makes them globally competent. Because of the potential that has been invested in Indian IT as a source of new consumer markets and cheap labor, some IT managers are proud of contacts with and abilities to deftly navigate the "difference" of India. Jan, the manager in Berlin with whom this chapter opened, boasted of being sufficiently versed in Indian culture to feel that he could at least tell to whom he was talking when he worked with people from India. "I can hear the difference between Hindi and Urdu," he said, telling me that he can differentiate between the two South Asian languages often associated with Hindus and Muslims respectively.[25] He further indicated that he cannot "distinguish between all the dialects, like Tamil." It seems almost impossible that Jan could pick up the difference between Hindi and Urdu but not between Hindi and Tamil (which is a South Indian language that sounds quite different from North Indian languages). With his evaluation, he brought home the importance of being able to claim cultural knowledge for the sake of being a good manager. At the same time, though, he also made clear that for him as manager, a deep understanding of differences within India was unimportant. That he could leave to his Indian subordinates.

Often, when discussing the particularity of Indian (and sometimes also Chinese) programmers, managers and European and American programmers would stress the university system. At a cocktail party in the United States after I had returned from fieldwork, an American programmer responded to a description of my project by saying that he notices Indian and Chinese programmers are mathematically minded and think of code as math, whereas American programmers think of it as a language and can therefore be more responsive to client demands. He suggested that checking in with the client more often—what is called "agile" programming—can avoid delays and miscommunications. But, because most Indian and Chinese programmers come out of a regimented university program, they are not taught to think that way along the lines of communication. On the other hand, according to this programmer, many American and to some extent European programmers are self-taught and therefore have a different approach, treating code as language, which to him meant something that is naturally communicative, there to be played with and improvised on.

Yet another way to divide the architect and car designer from the bee and the mechanic, the division of coding into language and math makes concrete a creative and repetitive approach to programming. The "East," defined by rote learning, is limited, while the "West," defined by poetry, expands. These differences, in keeping with a postracial imaginary, are carefully couched in national-cultural traditions of training, which allows them to be all the more effectively generalized. Such metaphors of difference, employed to explain to an ethnographer what the differences are between foreign and native coders, provide a frame through which participants in these worlds can explain and naturalize differences in experiences in the office to themselves and to others. As partially expressed codes for divisions of labor, they at once justify hierarchy and maintain the illusion of workplace meritocracy—where the best skills are rewarded by the best paychecks. They do so by expanding the scope of skilled labor to include the "soft" skills of human interaction and the "hard" skills of creative coding, thus rekeying the work of programming in two modes from which foreign coders are normally excluded.[26]

The Tale of the Turkish *i*

Within the framework of liberal tolerance, only a limited spectrum of behavior can be accepted without fundamentally threatening the stability of a democratic nation-state built on the idea of freely choosing and rational individuals.[27] In the case of Germany, Turkish immigrants are repeatedly framed as violating the principles of democratic society through their religious beliefs, "refusal" to speak proper German, putative associations with Islamic terrorism, and patriarchal practices toward women.[28] Indian migrants, on the other hand, may be framed as acceptably different.

A project manager named Björn, whom I met in the Mitte offices of Dash Technologies, a firm that builds specialized software to work with existing business platforms, worked on internationalization and localization, also sometimes called *globalization*. His team was charged with making all the programs produced by a parent company work across multiple languages, ensuring that there will be no mistakes or complications when keyboards, interfaces, and design elements move from one context to another. Because of the international nature of the work, he has built a team from South America, Russia, India, and China. When I asked for clarification by example of this programming of global fluidity, he began with an old case, he said, that still works as a good illustration:

When an e-mail program was first introduced, it used the icon for a mailbox that you would click on. The icon was round on the top and flat on the bottom, rendered with some degree of perspective. But this icon, which came from an American company, did not work well at all elsewhere. They rolled it out in Germany, for example, and no one would click on it. They all thought it was a breadbox. Eventually, after trying many other things, a group came up with an icon in the shape of an envelope. That was universal, worked everywhere, and people clicked on it.[29]

Localization and internationalization are about making programs work properly across different cultural and linguistic contexts, as the mailbox example suggests. For Björn, it was also a perfect location from which to notice differences in capacity parsed by nationality. Björn provided a second example but started off from quite an unexpected direction. "Indians," he exclaimed, "are so good at programming, but they will never ever have an internationalization center in India." In his opinion, Indians just are not interested in translating programs into other languages, not even their own regional ones. "Maybe it is because they are all so good at English, they think everyone should just learn that." Riffing on these problematic cultural differences, he moved on to the story of the Turkish *i*.

"This is an infamous problem because of what happened to a well-known cell phone provider. In Turkish, there are two different *i*'s, one with a dot on top and one without. A certain phone company did not make note of this difference when translating the texting software from English to Turkish." This company, which Björn did not want to name, was not even aware of the potential problem. They translated the text recognition software into Turkish so that the phone user could use predictive text software, which suggests words to the user as the user types. They only put in one *i*, even though users would clearly need two different kinds. "The issue is really quite serious," he concluded, "since if they used the wrong *i*, the sentence's meaning would completely change." In the project manager's story, this is exactly what happened. "One day, a man received a text that was supposed to say one thing but said another." I forget what the mistake was, Björn told me, "but it was bad because the man who got the text went into a rage and almost killed someone."[30]

The tale of the Turkish letter contains within it many kinds of stories; important among them are two cautionary tales of failure: one of the Indian coder to consider internationalization problems, and one of the Turkish cell phone user to act rationally in the face of an internationalization error. These two figures—the Turkish migrant worker and the Indian temporary coder—play off against each other as counterexamples of the productivity and danger of migrant cultures.

As if to underscore the rightness of his reading of Indians as good at code but not good at cultural translation, Björn told me about his old job, when he worked side by side with a developer from Tamil Nadu (in South India). It was 2004 when the Indian Ocean tsunami hit. He watched the coverage on the news and knew that his colleague was from an affected area. He went into work the following day and asked if everyone in his family was all right. His colleague seemed surprised. Yes, he answered, everyone in the family was fine, why was he asking? Björn said, because of the tsunami of course. His colleague told him that only the poor people suffered from the tsunami, and he should not worry. The poor people, he said, were not really full people anyway. Björn was shocked and dismayed. This was a sure sign that Indians did not really care too much about such things as the digital divide. Whatever might be said about the smug indifference of the Indian programmer toward the victims of the tsunami, for Björn, this was one more piece of evidence of insular thinking that helped him decide on the worth and the correct placement of his highly valued Indian team members.

Indians as Automata

On an Internet forum for German-speaking businesspeople, participants discuss the pros and cons of working with Indian programmers. Under the heading "Indian IT," a project manager relates a story of work that was outsourced to Mumbai. I excerpt a lengthy passage from this post to give the reader the narrative arc of postracial justifications of essentialization:

> I was asked to test a program that was allegedly already developed. The program was supposed to order financial information into a table, and

then as new material was entered in the table, automatically refresh each field or leave it as it was, depending on the calculation. My first test showed that the refreshing of the table worked correctly, but the data that was already entered into the table vanished when the table was refreshed. So, I did not accept the development and sent the whole thing with detailed reasons (in English) back to the developer in Mumbai (India). After a few days I received his extensive analysis of the problem with the conclusion that the functionality I required was not described in the original development contract. Therefore I should write a new contract with the required development described in it. "My good programmer" also cc'd my manager on this email. Everything must be done correctly! [*Auf cc hat mein guter Programmierer auch meinen zuständigen Manager gesetzt. Es muss ja alles seine Richtigkeit haben!*] In my answer I explained to him that he disturbed through his programming a functionality that was already working. He should simply program in such a way that what was already there remained undisturbed. . . .

I took some time to try to figure out if we were simply not understanding one another [*aneinander vorbeireden*]. But since I have been working on international teams with English as the project-language for at least 6 years, I had confidence that I could explain difficult cases in English. After a few days I received an email in which he questioned what he already had programmed. The point was that the programming contract did not describe what he was supposed to do with the data that was already in the table. He had programmed correctly to begin with, but now that the situation had changed, he had to start from the beginning again. This whole process had already taken 3 weeks. I then asked him as cynically as it was possible for me to in English, why he thought that it said that his program should calculate something. And why it did not say that the program after calculation should not do anything else. And if he had ever heard that sometimes circumstances are implicit in the description, without them having to explicitly be formulated. He agreed with me. After two more days of detailed explanation through Chat, he began working again. This part will surely be in the bill including these two days. I spent 3 or 4 hours on this during which I had other things to do. . . .

The development time [*Entwicklungszeit*] has now been extended by 8 weeks. How many (cheap) hours will be charged by the Indian company I do not know. For my part, I needed about double the amount of hours that I would need if I had been working with a halfway accomplished programmer in Germany. . . . Granted, this is an extreme example. For me, it is not necessarily a question of communications difficulties or cultural differences [*Verständigungsschwierigkeiten oder kulturellen Unterschieden*]. In the years in which I have worked with offshore programmers, most of them were just out of University and could program ABAP [Advanced Business Application Programming, used by the German firm SAP] but had no idea about business processes. . . . There are also good Indian programmers. But they usually work the same hours as we do, not offshore anymore, but here with us in Europe or the USA.[31]

The author of the post simultaneously masses his impressions around the poor working habits of specifically Indian IT experts while denying that culture or his own biases plays a role in the interaction. He relates the story as one of initial open-mindedness that was slowly replaced by frustration— until he has to intervene by using sarcasm to make the programmer work as expected. In the end, to forestall perhaps the charge of prejudice, he claims that there are also good programmers from India and separates those who are in India from those who "make it" to the United States or Europe.

The behavior he describes is echoed by those who respond to the post. Four individuals wrote lengthy responses to this post. The first response makes it even more clear how an image of an Indian IT worker who lacks sophistication and is more machine than human develops: "Indians—sorry if I generalize—only do exactly what one tells them. That is, they execute only like machines, no more, no less [*Sprich sie führen wie Maschinen nur aus—nicht mehr aber auch nicht weniger*]!!" Again, the writer is careful to mark his awareness that this might come off as a generalization but goes ahead and asserts the machinelike quality of Indian programming. This form of discourse at once rehearses the German overcoming of prejudice and elevates the author to "the ideal translator/interpreter of contemporary and past racism."[32] In this way, the judgment of Indian IT workers escapes the accusation of racism even as it uses probabilistic qualities of personhood to make general pronouncements.

Another response suggested that the problem was that the programming requirements were not written precisely enough. The writer gave the example of how the distinction between male and female could be rendered in several different ways: m/f, m/w (for the German *männlich* for male and *weiblich* for female), 1/0, or 1/2 and so on. Not specifying in the requirements exactly how this was to be written resulted in huge problems later on. This analysis is important because it moves in a different direction from the main thrust of this post, suggesting that responsibility lay with German assumptions about language and management practices that shifted blame to the overseas, outsourced workforce. Unfortunately, it remains an anomaly in a field otherwise crowded with repeated statements of the difference between those "over there" and us "over here." The final two responses add economic reasoning to the East-West dimension of these divides, noting that for big European and U.S. firms, using Indian programmers was a way to sink costs, while Indian firms soon realized that they could train their own people on the Western firm's dollar, and so they continued to send over their new people when they had to do on-site work.

In chapter 3, I show how Indian programmers working in German offices try to make sense of the demands of their managers at the same time as these workers criticize their treatment in the office. The perspective of the programmer in Mumbai who is at the other end of this story is not available to us. Yet, the second response I discussed contains a possible alternative transcript of events, in which the protocols are written unclearly, so the programmer tries to do only exactly what is written and no more.

The All-Hands: Racialization as Creative Content and the Dream of Replaceability

Back in the IT offices of Dash Technologies, we were called for the weekly all-hands meeting to the Oahu Room. The room names, each one for a different Hawaiian Island, fit into the overall ambiance of the workplace as a space that fosters imagination and creativity. The team members entered the room and joked about leaving cold Berlin for the islands—that they should begin to decorate the rooms with tropical drinks and palm trees. They are all looking forward to what Björn had christened "Pfannkuchen Freitag" (Flapjack Friday), when the team would roll up their shirt sleeves, remove their jackets, and spend an hour in the morning making pancakes for the office. This Wednesday, the all-hands meeting concerned the rollout of a new software product that had to be launched simultaneously in multiple European countries. As the project manager reviewed the progress his team has made so far, he repeated the team slogan for the project, "The

Internet is connecting computers, language is connecting people." Björn looked around the room and addressed each member of his team. He had staff from Russia, the United States, India, Spain, and Portugal in the room that day. In each case, he told them, they needed to be responsible for making sure there were no mistakes in the translation of the software into their respective languages. For my benefit, he asked two of his staff members to outline past mistakes in other projects. In Argentina, for example, the global version of a world map software application was translated into Spanish. But the Falkland Islands were marked as British in that version. Björn suggested that the head of the team in Argentina went to jail for treason over this. Another case occurred because someone "forgot one pixel" and the map of India left out Kashmir, but when the map of Pakistan came up, Kashmir appeared as part of Pakistan.

Asking a Hyderabadi programmer on Björn's team what she thought of her colleagues after the meeting was over, she said she "loves the work" and considered "the problems with global rollout fascinating." She was, echoing all the other team members with whom I spoke, enthusiastic about the team's international makeup. Being able to work with people from so many different countries was one of the primary perks of being in global software. This programmer had greater goals than being only a subsidiary member of the team. For her, too, international exposure would provide another reservoir of expertise in cultural differences and the international protocols of corporate programming work. As many Indian software developers told me, international "exposure" made them more attractive hires back in India. She eventually wanted to be where the project manager was sitting. To that end, she had bought a book to teach herself German at night. She recognized that although the team really needs her right now to translate between German and Indian offices on this part of the project, once the Indian office understands the workflow, she would be obsolete. She was eager to prove herself useful to the team for now by providing information about India and hoped, as they kept turning to her for this knowledge, she would be able to grow and expand her knowledge of management practices in a global setting.[33]

This striving may not yield upward mobility. Perhaps the greatest sign that she and other Indian coders will have a hard time moving up from their temporary positions came from Michael on one of our record-finding jaunts. He told me that the "holy grail" in the industry right now is to use social networking and crowdsourcing to do the work now done by Indian programmers. He himself was skeptical that this plan would ever come to fruition the way companies think it will, calling it "turning iron into gold." But the idea is that costs can be cut even further by using machine translation together with community members who would be offered discounted rates on the software for their services. The machine would translate, or produce batches of code, and then the translation, the original, and the source code would appear on a screen side by side. A community member would compare the two translations and correct the native language one, and then other community members would review the source code. When the same correction was made at least four or five times, the machine would learn the correct phrase and incorporate it.

Eventually, the Indian programmer as well as foreign language experts would be competing (and losing out against) such cost-effective models. In this future vision of labor, migrants are replaced not by a solitary machine but by a network of human machines. So far, the Indian coder, especially the one working in India, is still less expensive than the machine-human network.

In knowledge economies, the world outside the office is brought inside, precisely because the new economy relies so heavily on deep reservoirs of creativity: "Labor-power increases the value of capital only because . . . [of] its inherent connection to a productive cooperation richer than the one implicit in the labor process.[34] Because "culture" is a resource in the office, Indian programmers have a privileged place at the conference table. They are relied on as a crucial intermediary between Germany and India and are a valuable resource in producing new communicative competencies that might one day open India as a new market for the company's products.

At the same time though, the repeated layering of the inadequacy of Indian programmers for the sophisticated "culture work" that is required in translation projects creates an unofficial division of labor that keeps most Indian developers in the back office rather than moving them up as project managers who would command a higher salary and a permanent position with benefits.[35] The explanation of communication as fallible proffered in one of the discussion board comments is rarely taken up. Instead, most office communiqués operate as if there were a one-to-one correspondence between words and their meaning. Despite an awareness of the difficulty of translation as software moves across language zones, in interoffice communications, the reigning language ideology tends toward sense-reference predication, because everyone is speaking the same language, international business English.[36]

Modern types of office work appear interchangeable from the outside, because most cognitive workers sit in front of computer screens and keyboards. But in actuality, skills are more specialized, less easily learned, and less interchangeable than ever: knowledge workers "could never exchange jobs since each and every one of them develops a specific and local ability which cannot be transmitted to those who do not share the curricular preparation and are not familiar with the same complex cognitive logic."[37] The increased specialization is, in part, an effect of folding workers' outside interests into work itself so that workers are invested in work as never before.[38] The boundary between the work self and the home self blurs as workers' personal resources are drawn into the circuits of production. But it is precisely in drawing the biopolitical capacities of human life into the work process that workers become simultaneously individualized and *dividualized*, in Deleuze's terms, both more like themselves and singular and more a representative of a population to which they are made to belong.[39] Thus, while Indian programmers become less interchangeable and individually more specialized in their work, they also become a *type* of worker who fits in a shifting slot in IT economies.

Inhabiting Human-Nonhuman Interfaces:
How to Be Safe on Unsure Terrain

One evening, as I sat with him in the darkened offices, Mihir, a twenty-five-year-old coder and business graduate, turned to me and said, "The work is quite boring, you know—*just waiting* for some client to call in with a problem." Looking around the empty office, he began to link his work to his personal timeline. He grew up in Bombay (now Mumbai) as the son of a government worker and a pharmacist's assistant. Trained at the University of Bombay in computer science, he counted himself among the first recipients of the German green card. First, Mihir took a job with a small company in Regensburg, a city south of Berlin in the state of Bavaria, and then moved to another small company on the outskirts of Berlin after his six-month work contract expired. According to Mihir, Berlin is a big, open city, teaming with life, though not too full, like Mumbai. But Mihir realized that the imminent end to his current project meant seeking out new opportunities yet again.

Mihir's job was to test applications for a cell phone company. The company's ringtones had not been uploading correctly, leading to many customer complaints; he was on call to respond to them and fix the problem. Long after everyone else has gone home, he sat in the office hunched over his keyboard comparing lines of code across open windows trying to find the problem. He leaned back wearily rubbing his eyes and correlated the repetitive fixes he makes with the steps in his own timeline:

I was always good in maths. I went to King George School near my home and sat on the same bench as the guy who is now an important man at Wipro. At that time, I was not focused. I used to go and feed the stray dogs after school instead of studying. They were dangerous to others, but they never bit me until much later. Once when I came back home for vacation, I got bit. I got top marks and was thinking of studying architecture. My father was not against the idea but thought I should first study engineering for practical reasons.

Mihir did study engineering but was tired of school after so many years of studying hard and after-school tuitions (tutoring), of keeping up with his friends, and keeping his eye on his practical skills. He thought that when he finished this degree he would take some time to do something else and maybe return to architecture. But when he was finished, he noticed that all his friends were going for higher degrees because they would get better jobs and higher paychecks. "So," he said, "I went in for a business degree." While he was completing his MBA, his parents and some of his friends suggested he specialize in computers, since he was always so good at math, and in business school he specialized in technology and computer management.

On the weekends, Mihir has a ready smile and is brimming with talk of the latest Bollywood release, his next visit home, a new recipe his wants to try, or a restaurant he would like to visit. But at work, his spirits visibly sagged as the night wears on, his shoulders drooping and his skin assuming a pallid, jaundiced cast.[40] I asked Mihir, since he has not had formal training in computer science, how he knew so much about coding. He said he had picked it up along the way, because he had always been hired in development jobs rather than in management jobs, despite his management training. He compared himself with his friend from school, who got the job at Wipro. He had a straight course from school through computer science to

Wipro. But because Mihir was not focused and pursued (according to his own reckoning) meandering courses through life, he had become stuck as a low-level engineer.[41] He sounded tired and frustrated—just the opposite of how he is on weekend outings when he extols the pleasures of open spaces and easy sociality as an antidote to the stresses of the workplace. Yet, he also seemed to suggest that a return to his carefree boyhood days was no longer possible. The strays who never used to bite him now do, perhaps sensing he no longer is native to their haunts. Mihir has continued to adapt to current industry needs, remaking himself through his degrees into the perfectible white-collar brown-bodied laborer for the global economy.

One evening, he told me about the atmosphere during the day when his German coworkers and boss are around. He has made good friends with Sasha, who shares his worktable, sitting across from him in the hushed atmosphere of quiet concentration that pervades the floor. They go to movies together and have dinner; Mihir has introduced him to Bollywood film and told me that his friend bears a strong resemblance to Saif Ali Khan, a well-known Bollywood star. But his boss, said Mihir, was a different story.

Although at first the boss had been friendly, open, and curious about the lives of Indian programmers, lately he had begun to lecture them on etiquette in the shared kitchen. Mihir was hired as part of a two-person team from India; the other Indian programmer was an excellent coder but did not speak English very well. Mihir was often asked to explain things to him, including one day when the boss decided to fine this programmer for breaking a dish in the kitchen. Mihir thought that this action was over the top, but the boss started correcting their behavior repeatedly, telling them how they must correctly load and run the shared dishwasher. "I don't know how they do things in India," said Mihir's boss, "but here in Germany we place great emphasis on keeping things clean." For Mihir, these missives were not lessons in how to be a good coworker in a global workplace. Mihir understood these as signs of the boss's true nature—nice on the surface, but ruthless underneath. In the same context, Mihir told me that his salary was actually less than he was expecting because the firm was located just outside Berlin in the town of Potsdam, where according to labor laws, salaries could be set lower because the city was in the former East Germany.

Managing in the office requires "an *expertise* of the personal dimension of work. To administer work, it has become necessary to know, to calculate, to deliberate, and to evaluate."[42] I would add that knowing and calculating capacity based on the signs of race is part of this work of expertise. Race as an embodied marker of cultural difference is both valued and confining in the IT office. For the Indian programmer in Björn's office, this leads to a permanent remaking of skills in an attempt to add value to the office because of her race and to transcend the end of this knowledge's usefulness. In Mihir's case, the racialization of cognitive work leads to a profound destabilization because his boss appears to switch suddenly from opening and welcoming to punitive. As I have argued throughout this chapter, in the German context, talk about ethnicity is both outright and hidden, it is at the same time about the different qualities of different workers and about a general sense that cultural differences in the workplace reconfirms German tolerance and opens up new markets to business expansion.

A project manager who travels between the United States and Germany and is of Indian descent viewed these practices from the perspective of North American histories of discrimination. She told me that when she visits the offices of her multinational corporation in both countries, she is appalled by the way the Indian IT workers are treated. They are quite literally, she told me, put in a back room, hidden away from everyone else. She always tries to treat them as human beings, though, just in the way that she talks to them. After thinking for a moment, she admitted that they have no idea how they are coming across. For instance, they think nothing of bringing food from home and heating it up in the microwave, regardless of how it must smell to the others. She argued that to move out of the back room, Indian programmers would have to give up their habits and become aware of how they must appear to others. They would have to learn their footing on a terrain of useful and unwanted differences, what Smitha Radhakrishnan calls "cultural streamlining," if they are to move up before being moved out.[43]

In an online article posted on a website for Indians living in Germany, columnist Usha Amrit counsels flexibility as a response to unfamiliar workplace demands:

> In company recruitments in Europe a lot of emphasis is given to a potential candidate's social persona rather than just his or her mere qualifications and professional experience. I suppose, this takes more precedence if the candidate is an immigrant or foreigner. We [Indians] possess a certain inherent flexibility when it comes to working in diverse

environments. After all, it is not uncommon to find oneself working with colleagues from various parts of India, on an average in any work environment in India. For instance, your Tamilian boss pairs you up with a Bengali colleague and under your tutelage is a Bihari who works in conjunction with an Andraite while you are working on a project outsourced from a European company. . . . Working in an entirely foreign environment also requires knowledge and training of working styles that vary from country to country. However, I'd say given a rough survey of people across the world, we Indians with our innate flexibility are most likely to be at ease in having ourselves transposed and transported (given similar salaries and perks of course) to totally foreign work environments.[44]

The conversations and advice Indian programmers give each other on how to respond to questions about culture, questions of etiquette, and awareness of smells that might give offense are examples of cultivating what is taken above as an "innate" flexibility. They evaluate the "essential" quality of being Indian positively, all the while remaining within an essentializing discourse. Amrit's advice to roll with workplace norms so long as salaries and perks are adequate reminds me of Mihir's problems with his boss. He should obey the demands on kitchen etiquette but also look for another job in Berlin where his salary would increase. This type of advice, of course, ignores the way race is speculated on to produce both surplus value and a profile of employee worth more broadly across corporate software industries.

Producing Difference as Supplement: Rethinking Race in a Global Economy

Potsdamer Platz, where once stood a vast no-man's-land between East and West and earlier still Weimar's Mecca of dance, entertainment, and nightlife, now is home to looming corporate headquarters, a shopping mall, and a few remaining fragments of the Berlin Wall that gesture faintly at the immense divide between the socialist and capitalist Germanies that once defined this city. On one hazy May morning, I met Sasha at the exit of the U-Bahn on the west side of the large and busy square. Sasha was Mihir's friend and colleague from the office who really did look like a German Saif Ali Khan. We were not meeting to talk Bollywood movies, however.

Nor were we going to rediscover the art nouveau splendor of late nineteenth-century buildings like Weinhaus Huth, almost destroyed by Allied bombings. We were instead on our way to a conference on outsourcing, migration to Germany, and Indian coding expertise sponsored by Daimler-Chrysler and held at its gleaming corporate headquarters on the rebuilt city square. All the big-name German IT firms, including SAP and Siemens, would have representatives there. I was curious to see how they would present the green card and Indian IT to their constituency, an assembly of business professionals and local reporters. Sasha had been sent by his company to this IT fair to represent the company and network with other German IT professionals.

As we walked through the cool, damp air of a spring morning, I asked Sasha to tell me more about his background. He grew up in the West German town of Kaiserslautern (home to a U.S. Army base), which he described as a place he could hardly wait to escape. He came to Berlin for his university education, majoring in computer science at the Technical University. After graduating with a master's degree, he got a job at a small firm in Potsdam, where he met Mihir, who was hired on there as a temporary coder.

We took our seats in a spacious fourth-floor conference room with views of the shopping arcades below and examine our programs, awaiting the first speaker, a representative of Daimler. During the conference, the tenor of discourse around India and Indian IT was a mixture of the practical business strategy to be pursued by outsourcing "lower-level" tasks to Indian IT and the kind of difference and exoticism that could be a supplement to hard-headed business know-how. The first speaker discussed the mutual benefits of doing business with India. The way to approach Indian IT, he said, is to remember that it frees you up to concentrate on the things you are really passionate about and are good at. "Do what you do best," he intoned in English, "outsource the rest," echoing the theme of the CeBIT, or Centrum für Büro und Informationstechnik (Center for Office and Information Technology), expo that had taken place in Hannover a few months before. He claimed that Daimler was doing just that: the German head office provided strategic resources, and its partners in India provided the engineering talent to get the jobs done. In that way, he argued, both countries were winning out. He pointed out how the government's green card initiative was part of the same mentality, bringing Indian programmers to Germany to do the work that is needed by German businesses. They provide the talent; the business provides the leadership.

The next speaker, a manager from SAP, worked out of the company's Bangalore office. His tone was even more reassuring. Bangalore had much to recommend it, but there were three things holding Western companies back from moving all their business operations to the subcontinent: the political turmoil, the unpredictable weather, and the inconsistent access to water and electricity. He thought that German know-how could help the Indians in these areas and, at the same time, assured the German business-people in the audience that until such problems were solved—and who, really, can solve the weather?—the engineering talent of India would continue to be paired with German business talent.

These two presentations come to an end, and a hush fell over the crowd. People leaned forward in their seats as a white-shrouded figure with a long black beard entered the room, with a man in saffron strewing flower petals at his feet as he goes. The announcer exclaimed that we were very lucky to have with us today, by very special appearance, the world-renowned Indian guru and founder of the Art of Living Foundation, Sri Sri Ravi Shankar. It was an unexpected turn of events at a meeting otherwise dedicated to extolling the virtues of outsourcing as business process. The crowd of some one hundred men and women in formal business attire seemed relieved by the change in pace. They perked up and gazed at the stage, wondering what the guru might say. The man sitting next to me was explaining to his friend that Sri Sri was very hard to get a hold of, his schedule was very full, and there were hundreds of devotees in Europe alone waiting for an audience with him.

Sri Sri's organization, the Art of Living Foundation, has a divided mandate. It does meditation and empowerment work with prisoners. It also offers seminars and courses for business professionals designed to teach them breathing techniques called *sudarshan kriya*, to combat stress and increase longevity. Sri Sri had prepared a clever, punning message that played on the initialism IT. He delivered a talk entitled "IT—Internal Transformation." The audience should all think of IT in terms that go beyond "information" and "technology"; rather, IT could also and should also mean striving for internal transformation. He exhorted everyone in the room to keep this other meaning of IT in mind and "focus not only on the bottom line, but on their internal bottom lines." They should pursue not only success in business but also success in moral achievement. He smiled down on us all as he ended his talk, and the room erupted into enthusiastic applause.

I argue in this book that race in knowledge economies needs to be approached in its duality, as both a regimentation of labor divisions and worker management and an affirmation of liberal selfhood and a fecund source of communicative value. The response that Sri Sri Ravi Shankar's speech received demonstrates the importance of India as a source of value that floats—much like the derivative discussed by LiPuma and Lee—as the singular immaterial commodity of new economic networks.[45] The value of Indian coders can be similarly derived from the value of Indian culture. The former is valued for its cheapness, the latter for its distinction. As Susan Marchand relates in her comprehensive work on German Orientalism, although the relationship between Germany and India was complicated and changed over time, a strong strand of romanticism vis-à-vis Indian spirituality was woven through the history of German encounters with India.[46] It is this discourse that is at work once again in IT offices where points of Indian culture are matters of comment, discussion, and pleasure. As "internal transformation," IT refigures Orientalism so that it can be loosened from its moorings in India and fit within the confines of a business program. No longer strictly separating the spiritual and the material, the conference holds out the promise that the material can be infused with spirituality and that spirituality can be interdigitated with business concerns.[47] The morality of business, encapsulated in the terms that Sri Sri refashions, such as "bottom line" becoming "internal bottom line," is not undermined but preserved.

The conference perfectly encapsulates the two sides of the mobilization of race in cognitive labor. It is used to inaugurate a neat separation between front- and back-office operations and between the creative work that will be done in the first world and the rote work that will be done in India. The guru's speech highlights the *jouissance* that sticks to Indian culture when it is marshaled as communicative event. These two sides of race are not easily reconciled but instead form a constitutive contradiction in the development of capitalism. The confluence of the human and the economic gives pleasure by bringing basic faculties of the human in its communicative capacities in line with the sphere of production. The communicative capacity of race opens up a temporary resolution to the contradiction between working life and life as a value, suggesting that office workers can find satisfaction in their jobs to the extent to which their jobs can be suffused with both technology and transformation, both hard work and spirituality. Of course, this resolution is only ever temporary; when faced with the pressure of work deadlines, profit margins, the desire to generate leads or new business, and the pressing need to monetize those very communicative, human capacities, the balance between life as valued in its fullness and the value of a productive life begins to fracture.

The image of Indian IT workers that circulates in the offices is multifaceted, while the significance of their difference (from German workers, from other foreign workers) is at once recognized and disavowed as important to the way the office is organized. Indian programmers and programming work, from writing source code to testing existing products, are interconnected through these discourses of performance and exceptionalism. The labor of Indian programmers, as interpreted through repeated moments of noticing and remarking on their foreignness, at once ties them to cognitive economies and separates them out as having a particular role to play in them. The intraction of this human-technological unit proliferates (as Karen Barad and Bruno Latour might write) both kinds of people, as well as pathways for programming technology.[48]

In this chapter's opening vignette, the interaction between Jan the project manager and the office administrator of their firm was about the decal of Lord Venkateshwar in the entranceway. While the administrator, who sits up front and greets visitors, was worried that the manager might disapprove of its presence, Jan simply gave it and her a shrug and moved into the office. Such encounters gesture toward several kinds of inequality. The class difference between administrator and boss might be at issue, with each having a different attitude toward foreignness in the office. The office hierarchies are on notice, with the administrator subordinate to the manager and quick to distance herself from what she believes might be problematic. Jan's indifference signals a kind of acceptance of the supplements that an Indian workforce might bring to the office, and at other times, he is eager to learn what these additions might be. Such additions are tolerated because they do not harm the transaction of business but can enhance it by giving him the information to better manage an Indian workforce and, at the same time, begin to think of India as a new market for development. The sign of Venkateshwar in the entranceway may even signal his office's world-open, global attitude.

Within the official meritocracy of a postracial office, the race of Indian programmers can take on a number of different casts—the safe migrant, the limited worker, the valuable resource to open new markets and generate new ideas, the necessary supplement to Western materialism, and the alien automaton. In the dream of participation and virtual adventure promised by cognitive economies, the foreign IT worker should add color and promise new horizons of knowledge—and it is the concretization of office hierarchies that will produce this promise as a monetizable bet on the future.

As for Venkateshwar, it turns out that neither of the two programmers currently at Globus put the sticker up. They tell me it was put up by one of their predecessors who has returned to India. Asking them how they feel about it, they tell me it makes them feel good, as Venkateshwar in the entrance will ensure the success of the enterprise. Whether it will ensure their own success, however, remains an open question.

THREE

PROPRIETARY FREEDOMS IN AN IT OFFICE

In an old, refurbished lightbulb factory that houses the offices of Infotech, Srinu shepherded me toward the company cafeteria for lunch after my meeting with his boss. Along the way I took note of the architecture of this converted factory. The floor plan was open, desks were clustered together at intervals, cubicles had no doors, groups of engineers moved through the spaces like schools of fish among the shoals. The office was arranged so that workers could maximally share ideas, thoughts, and snippets of conversation. By producing new ideas and sharing packets of language, the office could take advantage of information, generate new leads, and be ready to respond quickly to new impulses.

The ongoing and continuous exchange of ideas is necessary to cognitive work. In tech offices, "the dialogic world is seated at the very heart of capitalist production."[1] Yet, at Infotech, everywhere there is a space of congregation, there is a sign warning people to keep their voices down. I noticed that despite all the architectural exhortations to communicate, the floor was quiet. Some signs get the point across by signing "STOP" in big red letters, with a message in English informing passersby they are in a work area. Some used a large printout of a smiley face emoticon saying "Shhh," holding an index finger over closed lips. Pinned to one divider was a bright yellow triangle with an exclamation point, the text underneath reminding the potential loud talker, "Leute arbeiten hier, bitte woanders plaudern," (There are people working here, please chat somewhere else).

In a hushed voice, I asked Srinu about all these signs. He replied, "Much of the business here goes on over the phone in talking to clients or to people in other locations. So they need quiet. And when the programmers are working on a particular problem, they need to concentrate." The pervasive conference zones, meant to bring people together and to stimulate new ideas, he believed, needed to be reconsidered. The signs got thicker as we approach the lunchroom, as did the hum of talk. Those cognitive workers who sit steps away from this most communicative space in the office, where the concentration required of minds and bodies always ready for new impulses can temporarily be broken by the banal rhythms of the stomach and palate, where ringing phones and tapping keyboards are replaced by the clink of silverware, had practically papered over their cubicles with missives urging quiet against the noise.

This chapter responds to the various framings of Indian programmers I laid out in chapters 1 and 2. In those chapters, I showed how the perceived abilities of Indian programmers in writing source code and maintaining systems are filtered through long histories of racialization and arguments for reforming European workers. Here, I explore how some Indian programmers use a political philosophy of free code to argue for the free movement of skilled migrants such as themselves. In doing so, they complicate the usual opposition between ownership and freedom implied in many free and open source software debates. This idea of freedom signals a departure from contemporary discussions of code as speech.[2]

The quiet spaces in the Infotech offices suggest that against a general exhortation to share and communicate freely, office workers produce islands of quiet calm in which concentrated work can be done. Indian programmers such as Srinu, Mihir, and Meenakshi similarly slow down the pace of work and insert themselves into the work process. They do this both to make a claim to own the code that they write—even if in a limited way— and to countermand the cognitive economy directive to be hardworking and always available. The critique many Indian programmers marshal of coding practices and migration regimes creates space within the office for a self-defined good life.

Anthropologists studying coding worlds address the way that code organizes social life and how the ethics of code evolves from the idea of a liberal public sphere. In the first branch of scholarship, code is taken to be part of an organizational infrastructure, an "algocracy," in A. Aneesh's terms, that governs through ordering allowable and barred actions.[3] According to this argument, code allows a further refinement in the techniques of governmentality, since it can channel human activity in particular directions. Code, in this literature, is folded into the study of physical and material infrastructures to explore new forms of (increasingly hidden) social control. In the second set of literature, code is a tool through which types of publics can be generated. In Chris Kelty's formulation, coders and others he calls "geeks" form "recursive publics" that create a shared moral and technical space through building layers of shared infrastructure and through talk about the ethical entailments of that infrastructure.[4] Similarly, in Gabriella Coleman's discussion of hacker ethics, coders pass through stages of technical and moral benchmarking in open source projects (such as Debian) that both promote group solidarity and leave open for future and ongoing contestation the boundaries and principles that govern that group of developers.[5]

My focus here is somewhat different. In this corporate setting, I separate out some of the practices of creating technical layers from a deontics of coding (what code ought to make possible) precisely because there are more schisms, dissatisfactions, and alternative perspectives to how code is organized in the workplace than there seem to be in open source and self-motivated (geek) projects.[6] I suggest here that thinking through philosophies of code is one way that short-term migrant coders create different kinds of relationships between people and coding work, not so much as a way to create social solidarity (as in Kelty's and Coleman's cases) but as a way to produce an ethic of individualized and universal freedom. As will become clear in the second part of the book, this ethic is one of the keys to understanding how the experience of work abroad is made commensurate with Indian middle-class sensibilities.

As knowledge workers, programmers capitalize on both their skills in writing code and the skills external to strict job descriptions that may be called on at any time. This chapter directs theoretical attention to the role stereotypy plays in corporate software projects, where, I argue, assumed qualities of migrant culture crosscut everyday practices of work and employee evaluation. For Indian coders who are the protagonists of this story, these extra jobs are often cultural and linguistic capacities that their employers value, like those that Meenakshi—the twenty-six-year-old graduate from Hyderabad's Indian Institute of Management—uses when she translates the bosses' demands into discrete jobs other programmers can execute. Meenakshi is the same age as Mihir, whom we met in chapter 2. Yet, while Mihir was disillusioned with the IT industry, Meena is optimistic. She enjoys the work and works under a project manager from Australia. She hopes to move up in the firm and eventually become a manager herself. Information technology workers like Meena must create and retain their value in these post-Fordist high-tech economies by making themselves indispensable to their employees. Sometimes, this balancing act requires that they counteract their positioning in the firm as exotic labor by using the counterexample of how code travels to unravel and critically apprehend the claims of technoeconomy control.

Eros and the Office

A midsize, 5,000-person firm in a formerly working-class neighborhood of Berlin, Infotech was the research arm of a large producer of hardware, drives, and processors. Its mandate was to integrate hardware and software functions and develop new applications for existing software platforms. Srinu, in particular, worked on the expansion of existing software into the fields of health and medicine. He was from a small town on the coast of Andhra Pradesh, on the eastern shores of South India, just north of Chennai, and had been trained both in computer science and in business management practices. At twenty-six, Srinu was thinking about how his job at Infotech might lead to a well-paid and high-status job back in Chennai or in Bangalore, and at the same time, he was thinking about how establishing himself in this way would allow him to get married and start a family.

The architecture of Infotech's offices recalls Gilles Deleuze's description of a society of control as a modulation of preexisting ways of life. In societies of control, disciplinary enclosures for the molding of docile subjects have given way to what Emil Røyrvik and Marianne Brodersen describe as "decentralized, relational networks type of reciprocal surveillance," prevalent in new economy workplaces:[7] The cafeteria, where Srinu told me about his family and shared with me his opinions on migration law, both continues and offers respite from these networks. Office workers sit at communal tables; they can choose food cooked by cafeteria staff or from a number of local restaurants around the office. Most workers seem to finish their meals together and then move off en masse back to their workstations, but some linger, deep in conversation or simply sitting on their own. No one minds the lingerers, since they could be working out a solution to a complex work problem—or they could be working on a project or having a discussion that is outside the parameters of work.

Like in other "no collar" offices, the open spaces in Srinu's workplace are designed to foster communication and creativity, thereby incorporating the critique of cubicle culture as inhuman directly into the design of the office.[8] The hope is that if workers are given free and open spaces, they will devise creative solutions to work problems and help open new markets that could not be thought of if the workers were disciplined more closely. At the same time, the proliferation of signs suggests a tension in the office. The smiley faces and warning signs, Post-it notes and stern admonitions to move conversations elsewhere try to create spaces of quiet fixity in an otherwise observant office, attempting to reestablish clearly demarcated boundaries between kinds of activities in a new economic order where the emphasis is on blurring borders. Knowledge workers themselves make the signs; it is not a disciplinary adjustment imposed by management to a worker-driven ideal of a transparent office. The signs suggest that resistance to the kind of control Deleuze describes may come in the form of trying to deflect "perpetual metastability" away from the individual worker, at least temporarily, and at least in some corners of the office.[9]

Programmers maneuver within the constraints of corporate work to create a space for a good and pleasurable life, what I call, following Bifo Berardi and Herbert Marcuse, eros.[10] Marcuse posited that in fully capitalist societies, domination had to be accomplished through channeling desire. While people in such societies were freed from want and scarcity, he argued, their instincts were channeled into perpetuating their own submission to endless cycles of production and consumption. Marcuse wrote in the "Political Preface" to the 1966 edition of *Eros and Civilization*, "The reproduction, bigger and better, of the same ways of life came to mean, even more clearly and consciously, the closing of those other possible ways of life which could do away with . . . the productivity of repression."[11] Marcuse called those other ways of life "eros" for the life-affirming instincts that he believed to be repressed.

In regimes of cognitive labor, according to Bifo Berardi, the nature of domination has changed. No longer repressive, domination works through hyperexpressivity, "an excess of visibility, the explosion of the info-sphere and an overload of info-neural stimuli."[12] We are incited, according to

Berardi's analysis, to produce and receive new packets of information and emotion almost constantly. Berardi finds the antidote to hyperexpressivity neither in a return to repression nor in Marcuse's liberation but rather in the channeling of expressivity into new pathways that help define and pose the question, what is a good life?[13] It is this sense of eros that I saw programmers trying to make possible through their coding practices.

Freedom in digital worlds is often described as freedom from restriction. Battles over regulation, intellectual property, and privacy online have pitched those who describe code as free speech against those who describe it as ownable property. These debates largely revolve around whether knowledge and communicative acts can be owned, since "knowledge is not just a good or resource, defined and delimited like standard goods produced and exchanged on the markets, but a dynamic entity and a cognitive tool pertaining to social groups that is crucial to both the individual and to social action."[14] This "second enclosure movement," or making of knowledge a kind of alienable (or separable) property, has required the development of legal instruments and persuasive moral arguments to fine-tune ownership over knowledge.[15] Accordingly, the politics of free software, indigenous knowledge rights, and intellectual commons have pitched ownership against fair and free use—the gradual enclosure of formerly shared knowledge behind corporate walls abetted by pro-business legislation.[16]

The "polymorphous collaboration, unrestrained plagiarism, and extraordinary cultural productivity" celebrated in open source coding projects often takes as its intellectual foil precisely the kinds of knowledge-owning practices that proliferate in the corporate worlds where Indian programmers work.[17] Indeed, at many points in their narration of their lives, these programmers agree with this basic critique of corporate coding. They suggest that the association between coding projects and bottom lines inhibits both their free play and creativity as coders and their ability to move freely through the world, hampered as they are by migration legislation. In equal measure, however, programmers fight for ownership of their time and their projects within the space of the office. These strategies suggest that, in practice, ownership and egalitarian sharing are not radically opposed but are entangled.[18] At the same time, these coders' practices of owning code suggest that the question of property needs to be reassessed from the perspective of privacy in a milieu that generally elicits sharing knowledge with the company.

Sometimes, programmers use one particular property of the code they write, namely, its ability to work across contexts and applications, in any environment, and to solve any problem (its "executable state," as Alexander Galloway calls it), to open a wedge between the conditions of work that they experience and the potential that their work should afford.[19] They then try to extend their relationship to that work to hold on to their jobs longer than their given contracts. They turn the strategy of creating private property out of office-owned code into a means of affirming eros by developing a theory of freedom that concomitantly affirms their right to own what they produce and their right to travel as uninhibitedly as the code does. Although freedom in coding worlds is usually articulated through an ideology of lack of ownership and freedom from restriction, Indian programmers pursue private ownership for the sake of eros. Thus, and rather spectacularly, Indian programmers often take up both sides of the debate on freedom and property in software and other forms of intellectual property. They claim both the right to own what they write and the right to travel freely across the boundaries. This dual sense of freedom is established by analogy with code that should transcend proprietary protections. The double right they claim suggests an alternative theory of freedom that is based on the right to live a good life rather than on freedom from restriction. This freedom would extend the freedom of movement to people at the same time that it recognizes the universal right to eros.

As Kant drew the distinction, coders work in the gap between what he described as freedom from interference and freedom to actively choose a course of life. For Kant, freedom was to be defined as "a warrant to obey no external laws except those to which I have been able to give my own consent" and thus constituted a positive freedom to decide on the law. In the current milieu, however, the negative freedom from interference Kant rejected provides the general baseline against which (and through recourse to ownership) more erotic—that is, containing polymorphous kinds of happiness—forms of freedom can be pitched.[20]

To help understand how privacy and ownership play out in writing code, a programmer sat down with me in Seattle and walked me through a snippet of code he was working on. Written in the programming language Java, it is a utility that will hide user information from display when it is being collected. The snippet looked like this:

```
public class LogUtils {
private static Boolean obfuscateLog=true;
public static void set ObfuscateLog (Boolean obfuscate Log) {
}
public static String obfuscate (string value) {
if (!obfuscateLog) {
return value;
else {
return "[obfuscated]";
}
public static String obfuscate (object object) {
if (!obfuscateLog) {
return object.toString();
} else {
return "[obfuscated]";
'      }
}
}
```

There is much that can be said about this snippet of code. For program-mers who use Java, several things will stand out, such as its being a work in progress that currently is set to hide all information as default. This will have to be changed as the program is further developed so that qualified users will be able to see the information that is relevant to their work. Even though it is bad practice, Java uses templates that name things the same, which may also be changed. Finally, there are several braces (that is, { }) that are currently not doing anything and will either be eliminated or filled with further snippets of code. For the purposes of this chapter, I want to home in on the private and public functions of this code. As it was explained to me, the code contains parts that can be freely accessed and amended by others who get this utility. These are the parts of the program that begin with "public." On the other hand, the parts of the code labeled "private" will be hidden from view and therefore cannot be modified. This distinction makes it easier to test a piece of code to make sure it is working correctly, because different parts of the code can be isolated and changed piecemeal. It also limits how people can use the utility, and therefore limits how it can be broken, because only certain parts can be changed in the future. Within this framework, private settings are a means of controlling access to the underlying source code, while public settings provide freedom from restriction. Within coding work, the positive freedom to make the rules and the negative freedom to be free from rules work together and are in tension with each other. They also provide one possible template for thinking through human freedom as entailed in both private and public functions.[21]

Protecting private areas of code resonates with other practices private programmers enact, such as saving money to buy an apartment so that a married couple can move out of their parents' house. Opening these private areas of code to changes also accords with programmers' desire to open up restrictions on how they can operate in the world of corporate coding work. As I recount in the remainder of this chapter, what code should do, ought to do, has done, and continues to do are all matters of serious contestation. When looked at from the perspective of migrant labor, the contradiction between free code and unfree people becomes apparent as a problem that needs to be solved by means of reforming the relationship between the private and public, obscured and visible areas of programming.

Indian Programmers and the Production of Semiotic Capital

I found that many people in Berlin's IT industry thought the world of code and the everyday world should line up according to a principle of performative action, that is, the world should behave as clearly or straightforwardly as code—the code does what it says and so should people and machines do what they are supposed to. But they often differed in their interpretations of how code behaved. Indian programmers on short-term projects stressed the freedom of code to move across boundaries and do many things, a condition they contrasted with their own constrained mobility. German managers and Indian managers who had successfully moved beyond the short-term work contract stressed that code was reliable and expected their employees to be the same. In their opinion, the code was something that should function in a timely manner and as promised, and they often analogized this expectation to Indian coders on short-term contracts.

Karin Knorr Cetina argues that the relationship between persons and objects of expertise (such as code) has at least two facets. It can be construed as instrumental, and it can be open to being continually redefined.[22] Similarly, Indian coders can be likened to instruments that are "an available means to an end within a logic of instrumental action." Or, they can be part of a "mutual communicative partaking" with the code they write.[23] In this latter sense, they are kindred with code, they take on what code provides them, namely, an example of how to move effortlessly through the world, to the extent that they immerse themselves in coding worlds. The former relationship was often stressed by managers in IT offices, while the latter relationship was often stressed by the Indian short-term coders with whom I spoke.

Most often, the critique of cognitive work pits freedom of creative agency against the channeling of that impulse. Tiziana Terranova, for example, writes that cognitive capitalism locates control "at two ends of the process: at the beginning, when a set of local rules is carefully put together and fine-tuned; and at the end, when a searching device or a set of aims and objects aim at ensuring the survival of the most useful or pleasing variations."[24] The creative impulses that came out of the workers' movements of the late 1960s, according to this critique, produced the potential for unprecedented modes of sharing and public organization located outside the sphere of capitalist production. But this human capacity, while still very much with us *in posse*, has been largely sequestered within "a thick net of hierarchical relations." In the critique of cognitive labor, freedom would be signaled by the production of "unrestrained invention . . . which hinges on a kind of latent wealth, or an exuberance of possibilities."[25]

While in no way wanting to diminish a call for invention that has undergirded many positive critical social movements, the divide between unrestrained creativity and creative control is clearly overstated. This becomes especially clear when we consider that office culture explicitly encourages blurring boundaries and producing communicative acts that may lead to productive activity in the future. In light of this fact, it may be that freedom is found in small acts of privacy that workers try to create when the company formally owns everything from their time to their ideas.

In a very different context, John Jackson's study of public space in Harlem makes a similar point. Describing the way that sidewalk space is used in everyday life by different manner of Harlemites from old-time residents to new townhome developers, he writes: "Residents' paths to and from, say, laundromats and corner bodegas, Chinese or Senegalese restaurants, their children's public school, and so on, become tiny patches of peripatetic privacy within an overdetermined landscape of market-based privatization. . . .

These intimate paths through public space are not equivalent to individual ownership in any simple sense. If anything, it is an ownership of space that money cannot actually buy."[26]

I think of the signs asking for quiet as establishing temporary privacy within the workspace that is not overdetermined from the start in terms of its uses. In other words, these islands of privacy are often used to complete something on deadline or drown out the exuberant creativity (and surveillance) of free-flowing conversation in order to control human activity and make it productive as a source of value to capitalism. But these private moments might also be pools of concentration that a coder may use to work on a problem away from the pressure of deadlines or for an office worker to check e-mail, read the news, chat with family and friends, and do many of the things not directed toward productivity. Creating pools of quiet might be a strategy to keep errant matter errant, that is, precisely to *not* make knowledge immediately appropriable by the office at large. Rather than there being a pure antimony between capital and its resistances, these temporary private moments point to the need both to disambiguate kinds of privacy within neoliberalism, as Jackson suggests, and to pose resistance as a counterconduct, emanating from the same techniques of freedom and privacy that knowledge work has built up as a tactic of capitalist accumulation.[27]

The next two sections turn to how the two sides of debates of intellectual property in software are mirrored in the ability of Indian coders to critique and strategize in the spaces of their labor. Indian programmers critique their limited ability to pursue work projects by comparing their lives with the possibilities inherent in the code they write, and they try to create small areas of temporary ownership of code throughout the workday. Of course, in the IT office, unlike on the street corners Jackson discusses, the space is already unambiguously bought by the company. In such a situation of clear ownership, where knowledge tilts toward the owners of production, these private moments both mimic and redirect technologies of corporate control.

Code Is Free, Why Aren't We?

I often heard Indian software engineers describe code in terms similar to the ones Meenakshi used one day, as "a set of instructions that tell a computer to do something." Similarly, she suggested, "it is the job of the IT worker to produce instructions that work in the time allotted for a given project."

In conversation with one another and with me, however, they often voiced the opinion that those who do not really understand how coding works often hinder them in this task. On this day, at the end of a long workweek, Meenakshi and Mihir were talking about their jobs and their job chances.

Mihir worked for a cell phone company debugging ringtones. In his conversation with Meenakshi, he agreed that, like a computer, the job of the programmer is to get the work done but pointed out the ways the "bosses," as he called them, get in the way. Mihir said, "With our skills we should be able to go anywhere to do the job. But we are not allowed." They disagreed about the bosses' role. Meenakshi told him that "the bosses have to answer to the clients and we have to do what they ask of us." But Mihir, working in a small shop of twelve people and with, in his opinion, an unfriendly boss, was less sympathetic. "We are free to do the work," he ended the conversation, "but we are not free to move up." Meenakshi aligned herself with the manager by stressing the unpredictability of client demands, thereby creating solidarity within the firm. Mihir, on the other hand, believed that Indians are continually frustrated by unfair migration regimes (a topic Srinu discusses below) and arbitrary glass ceilings. In making this critique, Mihir uses what he thinks of as the inherent properties of code as a negative example to illuminate his own restrictions. Many Indian coders I spent time with implicitly and explicitly make the argument that they too, like the code, should be able to go anywhere and use their skills to solve problems. They point out a contradiction between the freedom of code to cross boundaries and their inability to do so by aligning themselves as experts with the knowledge embodied in code.

Srinu was sitting with me on the short train ride from the neighborhood where we both lived, called Wedding, to Infotech's offices near Humboldt University. He talked about how he will have to adapt if he is to have more than a temporary job at his company. "I really enjoy the engineering side," he conceded, "but you get labeled an expert in a particular area." If you get pigeonholed as only a coder, it marks the end of your upward mobility. Srinu indicated that many Indian IT workers, instead of "moving up," are "moved out" to further short-term jobs or back home without a job at all. "I used to write code on the weekends just for fun," continued Srinu, "but I now spend my time studying marketing and using PowerPoint." He missed what he called "geeking out." "It's the fate of the manager," he said, describing his future work. "As you go up, you can't go into detail." He was willing to pay the price of leaving behind his geeking-out days because he wants to stay with the firm, get a better position and salary, and, above all, move from a temporary to a permanent position.

As he readied himself to leave the train, Srinu leaned over to me and said, "I have a story for you that you can put in your notebook." He promised to tell me at the end of the day. When we reconvened later at Meenakshi and Rajeshwari's apartment it was nearly ten o'clock; Srinu looked exhausted as he took off his smart overcoat and put down his briefcase. As usual, he had not eaten. Rajeshwari, twenty-eight and completing her master's degree in computer science at the Technical University of Berlin, remembered to leave some food aside for him. After filling his plate and wolfing it down hungrily, he turned to me and asked if I was ready for his story.

Two people, researchers and friends, both from India, were trying to go to a conference in the United States, in New Orleans. They both had similar backgrounds and qualifications. And they both applied for a visa to go to the conference. They were kept waiting until the last minute; each had bought a ticket for the trip and had prepared a paper. In the end, one got the visa, and the other did not. "With no explanation," said Srinu, "it's perfectly arbitrary and has nothing to do with reason or logic." His eyes were twinkling as he told me that, and as he asked, "Can you explain that? Will your work help solve that kind of problem?" I had to answer that I could not really explain it, according to logic, nor, as Srinu knew, would what I write do anything to change the situation. For Srinu, this was a clear example of the difference between how people and ideas are allowed, even encouraged, to travel.

The next day, as if to round out his narrative about the way technoeconomies actually frustrate and prohibit people from pursuing what makes them happy, Srinu mentioned yet another example of the lack of freedom. Walking to the subway in the morning, Srinu turned to me and declared, "You are working on migration and intermixing, but in my opinion, there is no real intermixing here. Real assimilation would mean people marrying each other and choosing to live and raise their families in different places." Srinu had in mind the way the Indian programmers were treated in the office where they work as cheap labor and as reservoirs of knowledge about India, limits on migration, and the restrictions his family will place on him to marry someone from home. I noticed how his remarks link the person, the politics, and the job as arbitrary blockages in the expression of eros.

Like the code that could be used to solve any problem, given enough time, resources, and talent, high-skilled migrants represent boundless potential that is restricted by arbitrary laws and people (such as visa-dispensing bureaucrats and business-oriented project managers) who lack the expertise to appreciate the importance of technical work. Information technology workers can create and command code, but they cannot partake in code's disembodied universal logic. The logic of code's unrestricted travel leads coders to think along parallel tracks: in terms of updating skills in what they think of as continuous résumé building and in terms of both reinforcing and evading the cultural, racial, and third-worldist suppositions that make Indian coders desirable as temporary workers. As Mihir told me on a night when I sat with him late into the evening, "With our skills in programming, we should be able to go anywhere we are needed, and we can solve many problems. All this—our work, our excursions, our travel—is, in some way or the other, limited."

While the short conversation between Meena and Mihir indicates considerable disagreement when evaluating management strategies, programmers were more in concert in discussing the inhibiting logic of migration laws. Although I recognize the speculative nature of some of the conclusions I reach here, I believe that often, by using code to think about the conditions of their own lives, programmers expose a neoliberal model of achievement that simultaneously rewards expertise wherever it is found and sequesters subjects within the concrete realities of embodiment and place in the name of rationalizing expertise. The reputation of Indian coders for having good back-end skills (that is, being able to code for long periods of time and get the job done quickly) often helps Indian programmers get their foot in the door in IT firms. At the same time, it can hinder what they can accomplish there. The strategies they use to move out of short-term jobs and beyond this reputation at once recognize and disavow the unjust logic of neoliberal apportioning of difference and merit that binds Indian coders and a particular type of coding. These strategies seek to move Indian coders out of the back room and into management positions. Like the snippet of Java code that makes some part of the code visible, public, and changeable and others obscured and private, Indian coders try to obscure some parts of their cognitive labor to be able to exercise more control and keep others from breaking what they've worked so hard to achieve.

The chapter began by wondering how programmers who are positioned within such complicated migration schemes and in the politics of labor divisions within a "polyoptic" office culture find room for maneuver. In the following example, writing bad comments takes advantage of the overriding desire on the part of project managers to get a piece of coding done on deadline to insert a programmer as irreplaceable expert on a project.

Bad Commenting

"One," said Bipin in his characteristically staccato delivery style, as he began to outline the problems with "spaghetti code," "it's an imposition on the next person who's going to have to pick that work up." "But two," he continued, gesturing toward the multiple open windows on his screen, "software, as it gets bigger, as more and more functionality that's interrelated is added, it becomes what programmers call a 'ball of mud,' or 'spaghetti code,' just impossible to disentangle." I was shadowing this thirty-four-year-old coder from Hyderabad in the office where he worked in the former East Berlin. It was after 9:00 PM and he was still moving through a section of code that according to the testers was not operating correctly. Bipin was one of the few married programmers I met in Berlin. His wife, Madhu, also a programmer, had managed to secure a job at another firm in the city. As Bipin told it, it is Madhu who has the hard-core programming skills and is highly sought after, so it is relatively easy for her to get a job. On the other hand, because he trained in IT management, he has been able to move into a fairly secure position managing his own team. Bipin and Madhu do not plan to settle permanently outside of India. Instead, they simply want to make enough money abroad to be able to buy their own apartment back in Hyderabad, as they put it, across the street from but not in the same building as Bipin's parents. This move signifies another arena outside the formal boundaries of coding where these Indian programmers pursue pools of privacy in an otherwise shared environment.[28]

On this evening, Bipin leaned back in his chair, taking a break from moving back and forth between the code and the comments that accompanied it, and took a long and satisfying gulp from the milky, sweet, scalding hot tea that always seemed to hover somewhere near his right hand. He explained to me why the job was taking so long. Someone had failed to put in complete source code documentation. According to Bipin, code should ideally be commented on so that it is legible and provides useful insight into the work that was done for subsequent teams continuing the project. The negative consequences of messy code that is not properly commented on can become monumental over time. Once you reach a ball of mud or spaghetti code, it becomes very difficult to change one piece without changing all others. It is hard to maintain correctly functioning code because all parts of the system are so interconnected. Over time, unregimented commenting can lead to a breakdown of the entire infrastructure of programming for a firm. Bad commenting makes up "the world of thick, unmanageable constraints" on the performance of code.[29]

Hearing the way bad commenting can build up over time and conscious of how late it was and how tired Bipin was, I imagined he must be really annoyed about the bad comments and asked him if he plans to talk to his group about them and try to find the culprit. Bipin, however, was surprisingly laid back about it.

Bipin was in charge of a team that adds on to an already existing software platform his company developed. His team was building more functionality into this platform and making it work with other types of software. There were weekly and monthly deadlines he had to meet, and he held an official "scrum" every Wednesday where he reported on his progress and heard from other teams about theirs.[30] The ball of mud impeded his progress. Yet Bipin was quite sanguine on the bad comments he had to wade through. He juxtaposed commenting with the ticking clock. "One," he began again, "comments are important in the long run, but clients often ask us to do things we don't know if we can actually do as fast as they want it. When it comes to putting in comments, they can be sacrificed to the pace of the job. And two," Bipin added, "if the boss sees we are getting the job done, that is more important." Finally, he linked bad commenting to extending a work contract. "Three, although leaving comments is a courtesy to other coders, doing so means you are also more replaceable. In a commercial environment, there is a disincentive to leave comments. You're more irreplaceable if you don't explain what you've done!"

Restricting documentation can be a subversive way to extend labor contracts. Because workers are on short-term contracts (most less than two years), if their work becomes tied closely with themselves as unique individuals through code that works and is produced on time rather than code that is well documented, they become harder to replace and consequently more valuable. If a coder fails to comment, then she is the only one who can understand the code and has become irreplaceable by virtue of making a very tight link between a snippet of code and her personhood. For Indian coders, the potential for further opportunities at a firm is in tension with the discipline of notation.

Bipin narrated the failure to comment comprehensively on coding as both a strategy for drawing out a work project and a by-product of the pace and expectations of migrant programming jobs. Bad commenting is a strategy that helps mitigate the risks of being removed from a project even while contributing to its overall instability. Bipin reminds us that the boss must see the work accomplished. In other words, the coder must produce code and must perform according to the standards of the project manager. Because of this, Bipin reported, there is not time to leave good comments. But this time constraint is improvised on and used by coders as a means of keeping their jobs for a little while longer. Failure to comment becomes a way of garnering longevity in a short-term labor market.

According to the system of classification that many programmers I interviewed deploy, programmers come in many different "types." Most divided programmers into planners and executors as a first cut into the different kinds of work style. One friend distinguished between programmers and coders, saying that programmers are those who have an overview and plan strategically and coders are those who just write code. He then flipped the metaphor, saying that he preferred to call himself a coder, because the programmers do not really do anything. For him, coding was worthwhile, although he says that in a corporate atmosphere it is programming that receives all the glory. This division is further made recursively between programmers who work by the seat of the pants, fix code, and move on (sometimes called duct tape programmers) and those who try to make beautiful, easy-to-read, and efficient code (perfectionists). These two categories embody very well the office conflict between getting work done on time and getting work done that can be extended, be built on, and create a robust infrastructure for a company. At the same time, flipping the valence of worth suggests that within the hierarchy between planners and executors, or programmers and coders, there is room for maneuver, strategy, and the elaboration of a counterethics of work and the enjoyment of life.

Bad commenting is a strategy for militating against replaceability that depends on exploiting the pace of the job. "The management of time in IT offices," as Aileen O'Carroll explains, "occur[s] within the constraints of externally imposed deadlines. However, unpredictability, the non-repetitive nature of the tasks, the dependence on technology or on others can lead to tasks taking much longer (or indeed much less time) to complete than expected, making it difficult to 'plan according to the clock.'" That very unpredictability, which "pits the task-oriented time of programming jobs against the homogeneous time of client-driven deadlines," is used by some Indian programmers to create two levels of work.[31] On the face of it and to management, they get the work done on time, whenever possible. Within the project and for the sake of their own position in the firm, they put in devices that may help them "own" the work they do going forward, so that a tie is created between themselves and the project and they become irreplaceable.

The exploitation of time pressure is not a strategy that is exclusive to Indian programmers but rather is endemic to an industry that relies on two radically different kinds of time, corporate clock time and the lived time of creative work: "The limits of the IT workplace are the limits to how fast, how often, how continuous the creative effort is, yet the creative effort is a process that resists compression."[32] There were moments, for instance, in which Indian programmers made promises of finishing projects quickly without knowing in advance if the project could be completed at all. When I asked one programmer about these decisions, she argued for a disconnect between the pace of the industry, the bosses' evaluation of her work, and her place within the company. "Often you don't know," this programmer opined, "whether you can do a project until you start it. But in order to get a contract, the bosses have to say it is possible, so we too tell them it is possible." Some programmers complained about their managers, who really had "no idea" of what was possible and what was untried. "They make all sorts of promises to the clients," Mihir once lamented, "but weren't themselves sure if the company could follow through." In turn, the programmers make promises to the managers that they themselves are not sure they can fulfill.

Despite the general contradiction between client-driven deadlines and project time, Indian programmers are particularly tasked with bringing work in on schedule, since they were hired especially for this purpose. This translates into staying very late at work. Mihir, for instance, was the only one other than his boss who has a key for the small firm at which he works. He was expected to come in after hours and on weekends. He told me that his German friend Sasha often asked him why he works so hard. And he was quite at a loss for what to say. He did work hard. All programmers noted at one time or another that German employees worked very hard but adhered to very strict coming and going times. At 3:00 PM on Friday, the office was deserted, except for the short-term migrant programmers who continued to work to fix bugs, cut code, and test software. "Indian programmers," said Meenakshi, "have a habit of working hard. But it is also what bosses expect." It was not rare to hear from Germans in the IT industry that Indians were suited to long hours at work, were better at abstract thinking, and did not mind the kind of asceticism that comes with those hours. They called them "the computer experts" and the "IT Indians" (*IT Inder*), highlighting their function as workers who program and their expertise at producing code.

The long work hours and abstract processes of computer work are clearly an expectation that falls disproportionately on Indian programmers precisely because they have been brought in as a labor force to produce reliable code on time. The history of Indian spirituality in the West provides an ex post facto justification for these expectations.

Appropriating Code's Freedom and the Ownership of Code

In their definition of freedom, many Indian coders describe it through analogies to their knowledge of how code works—the ability to move anywhere in the world pursuing their version of a good life. This position is simultaneously racially democratic, in that it provides a critique of migration controls, and profoundly elitist, in that the freedom of movement it prescribes is apportioned according to the merit one has as a programmer. Indian coders participate in a general culture of programming that balances sharing and cooperation with "an elitist stance that places an extremely high premium on self-reliance, individual achievement, and meritocracy."[33] Once they are elite, these workers will be in the position of getting the contracts. Ironically, they will then hear the same phrases from the new "not yet elite," telling them they can do the job on time and under budget. Some, like Bipin, will make allowances for the exploitation of time for the sake of security, while others will suggest that these workers have not lost their Indian mind-set, thereby forgetting the very practices that they themselves engaged in to get ahead: "Indian IT workers . . . offer a powerful embodiment of a new India in which each advances according to his or her individual merit rather than parochial categories." Such an ideology "gloss[es] over the inequalities of the elite education system in India," and workers "understand their own status as a result of their own hard work, talent, and effort."[34] Yet, this moment of possible erasure in which the structural critique of freedom and its limits gives way to the promotion of success as individual achievement is also the moment that can generate an alternative mode of freedom as eros, as in Srinu's comments about marriage.

The argument for code as free speech is undergirded by a legal argument stating that because code is a form of communication that is written and can have artistic properties, its expression, like that of speech, cannot be restricted. The argument for freedom of movement says that in the real world code is relatively unrestricted in where it can go, hence digital worlds are an example of a possible world in which people, too, are unrestricted in where they can go. In many cases, this latter line of argument has been dismissed as cyberutopian or cyberlibertarian, because it suggests that virtual worlds are inherently freer than embodied worlds.[35] But for Indian programmers, the claim is not so much libertarian as utopian in the sense of responding to an existing set of constraints with a set of better, but still imperfect, possibilities.[36] This claim takes the premise of a borderless world promised by information technologies and tries to make it real and concrete in practice. Like demands for true equality in situations of structural discrimination despite juridical equality, it reveals the hypocrisy of a system that so depends on the work of migrant coders but does not treat them as well as it does the programs they produce.

As Kavita Philip outlines in an important article, the major stakeholders in the free software–open software movement have become conservative over time, relying now on distinguishing between good and bad piracy. Piracy that must be defended is the creative reuse of ideas; that which must be policed is piracy that simply copies. But, as Lawrence Liang notes, piracy that is not creating something new is nevertheless "providing an entry point into the material for a large number of people who otherwise would have no access to it."[37] Philip posits that in such moments, "the possibilities of being a subject in this sphere are detached from the requirements of unique authorship . . . [and] the appropriative function is foregrounded."[38] In other words, for those made marginal to it, thriving in a knowledge-based economy requires appropriating the code in unsanctioned ways that do not correspond to prevailing definitions of good work.

Bipin's understanding of bad comments has this kind of sensibility about it. Duct tape code is not the kind of programming that would make most coders proud. As he mentioned, it leads to spaghetti code, code that is impossible to untangle. Such programming practices are not something that would be claimed by an author as would clear, agile, and well-written code. But it is a practice of appropriating the material properties of code for personal ends that provides continued access to the goods of the global technoeconomy for those who use this tactic.

Against the backdrop of the flexible workplace that encourages innovation and tries to channel it productively, Indian IT workers must strategically deploy the stereotype of the good Indian coder without allowing themselves to be reduced to being merely cheap, fast, and replaceable workers. At issue here is both making use of the ideological connection between India and IT work and making sure not to be trapped by the way it has been articulated. Often, Indian coders do so by trying to personalize their labor, by making the code they write part of themselves even in the midst of producing it for their firms. This is a form of proprietary freedom that is liberating and not reducible to the freedom of the market. In fact, it works precisely against such a neoliberal idea of freedom of exchange by holding something back from the exchange.

The creation of illegible comments is one instance of a different kind of autonomy, one that does not resist the management of work itself but rather rechannels that work away from its serial exchangeability and toward an anchoring of the properties of code in the body of the Indian IT worker herself.[39] In this way, it "devirtualizes" programming, pointing the temporary ownership of code back toward precisely those workers who otherwise cannot claim to own what they write. Like the conversations on the sidewalk, claims to temporary ownership of a commonly held good can be done in the name of increased access and equalizing social relations.

The demand some programmers make, that they should be able to circulate as freely as the code they write, comes up against the limits of freedom as defined in liberal digital worlds, where a difference between program and person is maintained as a way of staying within the bounds of a speaking liberal subject as the legal grounds for freedom of speech.[40] Sociological and anthropological studies of free software unfortunately often follow this lead, taking the "code as speech" antiproperty argument as synonymous with freedom.[41] This lacuna limits freedom to the particular and culturally local idea of maintaining an intellectual commons.

On the other hand, the mismatch between the ability of code to circulate and the ability of bodies to do so arises out of how Indian knowledge workers are situated in IT offices as expendable back-office laborers. Their demands for expanded visas or better quality of work are excluded from the demand for freedom of software precisely because admitting to these differences would widen the scope of freedom to such an extent that the very premise of free speech (without free people) as a legal precept would be questioned. The proprietary freedom evidenced here responds to the contradiction between Indian embodied difference as an expansive and proliferating sign and Indian bodies as needing to be managed, controlled, and limited in their movements. It holds on to a little piece of code not to monetize it but to bootstrap on that area of privacy and redirect its energies toward pursuing a good and satisfying life.

|| • ENCODING CLASS

The Indian middle class, sometimes referred to by the acronym NMC—or new middle class—has been analyzed as crucial to social, economic, and political life in contemporary India. Already important for its demographic dominance in government positions and presenting a normative model for good citizenship, the Indian middle class is newly important for its leadership in privatizing the Indian economy. In other words, what is "new" about middle-class Indians today is their orientation toward the market and their preference for defining themselves through commodity cultures and privatized pleasures rather than through government service. Theorists have rightly pointed out the new hegemony of this class, for the way it transmits to other classes a model for being globally Indian.

But what is missing in these discussions is a sense of the social significance of being a middle-class Indian. In other words, the category NMC is taken too literally, as if classes are best described as discrete units that make up a social whole, complete in themselves and without contradiction (except between classes). Even when it is clear that, according to income, buying power, and commodity ownership, the middle class in India is stratified, this translates in existing literature into making further distinctions among "upper" and "lower" layers of the middle class itself. Though this approach can bring into relief aspiration to membership in the middle class, it tells us very little of how it feels, what it means, and how one becomes a middle-class Indian.

Part I of *Encoding Race, Encoding Class* tracks the multiple ways Indian IT workers are racialized in global corporate software economies—as needed but unwanted migrants, as laboring bodies suited to particular kinds of work, and as sources of creative content for the creation of new value. Programmers both make use of and answer back to these forms of racialization by trying to climb the corporate ladder and by refusing the particular worker subjectivity that a cognitive office demands. Part II investigates how these workplace routines are sewn into practices of creating class affiliations. The opposition of Indian IT workers to work regimes in the office is elaborated in ways of inhabiting the Indian middle class.

By shifting the description from the category of the new Indian middle class to the question of being a middle-class Indian, I also argue that class is better thought of as a process than as a category. As such, establishing membership in this class is unfolding and continuous, while being a middle-class Indian may require negotiating between competing and conflicting ideas of middle-classness itself.

In the next three chapters, I explore how the programmers who are the protagonists of this story negotiate their loyalties to work, consumer patriotism, and family—all possible frameworks through which the new Indian middle class may be defined. Short-term programmers move toward what I have been calling *eros*, or a vision of the good life that is not wholly captured by any of these frames but at the same time does not directly contravene them. I hope to show thereby that while diasporic subjects are often thought of as living "in between" home and abroad, in this case it might be more accurate to say they are innovating new understandings of home and abroad, leisure and work, consumption and saving. In this way, their habitations of the Indian middle class are informed by and are in response to a much more general reorganization of life and work we tend to call "neoliberal."

FOUR

THE STROKE OF MIDNIGHT AND
THE SPIRIT OF ENTREPRENEURSHIP

A History of the Computer in India

A vital question which comes before any organization, before planning a computer installation, is—why go in for a computer?
—Charanjit Chanana, 1973

"I never realized that I had it running in my veins," read the first line of an e-mail that popped into my inbox in 2012. "Yes, the spirit of entrepreneurship," the e-mail from Adi continued. Adi had decided to launch his own start-up, a business based on an idea for a software product that was untested. The e-mail's subject line read "At the Stroke of Midnight!" After getting his master of computer science degree from the Technical University in Berlin, Adi married London-born Maya, whom he met through friends from Delhi University, where he had gone to college. Adi and Maya, in their early thirties, were a little bit older than most other programmers they knew. They had a two-year-old son, Krishna, and often talked about where it would be best to raise him—in England, in Germany, or in India. Because of Adi's degree from a prestigious university, their ties to England, and Adi's family network that included prosperous business professionals, Adi was better positioned than most to move out of the limited coding jobs available under the German green card. His e-mail was the first step in a series of messages that would ask family and friends to contribute funding to his venture. The remainder of the message said:

My parents have been quite versatile with their ambitions as they went about establishing a Textile Mill, a School, a Brokerage and Stationery shop, and finally a Financial Services firm. This fact was registered somewhere in my unconscious mind but I didn't realize it even as I went about serving the entrepreneur community as a volunteer.

Sareeta, at the stroke of the midnight, I will take a step—a step outside my comfort zone, a step into unchartered waters, a step into the unknown. It is a step that is taken with passion, with confidence, with humility, and with energy. It will be an adventurous journey but it is also risky. And today, I just seek your wishes.

—E-mail received January 2011, subject line: At the Stroke of Midnight!

I spoke to Adi a few weeks later by phone and told him that I found his "stroke of midnight" language evocative. I asked if he had in mind Nehru's "Tryst with Destiny" speech on the eve of India's independence. In this speech, made to the Indian Constituent Assembly on August 14, 1947, shortly before midnight, Nehru began:

Long years ago we made a tryst with destiny, and now the time comes when we shall redeem our pledge, not wholly or in full measure, but very substantially. At the stroke of the midnight hour, when the world sleeps, India will awake to life and freedom. A moment comes, which comes but rarely in history, when we step out from the old to the new, when an age ends, and when the soul of a nation, long suppressed, finds utterance. . . .

The achievement we celebrate today is but a step, an opening of opportunity, to the greater triumphs and achievements that await us. Are we brave enough and wise enough to grasp this opportunity and accept the challenge of the future?[1]

Adi confirmed that he had meant to reference the speech, saying, "The speech is about birth and a moment of change. Like that, this is the birth of something new for me." And almost immediately after drawing the link between the birth of a nation and the birth of an enterprise, Adi added, "The e-mails should do something to affect you. They are making an emotional argument to get you interested in the well-being of something. Like in the stages of the growth of a child." Nehru's language suggests the dawning of independent India is "but one step" on a path toward further development and, at the same time, positioned the independence of India as a "tryst with destiny," a culmination of a process started long ago and in some way inevitable. These two ways of framing an event, as progress over time and as a return to destiny, resurface in the way that Indian programmers in the diaspora narrate their relationship to the Indian nation.

Over the following weeks and months, Adi's e-mails, all with the same "stroke of midnight" tagline, outlined for friends and family the stages of his company as a child's growth. From the infancy phase to first steps, at each stage the child needed emotional investment from friends and family to nourish it and keep it growing. Adi was surprised at how well this strategy was working. "Only one person," he told me, "complained that you are asking me for money but not even telling me what the project is about. All others are willing to give even without knowing what I'm building." Asking him why he thought they gave so freely, he answered that for some of the older generation who had already made their fortune, it was a chance for them "to relive the excitement of the early days, to share in a dream." Perhaps Adi had tapped into a deep reservoir of feeling in his citation of Nehru's speech, which framed Indian prosperity as both something to be achieved through conscious effort and something bound to happen. In Adi's e-mails, he aligned the excitement of India's "birth" and with the birth of his company. He used the affect of Nehru's speech, including the rhetoric of new opportunity and the "challenge for the future" and combined it with his own spirit of entrepreneurship to open the purses of e-mail recipients.[2] Adi's gambit was a success. He was able to get enough support through these e-mails without ever revealing their purpose. Adi felt he needed to keep his plans secret because the idea was what was really driving the project; otherwise, someone else could take the idea before he got enough capital together for his start-up.[3] By using these well-known nationalist tropes along with the image of the company as needy child, Adi brought corporate technological change within the ambit of the developmentalist time of the postcolonial nation.

At an earlier moment during fieldwork, everyone was sitting in Meenakshi's front room drinking hot milky tea out of flimsy plastic cups. The conversation had started as a comparison of universities in the United States, Europe, and India. The contours of this conversation suggested that the West was clearly ahead technologically but that it was only ahead for now and that perhaps it was even stagnating. To illustrate this point, Bipin made a slicing movement through the air with his hands. The brain drain, he said, is a problem now, but it will not be an issue in the future. "Things are moving closer together. A global village." He moved his hands clockwise, intoning, "Things move in a circle. Now, Germany and Europe are at the top of the circle that India is so desperately trying to reach, and they are already moving toward that other place." He let his hands drop downward toward the bottom of the imaginary circle he had just arced out in the space in front of him. "India's high point was with Ashoka, and at that time in Europe there were only barbarians."

On this day, Bipin suggested that the IT revolution was like the coming of a new age of Ashoka, the third-century B.C.E. king who is most famous for his Buddhist edicts, carved on rocks and stone pillars spread throughout the Indian subcontinent. For Bipin, India was already rising, and the problems of the present and the past were destined to diminish with its ascension. The programming classes, according to his story, simultaneously should advance the cause of India rising and would ride on the wings of its historical inevitability.

These two stories encapsulate a continuous and changing relationship between the entrepreneurial subject and the nation-state, a relationship that has too often been assumed to have been sundered irrevocably with the coming of economic liberalization and globalization marked by "footloose" capital. In other words, while many scholars have stressed the ongoing importance of the nation-state, the way that the continued presence of the nation-state impresses itself on the new subjects of capital remains to be worked out. In India, the relationship between middle-class programmers and the nation-state emerges out of the intertwining of technologies, middle-class experts, and state power. This chapter follows the relationship between middle-class programmers and the Indian nation-state by showing how technologies of state enrolled elite Indians as their representatives in the construction of national sovereignty. Technologies like big dams and supercomputers produced an Indian middle class by mobilizing experts in a milieu where possessing a scientific temperament was a requirement for nation-building.[4]

Bipin's and Adi's narrative strategies confirm that development discourses do not disappear in postliberal India.[5] The liberalization of the Indian economy, normally told as a story of rupture dating to 1991, is more accurately parsed as an ongoing process, in which stories of national development and market liberalization participate.[6] Adi extracts a teleology of development and weds it to a narrative of entrepreneurial self-fashioning. Bipin sutures a circular discourse on time to the inevitable rise of India. These methods position programmers as drivers and recipients of national development.[7]

Resisting the "before" and "after" logic through which the story of the software industry in India is told can illuminate how this very history is taken up in everyday life as a means of self-making and class-making. In other words, by tracing the continuities and contradictions in the story of the computer in India across the dateline of economic liberalization (1991), I try to make sense of one important location for the formation of the "new" Indian middle class—the intersection of technical expertise, state power, and subjectivity. In what follows, I bring together several histories of the computer revolution in India and read them in relation to Bipin's and Adi's story of national development as sociotechnical entrepreneurship. While technical expertise remained central to national development from the anticolonial period to the present day, the attitude of experts toward the state shifted from working on behalf of the state to working to reform and even bypass the state on behalf of the nation. The continued reliance on the idea of technical expertise as an essential tool of governance allowed those who possessed these skills to pivot away from direct state service and toward the private sector. This is one meaning of what Bipin was expressing with his assertion that India is rising. Programmers' fates will rise with the inevitable rise of the nation, and at the same time, diasporic programmers also produce the conditions for this rise. Inevitability and agency are linked, the present is folded into the certain horizon of the future, and the conditions of present labor are understood as part of the inheritance of the "flexible and mobile performance of contingent identities."[8]

Technology and the Indian National Imaginary

A persistent concern of this book is self-fashioning on the constantly shifting terrain of contemporary capitalism. The longer history of linkages among science and technology and the Indian state can help tell the story of how Indian programmers come to inhabit the paradigm of a flexible and cheap worker even as they try to divert their futures toward more fulfilling roles. Beginning with Nehru's postindependence calls for educated technologists who would lead the nation in its game of catch-up to the West, Indian scientists have been the recipients of national support (especially through education), have held leading positions within government, and have played the symbolic role of leaders on the national stage. Technologically educated Indian elites built on government support throughout the decades after independence (particularly in the 1980s and 1990s) to tighten the relationship between technology as a good of and for the nation and their personal, familial, and class- and caste-based investment in technological knowledge.

The success of outsourcing and software services rewrote the globally savvy coder as a middle-class paragon of Indian citizenship. The moment in which the tie between nation and technology could be expanded to Indians overseas marked a significant reversal of the relationship between diasporic Indians and the nation. This signaled a turn to technoentrepreneurialism as a means of further developing Indian national imaginaries.

In other words, the Indian software and outsourcing revolution mirrored the emergence of an India organized around the rise of a new middle class that turned toward private sector employment as a source of new wealth and symbolic power. Information technology sector titans, such as Nandan Nilekani, Aziz Premji, and Vinod Khosla, were examples of this new kind of entrepreneurialism, embodying in their stories the switch in emphasis from manufacturing to services, from government employment to private companies, from India-oriented to world-oriented.[9]

Within India's outsourcing industry, programmers are asked to perform a globally accepted Indian difference that maintains the allure of brand "India" to outside investors at the same time that it satisfies a national imaginary of Indianness.[10] At the time of this writing and according to my informants, the path to middle-class success for young Indians leads to computer programming jobs, which are favored even over disciplines such as medicine. Computer programming is thought to be more lucrative and is more attractive because it is associated with the "opening" of the Indian economy to privatization. The programming sector is also aspirational for lower classes, with some researchers reporting that computer science is now favored in village education over English.[11]

Programmers link themselves with the rhetorical power of a national imaginary such that the development of the nation and the development of the self align. These practices of inhabiting technological know-how emerge from the extended involvement of the Indian state with technocratic knowledge. Programmers are inheritors of the technocratic imaginary of the Indian state yet find it wanting; they employ multiple repertoires of expertise that express "a further way to look" and can be understood as continuing a relationship, mediated by objects, between the expert and the state, "provid[ing] for the continuation of the structure of wanting."[12] Adi's "At the Stroke of Midnight" tagline betrays a structure of wanting that links the desire for India to move forward with personal desire of techonological objects. The Nehruvian ideal of freedom at midnight remains a strong argument but one that moves audiences toward private initiatives that are to stand in for public goods.

For Adi, Bipin, and other programmers I spoke with, their approach to national development withdraws support from a state they see as inefficient even while it reaffirms support for the Indian nation. When I asked him what he thought the government's role should be in helping poor communities in India, Mayur, who worked in Bangalore before applying for a German green card, told me that it was up to businesspeople and professionals like himself to grow the Indian economy, which would produce more opportunity for other people. The state, he told me, "should set up the basic rules, like establishing the laws of physics. And then get out of the way."[13]

Adi's idea for his start-up was a business-to-business (B2B) venture that he called BSure, which he pitched as a software program plus online and phone support that would function as a saved log of personal connections. According to his business plan, employees of a firm would fill in a simple form after each call or e-mail interaction they had with a client, listing both personal details (such as birthdays, interests, or hobbies) and business concerns. This would go into a database, so that the next employee who would contact that firm could pull up this information. For an additional fee, Adi's company would keep track of clients' interests and send them appropriate gifts, tips, and suggestions that would correspond to their personal interests. With the start-up funds that Adi was able to garner through his e-mail campaign, he was able to move to London. His next step, he told me, was Silicon Valley, where he plans to pitch the idea to venture capitalists. Adi is a success story within Indian programming economies. From his start as a student at Berlin's Technical University, he was able to stay in Germany long enough to find a few programming jobs and then, through this campaign and the money he had saved, to move to London, where Maya had family. He may be on the cusp of vaulting himself out of the middle-class precarity that I describe in this book. Yet, his story exemplifies how Indian coders inhabit a middle-class identity that coheres around a changed relationship to the Indian state and around a long-standing relationship to technology as definitive of elite-led national development.

Narratives ábouts the past both craft a story about what happened and a relationship between that story and the present moment. What is more, such narratives, far from only being the creation of professional historians, are the stuff of everyday life, where "we are all amateur historians with various degrees of awareness about our production."[14] Moments of "retrospective significance" occur when actors try to compose a narrative that looks back from the perspective of the present to craft a story of how that present came to be—such as when Adi and Bipin relate a historical relationship presaging rising India. Understanding these moments as part of "the processes and conditions of production" of history produces an account of the power of these narratives and of fissures and silences within them.[15] By tracing the palimpsest of these moments, history of the sociotechnical present emerges that recognizes multiple technical worlds in the making and how those worlds are linked, here, with the question of class.[16]

State Projects and the Emergence of a Scientific Elite

The history of software in India is often treated shallowly. The watershed moment of 1991 when India liberalized its economy marks in this narrative the beginning of the IT revolution in India. Liberalization reduced barriers to foreign investment, eliminated certain bureaucratic hurdles of arcane licenses and prohibitions that were the legacy of both colonial and early national legal regimes, and opened Indian markets to foreign trade and consumer goods. Complicating this story is a more recent body of evidence emphasizing that as much as a nascent industry was able to grow as a result of liberalization, the sponsorship and even protection of software services by the Indian state before 1991 and the long-term investment in science and technology higher education by the Indian state were also major causes of the rise of Indian IT.[17] These recent findings suggest that the development of India's IT industry can be understood as part of the developing idea of the state itself.

The early history of the computer in India shows how computers were integrated in national development projects while also helping soldify an ideology of national elites as leaders of the nation. While this association between technology, the state, and elite culture shifts after 1991 toward a new definition of both the state and the national elite that relies on private accomplishment to fund development projects, it nevertheless leaves technological expertise at its center.

A triangulation of technology, elite culture, and the state emerged in India's late colonial period as middle-class intellectuals began to shape anticolonial arguments through national identity. Middle-class Indian nationalists formulated an Indian nation whose positive attributes were both unrecognized and exploited by the colonial state. The elaboration of the scientific truths found in the Vedas and other scriptural texts became one pillar in an evolving riposte against assumed Western superiority. Bengali scholars such as Brajendranath Seal and Prafulla Chandra Ray codified notions of Hindu scientific progress that had been circulating in journals and pamphlets since the late nineteenth century. Seal's "The Positive Sciences of the Ancient Hindus" (1915) "identified a body of scientific knowledge and practices developed by the Hindus in the investigation of physical phenomenon," while Ray's two-volume *History of Hindu Chemistry from the Earliest Times to the Middle of the Sixteenth Century A.D.* (1902–9) read Sanskrit texts to "assess the achievements of Hindu alchemy from the point of view of modern experiments in observation."[18] Such works opened up a terrain of negotiation on which native intellectuals could press claims for membership in universal domains of knowledge and practice.[19]

At the same time that Indian middle classes were formulating an idea of Indian science that connected indigenous knowledge with national identity and elite cultures, the raison d'état of the British Raj was shifting toward managing India's resources. Partially in response to accusations of mismanagement from social reformers who linked famine, women's rights, and poverty to the failures of British statecraft, the late nineteenth-century colonial government refocused scientific enterprise away from what was called "systematic research" and toward utilitarian investigations. Science and technology were to find solutions to immediate and pressing problems, especially in agriculture and land management. Beginning in 1902, the newly created Board of Scientific Advice (BSA) shifted focus to the economic improvement of agricultural land and the development of industry. The instrumentalization of technology in service of the state sought out technical solutions to problems of productivity and socioeconomic organization: "By the beginning of the 20th century, colonial power was no longer about bringing the light of Western reason and Christian truths to the dark corners of the globe, but about the scientific and technological reconfiguration of these dark corners. As an incarnation and instrument of the technological will, the colonial state became inseparable from the configuration it had brought into existence. Not surprisingly, it also emerged as the site for the definition and determination of India and Indian interests."[20]

The establishment of a postindependence technoscientific apparatus for the sake of benefiting the citizens of India was centrally important in the years leading up to and in the decades after 1947. Problem solving through technical means created a kind of contract between the citizenry and the state, whereby what Srirupa Roy calls the "needy nation" and needy citizens were invoked by the Nehruvian government as a means of reinforcing state power. The sovereign certainties of colonial science gave way to the postcolonial management of development through technology, which "presented the task of nation building as perilous, uncertain, and above all incomplete without the willing partnership and active participation of the people."[21]

In the decades after independence, the nation and its citizens were constructed as having problems that science could solve, while the state was constructed as needing its citizens' expertise and "scientific temperament" to succeed.[22] Both the state and its citizens were defined as lacking the knowledge that scientific expertise could provide. Out of these citizens a small cadre of elite scientists would be trained to lead the nation at the same time that all citizens needed to develop an attitude of openness to rational inquiry that went beyond the expertise of scientists themselves.[23] While the ideological rhetoric of the nation shifted from colonial to postcolonial regimes, the need for a strong technoscientific state apparatus remained unquestioned.

From the 1950s through the 1980s, computer technologies fit into this overall framework of technoscientific management in two critical ways. First, machines were prestige objects that signaled the state's internationalism. Second, they were technical apparatuses to be used within a general framework of problem solving. Crucially, Indian elites participated in both projects by brokering the provision of computers to India from abroad and by integrating machines into already existing scientific enterprises.

The drive to computerizing existing research programs was led by Homi Bhabha in Bombay and Prasantas Chandra Mahalanobis in Calcutta, both well known as leaders of India's technoscientific establishment. Mahalanobis founded the Indian Statistical Institute (ISI) in 1932 in order to "increase the efficiency of human efforts in the widest sense."[24] While employed by the Raj, Mahalanobis used his statistical methods largely to study cash crops such as jute and to compute food yields as related to famine, such as rice. After independence, the ISI produced yearly statistical data on the economy, agriculture, and population health of the country to govern national planning.[25] Bhabha used computers in his nuclear research programs at the Tata Institute of Fundamental Research (TIFR) in Bombay, which he founded in 1945. They were integrated in nuclear reactor electronics and control systems. The machines at TIFR were time shared and used by scientists from government labs, educational institutions, and private organizations. During the late 1950s, a battle for computer resources began between Bhabha and Mahalanobis. Each wanted to establish a national computer center in order to have increased access to the computing power the government of India could provide through imports from the United States and the USSR. Bhabha effectively won this battle by negotiating independently with American suppliers, especially IBM and CDC (Control Data Corporation), to supply machines for TIFR.[26] These early uses of computers in India set a pattern: limited governmental resources, reliance on importing machines from the United States, the USSR, and elsewhere, and the integration of computer technologies across a wide range of national-developmental programs, from economic data collection to nuclear experimentation. At the same time, throughout the 1960s and 1970s, considerable emphasis was put on the development of Indian machines and especially on developing programming skills. Much of the training in programming at this early stage was developed in conjunction with overseas research institutes, especially the University of Illinois in the United States, a pattern that would yield the transnational connections important to the expansion of Indian software services in the late 1990s.

The history of computing in India from the 1950s through the 1980s was dominated by the investment of government in technologies as a means of statecraft, the cross-border connections of the scientific elite and the corresponding ideology of development that they and the government promoted, and the evolution of improvisation and ad hoc construction by individual technicians in the face of resource shortages. Early efforts by researchers to build computers often involved a great deal of improvisation as necessary parts were frequently bought from markets selling post–World War II remainders in Chandni Chowk in Delhi and Mohammed Ali Road in Mumbai. In India, this tradition of improvising machines from local parts bazaars is a major part of the way digital cultures work in South Asia. Although this topic is ancillary to my book, traditions of bricolage no doubt hold important insights for understanding computer cultures in India.[27] In this discussion of relations between elite transnational coders and the history of science and technology, I want to emphasize the way certain contradictions in the way computer technologies were integrated into the state's technoscientific enterprises were themselves subject to improvisation, as middle classes fashioned themselves first as technocrats in the service of the state, and then as entrepreneurs in service to the nation.

The state's investment in computer technology consisted of brokering deals to get supplies of computers from overseas and in using international collaborations to build training institutes, including the Indian IITs. Histories of the Indian Institutes of Technology suggest that in addition to institutional support from the United States at IIT Kanpur and Kharagpur, the USSR at IIT Bombay, and Germany at IIT Madras, the establishment of the IITs depended on the circulation of Indian national elites who had been trained overseas and then helped broker agreements and staffed the institutes in India. Devesh Kapur has argued that the emigration of elites to the United States and elsewhere acted as a release valve in the political arena, allowing other groups to enter political society at the same time that for the old Brahmin-dominated elites it "changed the locus of privilege from political power in the state to economic power in the private sector and outside of India."[28] This suggests that there was a transnational character to Indian professional technologies (such as medicine and engineering) long before the liberalization movements of the early 1990s. It also confirms the domination of computer science in India by upper-caste Hindus. After 1991, overseas elites were folded into a narrative of state as its ambassadors and representatives in a global economy in which increasingly private institutions and actors furthered state power.

The IITs: Embodying Postindependence Contradictions and Establishing a Technoscientific Middle Class

Authors trying to explain the success of Indian programmers often turn to the Indian Institutions of Technology, the IITs, which have justifiably become famous for graduating several leaders of tech companies in the United States and in India. Yet it is also very much the case that most programmers working in India and overseas have not graduated from one of the IITs.[29] Programmers attend regional institutes and colleges and also supplement training in engineering and related fields with certificates in programming languages from private institutions. The IITs might be better understood from within the longer history of the computer in India that I have been tracing as embodying the sometimes contradictory framings of technological elites, the work of the nation, transnationalism, and citizenship.

According to reviews of the history of IITs conducted by Ross Bassett, Patrick Kim Sebaly, and Stuart Leslie and Robert Kargon, the institutes were set up with the cooperation of the governments of the United States, the USSR, and Germany and financed largely by the government of India.[30] The internationalism pursued in the grounding of IITs was in fact similar in nature to that pursued in other areas of technological development, including building the country's nuclear technology and provisioning TIFR and the ISI with computers. In all of these cases, supplies of materials, knowledge, and outside expertise were to be secured from as many sources as possible, in keeping with the official policy of nonalignment during the Cold War. Competition among foreign powers, especially the United States and the USSR would help assure that Indian needs would be well met. The American impetus for investment, for instance, fit squarely into a post–World War II development paradigm. Of the MIT experts who were engaged in founding IIT Kanpur, Leslie and Kargon remark that their agenda was "to train the future engineers and engineer-administrators capable of leading developing nations to modernization. Having spent a decade perfecting engineering at home, they welcomed the opportunities afforded by the Department of State, by the Ford Foundation, and by businessmen and political leaders in developing countries to share their success abroad."[31] Similarly, Soviet assistance at IIT Bombay and German assistance at IIT Madras were governed at least in part by the desire to export Soviet and German educational models to the developing world. The result of German consultation at IIT Madras produced training that integrated practical workshops and hands-on experience while Soviet experts developed specialized courses of study on the graduate level at IIT Bombay.[32] On the whole, the IITs were based largely on an American model of education, which would move the Indian technical education system away from the training of technicians and toward the creation of general, conceptual knowledge and collective problem-solving skills. This would be accomplished through a curriculum stressing basic sciences, along with humanities and social science studies, and the latest and most up-to-date technologies, including computers. The first director of IIT Kanpur, P. K. Kelkar, believed that "a scientific foundation could provide the basis by which teams of diverse experts could collaborate to solve complex problems." He believed "the American reforms were based on anticipating a 'complex and challenging future' and the need to prepare for it," which was also the case for India."[33]

The founding charter of the IITs was the 1946 "Development of Higher Technical Institutions in India Report," also known as the Sarkar Committee Report. It is an interesting document, not least because it displays so clearly the ambivalences around what a technical education for Indians would look like. The mandate of the commission was to establish the best possible method for training engineers and other technologists for postwar and, soon, independent India. The first lines of the report capture the burgeoning sentiment of urgency in the pursuit of development for India and the conviction that these projects would have to be led by the nation and its citizens and not by outside forces: "In view of the certainty of an appreciable increase in the demand for higher specialists in Industry," wrote the committee, "a rapid expansion in the facilities of Higher Technical Education is a pressing necessity. It is evident that apart from any other considerations, the calls of reconstruction in Europe and elsewhere, and the enormous industrial and Governmental undertakings completed in Europe and America to provide full employment, will make it difficult, if not impossible, to secure from abroad, the services of the right type of engineers, architects, technologists and planners etc. to carry out India's postwar projects."[34] Framing the choice as one between setting up one main institution with several branches "possibly on the lines of the Massachusetts Institute of Technology" or several regional institutions, the committee ultimately recommends establishing "not less than four" institutions, in each of the cardinal directions.[35] They superimposed thereby onto the physical and cosmological topography of India a technological map of state. In the very plan of the IITs, the geography of India and the technological imaginary of the Indian state mutually reinforced each other.

Reading through the report, however, some of the contradictions in this imaginary of India come to the surface. The dissenting opinions of committee members Dr. Nazir Ahmad, Office of the Indian Tariff Board, on the one hand, and Brigadier R. D. T. Woolfe, controller general of inspection, MGO Branch GHQ New Delhi, on the other, make for particularly compelling reading. The committee found that "the existing facilities of higher technical education in India are inadequate . . . to satisfy India's post-war needs for high grade technologists." Foregoing a "normal" process of investigation and survey due to this pressing concern, the committee wrote that "the needs of the present situation are so apparent and urgent that a solution cannot be deferred pending such a survey."[36] The sense of expedience carried the committee past considering what these needs might be and why they would be best addressed by four new institutions. In his dissent, Ahmad, for instance, suggested that there was little attempt made to assess existing facilities and how they could be developed. He further pointed out that creating four new institutions would leave a gap between the number of "trained men" and the requirements—estimated to be several thousand— of the country. Rather than creating institutions ex nihilo, Ahmad suggested developing what already existed, a method "which has already been followed in Europe and America." He further warned that "if this process is not followed, the existing institutions would stagnate and decay while the newer institutions will work in an atmosphere of isolation."[37] Ahmad went on to suggest bolstering the resources of historical institutions of higher learning, especially because he felt that the proposed IITs located in only four places and for the most part in urban centers would remain beyond the reach of most Indians.

If Ahmad was concerned with the education of rural Indians and the development of existing programs, Brigadier Woolfe's dissent proceeded along entirely different lines. He complained in a letter to Dr. Jon Sargent, educational advisor to the government of India, regarding technical education in India, "There can be no doubt that the scientist members of the committee steered the discussions very ably into channels with which they were familiar."[38] The result of the scientists' influence was a plan, according to Woolfe, to train chemists and engineers in "the very industries which come into conflict with overseas competition already developed on much more efficient lines than India can ever hope to achieve."[39] No doubt he had in mind the British and other European industries that had been able to produce in the colonies markets for their finished goods and intellectual commodities. The letter goes on to suggest a better application of resources would be to train technicians (as opposed to general practitioners) for the specific industries of jute, cotton, silk, lumber, fuel, mining, and pharmaceuticals. Woolfe was envisioning in the main a continuation of the British practice of training specialized executors to produce the raw goods and materials of Empire, and he certainly had one eye on preventing competition for European knowledge from possible colonial upstarts.

The findings of the Sarkar Committee and these dissents collectively embody the ambivalences around technologies of state that would characterize the postindependence period and after. This period witnessed negotiations over what the technical enterprises of state should be and what kind of contribution the technological elites being trained in India would make to the newly formed nation. Finally, the internationalist aspects of technological projects embodied both the objectives of large-scale development projects and the equally broadly imagined paradigms of a sovereign postcolonial state.

Itty Abraham has argued with regard to India's nuclear projects that the keen interest and energy devoted to developing nuclear energy has to be understood as part of a postcolonial desire to claim national sovereignty on an international stage, creating of nuclear technologies a visible sign of the power of the state itself. Dams, steel mills, and nuclear tests are some of the most visible fetishes of state power.[40] Yet, a similar argument could be made for investment in the IITs and in computer technologies. The urgency expressed in the first few lines of the report represent in this sense a riposte to Woolfe's more tepid claims for India. In the immediate postindependence period, the state and its leaders were set on countering, in numerous fields, the idée fixe that India would remain hopelessly stuck behind areas of the world that had taken full advantage of a very long colonial engagement.[41]

It was also clear that those trained in the new technical institutes were to play leading roles in these transformations; they were to be incorporated as experts into the technical apparatus of state.[42] But it remained underdetermined exactly how they were to fulfill this role, as Ahmad's dissent points out so clearly.

Elite technological institutes were given the simultaneous mandates of producing cutting edge research for an international audience and of developing local talent and local resources. Nehru's vision as expressed in numerous speeches from the late 1940s through the late 1960s often stressed the latter, envisioning a cadre of graduates who would bring a technical, modernist mind-set to all of India.[43] It fell to India's scientific establishment to create, as he urged the graduates of Administrative Staff College in Hyderabad in 1958, out of the agricultural laborer, "a technical worker, even in the field."[44] In this vision for India, the scientist-technician brought together knowledge and morality in an idealized fashion. "The scientist," Nehru exclaimed in a speech at the inauguration of the forty-third session of the India Science Congress on January 2, 1956, in Agra, called "Scientists and an Integrated View of Life," has to deal with the problem of "the betterment of the Indian people, raising their standards, increasing their wealth, removing inequality, and so on and so forth; planning, if you like, in its widest sense to help in that process." Given the scientist's duty toward development, Nehru asserted that "the scientist ought to have, and I believe has, a somewhat greater freedom of functioning and of directing people's thoughts, because the politician is suspect."[45] The presentist framework of Nehruvian moral development made all historical inheritances amenable to intervention. "To put the point perhaps overstarkly," writes Uday Mehta, "the challenge of caste injustice becomes analogous to that of building industry or large dams. They are all challenges in which the state draws and leans on the guiding primacy of science and social science."[46]

The dual mandate of achievement and development for elite classes did not always fit neatly together. As Ahmad predicted, the graduates of elite institutions such as the IITs often found their closest interlocutors and colleagues among other technoelite groups who were frequently working in high-tech positions overseas.[47] Despite, or perhaps because of, the lack of clarity about how nation, citizen, and technology were to be woven together, consensus moved instead toward promoting the needs of state through technical solutions. While in the 1950s and 1960s these solutions took the form of large-scale investments in big development projects, beginning in the late 1970s and 80s, the state additionally turned to privatized industries and transnational networks of technoelite power.

Computers as Development: Expertise as International Connection

During the 1960s and 1970s, Indian computing depended on the training of experts in institutions such as the IITs, the implementation of computer technologies in government-backed development projects, and the importation of computers and computer components from overseas suppliers. The ISI, for instance, initially rented machines for its statistical work at a rate of approximately eight to nine lakhs per year ($114,250–$128,570 according to the 1970 conversion rate). In 1961 to break this cycle of spending, Nehru asked IBM to manufacture the model called 1401 and to train computer operators in India.[48] The manufacturing and sales methods used by IBM would prove controversial, leading to the company's eventual ousting from India in 1977. In *The Long Revolution*, Dinesh Sharma provides the following summary of the company's standard operating procedure: "The operation ran something like this: old or discarded machines were brought in from the US and other markets; they were stripped to the base; all parts were tested, whatever was not reusable was thrown away, whatever was reasonably good and reparable was repaired, and the machine was rebuilt from almost the component level."[49]

These refurbished machines, often already obsolete in the United States and Europe, were then to be leased with maintenance and service packages that would be paid monthly. This practice, widely accepted in the global computer industry through the 1960s, came under increasing scrutiny in the first half of the 1970s. A report compiled by the Electronics Commission of India in 1975 found that when 1401s were being installed in India, minicomputers with the same capacity could be had elsewhere for one-quarter of the cost, and a slightly more powerful computer could be purchased for $1,200 while IBM was charging $20,000 in annual rental for a single computer.[50]

The political maneuvers between the government of India and foreign multinationals during the early part of the 1970s deserve their own treatment, and indeed, assessments of this era of protectionism have been anything but sparse.[51] A reading of this literature as regards the computer industry suggests that both the high-profit business practices of companies such as IBM and protests against the automation of work by banking and railway unions led to a reassessment of IBM's business practices in India.

Notably, the newly modified Foreign Exchange Relations Act (FERA) of 1974, which rewrote provisions originally set down before independence, limited foreign ownership of Indian corporations to 40 percent.[52] IBM was given two years to comply with the provisions of FERA. In the meantime, the government's Public Accounting Commission Report made the argument for protectionist policies more acute by concluding that "the import entitlements facility given to IBM . . . enabled it to dump in India what was largely junk, that is, machinery and gadgets which had hardly any market elsewhere in the world, yet to earn excessively high profits without making any or significant contributions towards India's attainment of self-reliance in critical areas of computers."[53]

The ensuing history of IBM (and also Coca-Cola) pulling out of the Indian market is often related along free market versus socialist interventions or in terms of uneven development as a continuation of colonialist strategies. While the era of import substitution can certainly legitimately be read as a case in the study of nationalist economics, it is also the case that polemical arguments about whether protectionism or open markets lead to more development remain ahistorical, generalizing from a very particular context to an ideal type that cannot hold across place or case.

What is clear in the history of the computer in India is that the 1977 departure of IBM from India in no way extended to a questioning of computing or technology in general.[54] Throughout the 1950s–1970s, it was a shifting mix of nationalism and internationalism, global expertise, and national development initiatives that consolidated the position of the elite technical classes as a model and agent of the technologies—from steel plants and mining to finance and computing—of human development.

During the 1970s and 1980s, the mandate for technological development in India began to move in two opposing directions. While technologies of state were still meant to better the people of India, the locus of development during this period moved uneasily between two Indias, rural and urban, indigenous and cosmopolitan. Often glossed as the distinction between *Bharat* and India, these two Indias were largely interlinked in practice but increasingly distant in the rhetoric of statehood as powerful farmer's unions and wealthy landholders mobilized political support around the countryside in opposition to the cities. Indira Gandhi's political career was in many senses sustained by appealing to a popular imaginary of the countryside as Bharat, dividing the political sphere and its citizenry into a Manichean duality that could be recursively applied across the populace.[55] Within this framework, the computer was called on, as in the 1950s and 1960s, to aid in carrying out calculations and developing new solutions for already existing research, the building of utilities, and industrial projects. Indeed, many of the developments that are commonly associated with postliberalization India, such as software technology parks (STPs), have a much longer history. It was under Indira Gandhi's third term as prime minister that STPs first garnered governmental support, with the idea that they would produce software exports for which investment in special export processing zones and satellite technology could be justified.[56]

To this mandate was added another, the goal of developing an internationally networked system of machines that would link together the "developed" and "underdeveloped" worlds. As the UN Development Decade Report for 1970–80 had it, "As international computer networks and computer reporting become established during the next decade, developing countries will find computers necessary as a ticket of admission."[57] In the Indian context, the dual mandate of using computer technologies to better the lives of the poor and of staying abreast of the latest technological development with an eye toward maintaining that necessary "ticket of admission" on the international stage led to several only partially acknowledged contradictions. While government policies continued to pursue technologies from abroad, for instance, workers in the banking and railway sectors went on strike to oppose their replacement by machines. And, although the stated aim of computer research continued to be framed in terms of service to the nation, the practices of India's technoelite continued to look toward the United States for training and employment. Indeed, it was in the 1970s and 1980s that Indian computer engineers began to set up the international networks that would become the outsourcing industry two decades later. Companies with founders who had been trained in the United States were able to create business that relied on labor arbitrage, taking advantage of the cheaper cost of technical labor in India, throughout the 1980s.[58]

The split between middle classes that looked toward major metropolitan areas, research centers, and networks of diasporic Indian elites in the West for self-development and the ongoing moral discourse of development through computer technology would only be resolved during the era of neoliberalism in India, when the moral authority of development was folded into the practical advancement of the private individual. It was when moral governance began to be conceived of as a matter of care of the self as care of the nation, of good conduct as a means of conducting the development of the nation, that the elite technical classes of India could become vessels of national development by virtue of pursuing their own privatized advantage.[59]

Software for the Indian Nation

In 1991 the high-water mark of market liberalization in India reformed industrial policy, abolishing industrial licensing for all projects except human health, the environment, and those considered strategically important (such as mining), and doing away with 40 percent foreign ownership rules. These measures rested firmly on the links made between the state, technocratic reason, and technical elites. Summarizing the layered history that led to India's IT boom, Ramachandra Guha writes:

> Some of the credit is certainly due to the reforms of 1991, which opened up foreign markets for the first time. But some credit must also be taken by Rajiv Gandhi's government, which gave special emphasis to the then nascent electronic and telecommunication industries. Moving back a decade further, the Janata government's expulsion of IBM allowed the development of an indigenous computer manufacturing and maintenance industry. But perhaps the story should really begin with Jawaharlal Nehru's government, which had the foresight to set up a chain of high-quality engineering schools and the wisdom to retain English as the language of higher education and of interstate and international communication.[60]

Indeed, several recent analyses have tried to contextualize the reforms of 1991 within a longer history of government support and intervention in the IT industry in order to argue that a mixed rather than free market economy is what ultimately produced India's IT boom. Murali Patibandla, Deepak Kapur, and Bent Peterson, for instance, argue that the high level of skill in software in particular came out of import substitution policies on hardware.[61] Because imports of hardware were blocked except for the purpose of developing software for export, attention turned away from producing hardware for overseas markets and toward producing software that would run on locally produced machines, such as the IBM 1401, left behind after

1977, and new machines being produced overseas, for which government initiatives such as STPs were built. In other words, even in the industry said to most benefit from the turn toward privatization that the 1991 reforms supported, rumors of the demise of the power of the Indian state are highly exaggerated.

As I have been arguing, these debates on the advantages or disadvantages of free markets have tended to obscure what is an important but not unchanging problematic that extends across the history of the computer in India: the tight but ambivalent relationship between technoelite classes and the development of state power. The narratives of Bipin and Mihir betray much of this ambivalence. Perhaps what has produced the most significant sense of change for this generation of technoelites is the strategy for pursuing the goals of national development and the corresponding sense of the milieu in which they are to be pursued. If their parents' generation—the generation of Nehruvian scientists of state—was to provide be representatives of the state and teachers of the nation, this generation is meant to serve the nation and incorporate in themselves the qualities of a new, privatized state power—adaptability, growth, and openness to foreign investment. Commenting on the continued, if altered, significance of attachment to national development among IT professionals, Chris Fuller and Haripriya Narasimhan write:

> Older people do not expect the younger generation, including their own children, to want to work for the state, rather than better-run and better-paying private companies. In itself though, this does not amount to a retreat from Nehruvian ideas of progress, let alone from any patriotic commitment. Many older informants, including those who worked for the government, tend to insist that the state has become corrupt and no longer serves the nation and people. Moreover, everyone who favors economic liberalizations and globalizations also argues that they are the best means to national development and prosperity, which the bureaucratic state and the old "permit raj" failed to deliver.[62]

The salient point is that the institution of neoliberal forms of governance, which include privatizing industries and relying on nongovernmental entities to foster development, does not correlate with a decrease in state power as much as with a restructuring of how state power operates. And, similarly, those who most benefit from privatization of industry, including

IT professionals, have not retreated from the nation-state but have come to inhabit a new sort of relationship with state power. This relationship continues to be articulated through the medium of technology.

Of Partially Fulfilled Contracts: From Technoelites to Tech Entrepreneurs

In chapter 3, the code that programmers write was considered a means of exchange rather like the partial terms of extended contract that might be called "taking while giving," of maintaining attachment to the code itself as a valuable object even while producing code in the service of one's employers.[63] In the transactions around code as it is deployed in the workplace, the Indian programmer is simultaneously tasked with producing workable software solutions within the parameters of any given project and, through her very presence in firms, the speculative capital that marks a firm as adequately global. One strategy that coders pursue is to attach part of the value of code to themselves—to make code to some degree "inalienable" from themselves—even while they produce it as a product that can be alienated from their labor.

The creation of bits of code as inalienable wealth is a risky strategy that is encouraged by the politics of culture in the IT workplace. The IT industry tries to capitalize on the perceived value of the Indian coders. It is risky because it can all too easily lend itself to an overspecialization, turning what is a willingly mobile orientation to the world to an unwittingly fixed one. As Srinu explained, "Getting labeled as an expert in a particular area" prevents upward mobility. Though it is precisely this expertise that got him his job in the first place, if he does not show his versatility he will become stuck in one place and might eventually inherit a role that is about to be terminated as a project ends.

A similar set of constraints applies to the tie between technologies and national belonging. Though the assumption has been that diasporic Indian middle classes have decreasing attachments to the idea of India and have replaced Nehruvian allegiance to the state with an allegiance to their own bank accounts, this ethnography suggests this line of reasoning is unfounded. Rather than framing the question in terms of patriotism tout court, it is better to ask how newly emerging relationships between the state and its subjects reimagine the state itself and how national development can best be served.

Mayur, who believed the state should set rules and step aside, said he has "thought a lot about" what the role of IT should be in development for India. The state, according to Mayur, should "support projects without profit potential and projects tangential to profits, with long ROIS [returns on investment], like transportation. For everything else, government should keep hands off." Mayur reimagined state power as taking on infrastructural projects that could not be accomplished by industry because of a lack of profit motive. Meanwhile, the life chances of ordinary Indians will be assured by expanding the reach of the market. I asked Adi and Bipin, who had been listening to our conversation, if they had thought that the IT industry had improved the lives of the lower castes and classes in India. Adi pondered the question a moment, but Bipin provided a ready answer for the both of them: "Yes, definitely, it's produced opportunity."

If one asks programmers if they think of themselves as Indian, they will say yes. Ask if they are proud to be Indian, and the answer is just as unequivocal. But they know that being proud to be Indian also includes being cognizant of the failures of national development as well as the hubris of the state's promises of the same. Ask programmers how they can best develop and serve the nation, and their answers mirror closely the rhetoric of neoliberal globalization. Their job is wealth creation and the creation of opportunities—two things that the government, in all its inefficiency, has been unable to produce.

The programmer's relationship to the Indian nation-state might be called the attitude of a party to a partially fulfilled contract. Programmers recognize that their very ability to generate wealth is due in large part to "brand India" as an IT powerhouse, yet allegiance to this brand has not yielded the promise of a good life. This good life, evoked but never fulfilled in the Nehruvian vision of industrial growth, was symbolized by the rationalization of technical processes, clean streets, wide avenues, and green spaces—the trappings of an Indian middle-class lifestyle that IT workers try to enjoy in life abroad and in new housing developments at home.[64] This dance of closeness and distance from the nation-state makes IT workers ambivalent partners in creating an India that like the workers themselves is high tech and highly adaptable.

Different expert lifeworlds produce a diversity of epistemes that only appear to be unified as "science" as an aftereffect of their description as a culture of science.[65] In the historical relationship that emerged between expertise, the Indian state, and computer technology, three repertoires of expertise emerged linking the individual expert to the state. In the first, the state needed experts as scientists to produce knowledge and attitudes toward progress that were rational and could be transmitted to all citizens. In the second, the expert and the people were more fully divided, and the expert was needed as a link to international prestige. During Indira Gandhi's and Rajiv Gandhi's times as prime minister the divide between elites and the people devolved in the software industry into protectionism, which led to the elaboration of software and coding skills to be used on local machines, and international collaborations with Indians overseas. Third, the personal success of the computer expert stood in for state expertise, at the same time that success in the private world became the avenue for building national wealth. Rather than these three dominant arrangements of technological expertise and state power simply being divided into separate historical periods, they provide overlapping alternatives for Indian programmers to link themselves to—and distance themselves from—the power of the state.

These repertoires of expertise are mobilized by programmers in several ways. Adi uses the expert as scientist to appeal to older generations to contribute to his business venture. Bipin, on the other hand, makes a less straightforward evaluation of the relationship between India and its citizens. He links the time of Ashoka to an approaching future that is fated to come into being. He thereby both links his own fate to this coming success and delinks himself from active striving on behalf of the state. If the turning of time fails to come, it may even be the fault of the state for holding back the inevitable.

Many commentators on diasporic Indians accuse them of being disloyal to the nation-state for choosing a successful life abroad instead of a life of service in India.[66] At the same time, in many Indian government publications, the successful programmer abroad is lionized as a model subject for a new India. Meanwhile, surprisingly little has been written on how these experts conceptualize their own relationship to the state. If, in 1973, the review of computers in Asia could begin by asking what a computer was good for, in the new millennium, that question would no longer be posed. Computers were squarely part of the apparatus of a successful India, and the eradication of Indian ills would be solved by IT's thought leaders.[67] As programmers navigate their relationship to national trajectories of development, they are able to bring together the story of their own striving with the narrative of national well-being because of the longer histories of technological expertise that subtend both these narratives. As computer-aided statistical and atomic science projects enrolled programmers and other Indian class and caste elites as experts, they consolidated expertise and the representativeness of these very elites as national subjects. In doing so, they established parallels between individual growth and national development. Entrepreneurial projects pursued both within India and transnationally could then filter programmers' experiences abroad through this doubly located Indian national imaginary.

FIVE

COMPUTERS ARE VERY STUPID COOKS

Reinventing Leisure as a Politics of Pleasure

Lowering the gas flame and blowing over the surface of the tea just before it boiled over, Meenakshi turned to me, "Cooking is like programming," she said. "You give the computer a recipe and it follows it." We were standing in her kitchen, where I had seen her whip up lemon rice, egg pakora, puris, and all different kinds of vegetable dishes without ever cracking a book, all the while keeping up an easy banter with me and whoever else was in the kitchen. "But you don't use a recipe," I exclaimed, wondering why she might think of cooking as following recipes, since she never used them herself. She tipped the pot and poured the tea expertly into two small plastic cups smiling indulgently. "That's different," she teased. "I don't need a recipe. But the computer is a very stupid cook." .

The kitchen had become a place for us to have easy conversation that meanders from work to home to the habits of Berliners. Meena knew I was trying to understand "this whole programming thing," as I sometimes put it, and she would test out different ways of explaining to me how her job works. On this day, Meena began by describing how computers follow source code like cooks follow recipes. She explained that writing code is analogous to writing a cookbook for machines. Meena did not consider herself a recipe follower. She was instead an author, an expert in thinking through the steps of making something, someone who wrote these steps down in a program for the "stupid" cooks, who simply follow along. A computer, she said, "will always do what you tell it even if it will not work."

The slow pace of cooking, the daily ritual of making tea, allowed her some distance from the computer as executor of commands. I was struck by how she unraveled the threads that bound her to an expectation of straightforward, unthinking performance in the office.

The practice of making tea the way she does, watching the pot for the tiny indications that it is about to bubble up and quickly turning the dial to shut down the gas flame before it boiled over, is an expert technique that would be difficult to write down in a cookbook. It is not timed, it is sensed when she hears the milk making a slight hissing sound. It is not observed but glimpsed in the tiny bubbles that ring the pot. Wait too long and the milk boils over; too soon and the tea is weak and underbrewed.

Contrasting these two kinds of cooking, the improvised and the directed, separates home from work and lifts programmers away from their reduction to "stupid" machines. Habits and practices cultivated in the kitchen relieve the constant pressure of succeeding in programming economies by following narrow conceptions of programming labor. In this instance, Meenakshi framed her expertise in opposition to the stubborn materiality of the computer—hers were expanded competencies. In such reflective moments of human-object intra-action, programmers like Meena distance themselves from machines.[1] Such assertions of expertise tilt knowledge toward its "changing, unfolding character" and away from its self-contained, complete, and inert nature.[2]

In the living room and the hallways of the apartment that she shares with Rajeshwari, Meena has hung handmade signs and phrases urging confidence and good spirit. A bubble of paper with an inked phrase, "Just believe and all things are possible" floats above "Behind every ambition is effort and behind the effort is someone trying hard"; the back of the bathroom door tells us, "Every day gives a new hope," and on the way out the door, the last thing she sees is a photo of a dolphin leaping from cobalt blue waters. Meena said the phrases and images keep her moving—they are reminders of what hard work can bring. These phrases transform the home into a space of preparation for work, where responsibility for molding the soul and the body for the rigors of long workdays, of training desire to find fulfillment in the office and in the horizons of a future just out of reach, rest on the shoulders of the workers themselves.

I asked her where she finds and how she chooses these sayings, and she pulled from her bedside table a copy of the autobiography of Neil Armstrong. Meena was a fan of autobiography. She told me she often copied out phrases from these books, carefully choosing ones that express faith in the future and tenacity for the present time. How did Meena reconcile her commitment to preparing herself to work through self-motivation and her distancing of herself to the way she is positioned at work through her expert cooking practices? This chapter explores the spaces of parks and kitchens, sitting rooms, and homes as places where new relationships between leisure and work are emerging. To do so, I take critical distance from prevailing ideas of neoliberal self-fashioning and self-improvement to argue for a doubled relationship that takes place in these spaces that makes leisure both a site for the production of laboring subjects and a site for the production of alternative practices of selfhood I describe as *eros*.[3]

Meenakshi was not a person who often simply followed directions. As we moved through the deepening afternoon light in her apartment, the damp winter curling around us and pulling us toward the warmth of the kitchen, Meena unfolded her tale of how she ended up in Berlin. Meenakshi, whom her friends call Meena, came from a landholding family just outside Hyderabad. While her grandfather once presided over green fields lush with barley, rice, and cotton, her father took the family to the sea, trading in fields for fish tanks. The family now owned an aquaculture farm producing fish and prawns for domestic and overseas consumption. Meena is one of two daughters; her older sister studied medicine, whereas she decided to go the information technology route, studying computer science and management.

A mixture of desire and anxiety led her to study programming. She would look out over the cool deep wells of wriggling aquatic life, the farmworkers balancing adroitly on wooden planks that ran along the tops of the tanks, and think that she wanted to be as successful as her sister. But, she believed, becoming a physician would not suit her. It seemed that everyone she knew was "doing the IT thing," so she studied computer engineering and management. Nearing the end of her degree, she had another decision to make: to work locally or to go abroad. Again, it seemed that everyone she knew was going or trying to go "for foreign." Although she loved her family, Meena wanted to get away from the family business for a while. It was expected that she would marry soon and that her future husband would eventually take over the fish farm. Working abroad for a few years might take some of the pressure off, since Meena was not ready for the married life just yet. Like Madhu and Bipin, Meenakshi used the German green card to create a private area of individual control within global coding economies that she could leverage when she returned home. After completing her education at the Indian Institute of Management, Meenakshi decided to apply for a job with Software Solutions Global, headquartered in Germany. She had rarely been outside of Hyderabad and its environs, but after seeing the company's profile in one of her courses, she thought a job with SSG would better her résumé. So, after a brief phone interview with her future employers, she bought the plane ticket that took her to Berlin.

Her decisions fashioned Meenakshi as someone who does not follow instructions but improvises on them. She and other programmers resisted the instrumentalization of their cognitive labor by emphasizing their "capacity to unfold indefinitely."[4] In her leisure time, Meenakshi undid some of underpinnings that fashion programmers into "the tools and commercial goods which are ready-to-be-used or traded further" by trying on the possible alternate worlds she might inhabit.

Variously decried as the end of free time, overwork, or the indefinite extension of the working day, most accounts of the relationship between leisure and work under late capitalism posit leisure as a fading value and experience in the world. Against this position, this chapter argues for a multifaceted relationship between leisure and work, where leisure gains in significance in three ways, only the first of which explicitly links productivity and leisure directly as a way of valorizing the subject "in leisure and reproduction."[5] First, leisure time is used to recuperate and prepare for work, in part by developing skills and qualities of self that can translate to the workplace. Second, spaces of leisure are also spaces in which an alternative ethic of pleasure, or eros, can be developed as an explicit antidote to the claim on leisure by work. It is because leisure has been conceptualized as wanting to be made productive that it becomes available for appropriation and reappropriation for a politics of eros.[6] Third, spaces and times of leisure are sites of experimentation in building an Indian middle-class lifestyle. These experiments with forms of life emerge from spaces of leisure that support cognitive labor and redirect its energies.[7]

Shezad Nadeem's account of outsourcing to India traces what he calls "consumer patriotism" that works to bridge the space between the hope for future prosperity and the reality of the daily grind of work. Such consumption, argues Nadeem, shapes aspirational Indian middle-class identity through objects imagined as Western, like coffee, cigarettes, pop culture, the idea of upward mobility, and open displays of wealth.[8] Nadeem calls such consumption a "consumer-oriented mimicry that has emerged as an integral component of class and personal identity."[9] This analysis dovetails with several recent accounts of the new Indian middle class stressing how class is defined through consumption, which has replaced government service as a mainstay of Indian middle-class identity.[10] While it would be easy to subsume what I analyze here as the pleasure of leisure within consumer patriotism, leisure in the stories recounted below is neither a straightforward appropriation of a Western lifestyle nor a continuation of the politics of consumption through the consumption of time. Rather, the very meaning of consuming time as leisure is revisited in a situation in which the boundaries between work and leisure themselves are blurred. In the end, I argue that trying on forms of life (often through consumption) is more important than consumption in and of itself as foundational to Indian middle-class identity. It is this sense of experimentation, and the right to experiment, that no doubt will be picked up, transformed, and appropriated by others within the national and transnational imaginary of India.[11]

In the office, Indian IT workers have to simultaneously exploit and transcend racialized assumptions that reside in Indian programming. They do this by elaborating a practice of ownership that is appropriative—it exploits the time frame of client-driven projects to temporarily own the code they write in order to extend their time on the job. Strategies of pursuing freedom as ownership occur within the ambiguity and undecidability of race discourse as it comes to ground in evaluations of new kinds of workers, where Indian IT workers are both devalued as grunt coders and revalued as sources of local knowledge. As I argued in chapter 3, these practices leave behind a trace of an alternative theory of ownership that creates spaces of privacy for the sake of freedom in an office overdetermined by the logic of innovation through knowledge sharing. After work, Indian programmers begin to unravel the demands on their time and demeanor in the workplace in similarly finessed ways. They use times and spaces outside of work to make themselves ready for the working day even while they try on lifestyles and play with forms of life that are then embroidered into an idea of the Indian middle class.

Meenakshi later explained to me that Neil Armstrong's story has particularly touched her because of the way it marries science and belief. He embodied for Meena the fusing of religion and science through the trope of future transformation. When Armstrong was walking on the moon, according to Meena, his disbelief in God and the spiritual realm of life turned into its opposite. Her religious practices, including daily *aarti* (prayers), special prayers at particular times of year, and festival celebrations, maintained her focus on the all that she needs to do to achieve success in this brutal industry. It kept her mind concentrated in order to learn new programming languages and to always be on the lookout for new opportunities. Her phrases and books are types of work on the self that tune it to the hum of an economy that values initiative and acceptance, focusing on the long horizon of the future and accepting the uneven present.[12]

The two ways that Meena uses her apartment incline toward a reconceptualization of the times and spaces outside of work as both the location of producing knowledge economy workers and the place for trying out new ways of inhabiting that world. An Indian middle-class imaginary emerges in the evolving, dialectical relationship between the two.

Leisure Reconsidered

In *A Grammar of the Multitude*, his treatise on the shifting categories needed to think about and imagine alternatives of contemporary capitalism, Paolo Virno describes the qualities demanded of workers today, contending they must be "accustomed to mobility, to be able to keep up with the most sudden conversions, to be able to adapt to various enterprises, to be flexible in switching from one set of rules to another, to have an aptitude for a kind of linguistic interaction as banalized as it is unilateral, *to be familiar with managing among a limited amount of possible alternatives* [italics mine]."[13]

Virno points out that the development of these characteristics takes place outside the office. Spaces and times outside work become, he notes, the sites where discipline in the arts of flexibility is cultivated. Rather than the workplace being the site where workers are formed, they form themselves before and after work to fit the model of an industrious, entrepreneurial self-starter.[14] Thinking about how IT workers use and conceive of spaces and times before and after work, I realized their practices require revisiting both Virno's formulation and more traditional approaches to the study of leisure.

Leisure and work have been linked since the advent of industrial management practices. Leisure, according to studies by Chris Rojek and others, has since the late nineteenth century presented itself as a release from work, a utopian space of individual freedom that, as the Latin root of leisure, *licit*, connotes, promised to allow what was barred from expression at work.[15]

The sociological studies of leisure that began in the 1920s to investigate the spaces and activities of life after work, such as Siegfried Kracauer's *The Salaried Masses* (which I discuss more fully later on), demonstrated that leisure activities were often both overtly and subconsciously organized by work.[16] Leisure reinforced workplace rituals and hierarchies, all the while retaining a feeling of release from the demands of the workplace. Leisure was also conceptualized as a kind of commodity itself—to have and consume leisure was to become a member of the upper or leisure class. For Thorstein Veblen, for instance, leisure is a conspicuous wasting of time in order to confer on the subject rank and distinction, a consumption of time that has its correlate in the consumption of luxury goods.[17] In Veblen's account of leisure, the pursuit of the markers of high status was an all-consuming passion that transcended class interest, such that lower classes emulated the consumption practices of the rich while the rich consumed luxury goods and quite literally wasted time to set themselves apart from the working classes.

By and large, the critical response to leisure has been twofold: first, to draw out explicitly the way that leisure-time activities are structured by the subject-making demands of capitalism and, second, to draw out leisure as an arena of distinction. Autonomist Marxists suggest that, against both the sociology of leisure and the critique of leisure and status making, work and leisure are no longer categories of binary opposition. They are instead linked horizontally through habits that have full right to expression in each world. Just as work is brought home and work time expands into leisure time, leisure abides in the workplace through parties, contests, telecommuting, casual Fridays, and flexible work hours. At the same time, when the very lines between work and leisure are blurred for the sake of generating new productive influences, the forms of life after work I discuss here are ways of experimenting with multiple kinds of emergent habitations of a *neoliberal* modernity.[18]

Accounts of late capitalism and subjective experience often seem to suggest that the whole of human experience has been colonized by work. Working longer hours than ever before, with the ability to work anywhere, the contemporary office worker "ought" to work everywhere and always. Bifo Berardi makes this connection explicitly, writing "the reasons behind the new love of working are to be found not only in the material impoverishment derived from the collapse of social warranties, but also in the impoverishment of existence and communication. We renew our affection for work because economic survival becomes more difficult and daily life becomes lonely and tedious: metropolitan life becomes so sad that we might as well sell it for money."[19]

Although the description of the cognitariat that Berardi develops seems to describe so well the link between Indian programmers and the world of work, we have already seen in previous chapters how it fails to adequately engage difference and race. Here, the critique of knowledge work again does not accord with the experience of most Indian programmers I met. Rather than their metropolitan lives being sad, they were exuberant; spaces of leisure were also profound spaces of pleasure.

A more adequate accounting of this discrepancy argues that leisure time is not colonized by work but rather exists in a multiple and dispersed relationship to work. If the new reality of work and leisure inclines toward blurred boundaries and "perpetual metastability," then it is a misrecognition of that blurring to suggest that work can colonize leisure.[20] Instead, there is a relationship between work and leisure that moves through many possible iterations, from opposition to collusion, from respite to continuation.

Self-Improvement: On Jogging

Not long after my conversation with Meena about computers and cooking, Mihir and Meenakshi decided that we should go jogging. They were taken by the idea of waking up early every morning before work and going for jogs in a nearby park. Given the long work hours that everyone was engaged in, I was skeptical that this plan would ever materialize. But sure enough, the following morning at 5:30 AM, I heard my buzzer ring. I hurried downstairs, the lines on my face still visible from the pillow on which I had slumbered, an unhappy fact Rajeshwari and Meenakshi, waiting for me at the door, were only too glad to teasingly point out. There followed a valiant three and a half weeks where just over a half dozen of us would struggle out of our beds and make our way to the park early mornings. Meena and Mihir would jog, the rest of us were content with walking. Eventually we all succumbed to the need to sleep over the need for fresh air and exercise. The walks moved from being an everyday affair to a weekend activity.

Over the course of this month I began to wonder what would make programmers go jogging so early in the morning, despite the evident fact of their long work hours and at times extreme tiredness. I asked Mihir and Meena what had possessed them to jog in the morning in the first place, and their answers were telling. It was partly a competitive, flirtatious thing, Meena said, "since both Mihir and I are good at sports, we wanted to see who was better." But also, added Mihir, "there is the enjoyment of the park itself."

Humboldthain Park is a unique Berlin institution, urban and wild, the shards of historical memory partly visible around every corner, pushing up out of the earth, mussing up evidence of well-laid-out and beautiful city planning. The park was built on top of an old World War II bunker that was filled in with debris to form two sylvan hills. A formal rose garden was carved out of the rubble of the gunnery platforms. Beneath the entire complex, a labyrinth of tunnels led from the vast armories of the bunker out onto the surrounding streets—the entrances to these passageways still visible and accessible from the sidewalks on regularly scheduled bunker tours. In the mornings before the sun evaporated, fog hung over its hills, and Humboldthain was cool and fresh. Meenakshi pointed out that these early morning walks were one of the few times that they could enjoy the calm space of the park, and this was another reason for getting up so early—to enjoy the clean spaces that the city had to offer. Then, there was also the element of training.

"Taking rounds in the morning" said Mihir, "will increase the ability to concentrate, the mental capacity. If you are fit in the body, you'll also be fit in the mind." He echoed Meenakshi's sentiment about the sayings on her wall. Their answers point to the way that jogging "went with" the IT lifestyle. Working hard during the day, using the abstract faculties of the mind, needed to be complemented and countered by a morning jog that would be a locus of enjoyment, a respite from work, and at the same time would hone work skills. Jogging prepared the body and the mind for the office; it was a form of self-improvement that was explicitly conceptualized as training for being a self-managing subject who works on herself to develop

monetizable personal competencies. Linking jogging explicitly to competition, Mihir allegorizes the IT job market itself and the ultimate prize of a
permanent position.

Meenakshi and Mihir explicitly thought of themselves as being in competition with each other; others were in competition with their own tiredness. As in the office, those with the best skills and most flexibility would
prevail. Jogging was both the testing ground and training field of success.
As may be well known, jogging is not a particularly well-developed pas-
time outside the United States. In Berlin, Americans and others who
jogged were regularly met with curious stares. One student I met while in the
field told me that one day while jogging past an older woman, she clutched
her purse tightly to her chest, looked aghast, and called after him, "Warum
rennst Du?" (Why are you running?). She was afraid, perhaps, that he was
being chased. In India, too, jogging is a recent phenomenon, limited to the
young, elite classes. In Mumbai, around Five Gardens Park, young men jog
wearing shorts and sneakers, with headphones on, while the middle-aged
walk "rounds." In training themselves in the arts of bodily fitness and
mental concentration, Indian programmers create for one another examples of how to inhabit a new lifestyle emblematic of the ethic of working
hard and at speed that was a demand of the industry.

"Sport," write Niko Besnier and Susan Brownell, "presumes an audience."[21]
Programmers performed for a projected future audience of office colleagues,
who could be told of their activities as a badge of similarity, vaulting them
above other workers into the body-conscious class of IT managers. Yet, as
the gradual slowdown of jogging to walking suggests, the drive toward hard
work could not stand up and was at least partially subsumed into the slower
pleasures of the leisurely stroll.

What is the relationship between work and leisure, the home and the
office, that was being elaborated here? Can the way that houses and parks
are used be unpacked to reveal something about the conditions of life and
work in programming economies? Bifo Berardi suggests that cognitive
workers should be seen "from the standpoint of social corporality," stressing not only the cognitive but also the embodied realities of these workers, a
two-sided relationship between virtual labor processes and a host of other
needs that he describes with the term cognitariat.[22] Can the activities of
leisure reveal something about those other embodied needs that are not
met at work but are still very much related to the world of work?

To answer these questions, it may be worthwhile to take a short detour through an earlier examination of work and leisure. In the 1920s, Siegfried Kracauer undertook a study of white-collar workers in Berlin, which he called *The Salaried Masses*. Kracauer describes the organization of the office in strict hierarchical terms, lingering on the divisions between upper and lower managers, the rooms full of young women typists, the strict order and evident classifications marked by title, size of office, quality of furnishings, clothing, and demeanor. In these offices, personnel were organized in divisions and units, their desks precisely following one after the other in neat rows, the discipline of the workplace like the discipline of an army.

Leisure time was a somewhat more complicated affair. As Kracauer outlines, time outside of work was both a respite from the working day and organized along the same lines as the workplace, so that it became the training grounds for increased workplace efficiency. He describes the sporting life organized by companies, where company teams met each other as if on a battlefield. Among managers and for some workers, such activities built solidarity and trained them to be healthy and fit for the office. These teams and outings sponsored by companies to include families were, in Kracauer's estimation, designed to harness the collective energy of workers that might otherwise be directed toward unionization and collective bargaining. The "company community" provided an outlet for collective energies that aligned with the interests of a firm. Kracauer quips, "Sports associations are like outposts intended to conquer the still vacant territory of the employees' souls."[23]

Clearly, the conceptualization of the worker's "soul" as subject to manipulation by capital long preceded current formulations of the soul as having finally entered into the work process. Resonances can be noted, for instance, between Kracauer's account and Mihir's and Meenakshi's ideas about jogging, especially as they relate to preparing the body and mind for another day's labor. Like Kracauer's white-collar workers, these cognitive laborers jog to make themselves ready for another day's work, positing that the exercise, discipline, and fresh air will sharpen what is their primary work tool—the mind.

Unlike under industrial capitalism, however, Mihir's and Meenakshi's training is self-organized. For early twentieth-century office workers, the company encouraged and organized sports; in the early twenty-first century, the high-tech company may make space for free-time pursuits through flexible work schedules. Yet often, when work schedules demand eighty or more hours a week of cognitive labor, these activities must be put on hold—a situation that in Germany at least sometimes fell to Indian coders, who were expected (and assumed to enjoy) putting in long hours at the office.

The deep investment in these activities suggests that sports and enjoyment are related to work as promises on the future. In Kracauer's world, leisure-time activities were organized as if in a factory at the same time as they were meant to replenish workers for another day of labor. In the twenty-first century, the idea that leisure time can replenish the worker is retained, but making leisure time productive is largely the responsibility of the worker herself.

Yet this, too, is not the end of the story of leisure. When jogging fell victim to the pace of work, the conviction that these and other similar activities were important remained for most Indian programmers. Walks replaced jogging after work and on weekends; some began daily meditation. These were all practiced to sharpen the mind to better hold up at work but also as part of a politics of pleasure and a spacing of leisure away from the demands of work. The walks, at a slower pace, without the competition, incline toward a slow appreciation of the space of the park. Enjoying the park is an example of how leisure—once explicitly conceptualized as a sphere of self-improvement to make oneself a competent and successful knowledge worker—can be redeployed toward more open-ended and oppositional ends. Such practices may be akin to what Judith Farquhar and Qicheng Zang describe in their discussion of the Chinese quality of *yangsheng*, or life-cultivation arts, where "the resources that can be mobilized in the service of the good life yield both pleasure and strength."[24]

When the autonomist Marxist Bifo Berardi takes up the idea of eros from Marcuse's *Eros and Civilization*, he aspires to divorce it from its repressive connotations, that is, from the association of domination with the repression of pleasure and freedom with pleasure's liberation. Because, according to Berardi (who here follows Jean Baudrillard's analysis of capital), "the ideology of liberation corresponds to the full domination of the commodity," liberation cannot signify freedom from oppression. Instead, expression of impulses rather than repression feeds capitalist production. Like any commodity, signs produced under cognitive capitalism respond "to the abstract logic of value production." For Berardi, a "generalized compulsion to expression, rather than repression" results in the overproduction of signs.[25] If eros—as the pursuit of pleasure and the good life—is folded into capitalist expression in this way, then one may legitimately ask, what is left of eros as a political concept? Indeed, because Berardi posits expressivity as wholly given over to capitalism and correspondingly posits the cognitive laborer as she who most clearly gives voice to the folding of expression into work, he ends up recapitulating an empty and meaningless sphere of pleasure, in which one may as well work, because the pleasures of expression that once characterized metropolitan life are impoverished. The saving grace of eros, for Berardi, may not come from liberation but nevertheless comes from without—from channeling desire into other, more utopian pathways. Yet, from thinking about the leisure practices of actually existing cognitive workers, I have come to think of eros as a much more open and ambivalent concept, capable of being deployed simultaneously as oppositional to "the general compulsion to expression" and as conducive to forming an embodied middle-class imaginary through pleasure. This makes eros part of a critical utopian project (which I discuss more in the conclusion) that is neither free of capitalist constraint nor completely within the control of workplace demands.

Perhaps, then, the conviction that work will finally conquer the soul, unearthed by Kracauer and again, decades later, by Berardi, is overstated. Such a recurring fear might indicate just as equally the continued reworking and reimagining of the relationship of work, leisure, and the human soul, rather than colonization of the soul by work.

Bodily comportment has long since been part of the techniques of political authority in South Asia. Precolonial Yogic and Sufic techniques of asceticism, meditation, and breath control were said to develop fighting ability and supernatural power in their practitioners. During the colonial period, these legacies were reinterpreted by reformers such as Swami Vivekanana, Aurobindo Gose, and Hazrat Inayat Khan to offer up an indigenized version of Victorian bodily discipline that could frame Indians as morally, scientifically, and physically superior to British colonizess. In doing so, such reformers blended British codes of conduct and textual sources in such a way as to "purify" these traditions by ignoring, for instance, folk practices that included opiates and multiple crossings between religious communities.[26] Such neo-Yogic practitioners also made bodily discipline a safe mode of expression for middle-class subjects to the degree that they divorced asceticism from violent rebellion on the one hand, and class, religion, and caste mixing on the other. A different trajectory of these same developments made its way into the nationalist *swaraj* (self-rule) philosophies of Gandhi and the martial exercises of the Hindutva cadres of the Rashtriya Swayamsewak Sangh (RSS).[27] The jogging practiced by these programmers can thus be fit into a genealogy of bodily discipline that at once critiques dominant modes of power from the West, allows for experimentation with forms of selfhood, and solidifies the lifestyles of those who are economically successful.

In Joseph Alter's discussion of wrestling in North India, he makes the important point that physicality is linked to critique. By mobilizing practices of the body, wrestlers at once recall a utopian good rule where kingship, health of the nation, and responsible citizenry were aligned and a critique of the "babu" state run by corrupt and effeminate bureaucrats. In the reformed nation imagined by wrestlers, "developing a moral physique taps into the vital energy reserves of the human body and directs this energy to productive and virtuous ends."[28] Though they would be placed by wrestlers on the "babu" side of this equation, programmers are involved in a similar project.[29] They link programming and physical effort at "the level of the whole self" to develop themselves into hardened and heroic global cognitive laborers.[30] Their resolution of mental and physical modes of being is ambivalent precisely because they cannot fully endorse the way physical exercise is folded into the politics of the firm. The ambivalence around leisure time recalls Priti Ramamurthy's discussion of perplexity, "the puzzlement of people as they experience both the joys and aches of the global everyday."[31] Even while conceiving of pleasure (in jogging, for instance) as shaping the body as an orientation toward future work, sites of leisure can be appropriated to support the joy of life after work, which also is integral to being middle class.

Excursions

In weekend outings, the organization of potential as a productive force in contemporary capitalism is reappropriated as the pleasure of experiencing a thriving European metropolis. "The weekends and after work are for enjoyment and relaxing," Mihir told me as he suggested, over my objections, that we all celebrate his birthday on top of the old German bunker in Humboldthain Park at midnight. "We work so hard during the week, we should have some fun." While I love the park, I was not sure it was entirely safe late at night. The only people I had seen there after hours had been drinking heavily from liter-size cans of cheap Köstritzer beer and generally had one or more large dogs with them. Ignoring my warnings, he went ahead with the plan. His friends bought a birthday cake and candles, and we all began the walk to the park shortly before midnight. At least someone had managed to bring a flashlight. I seemed to be the only one at all concerned that this might not be such a good idea, but the plan went well, except for Rajeshwari, who in the trek up the hill in the dark lost her passport. She would spend most of the following weeks in embassies and migration offices trying to reestablish her paperwork. We reached the top of the bunker, pulled out the cake, and lit the candles. Mihir blew them out, the teetotalers drank sparkling fruit juice, and the partakers champagne. We took one last, lingering look out of the darkness onto the lights of the city twinkling below and then headed back down to our homes.

Continuing the conversation the next day after work, Mihir revealed that the pleasures of Berlin were an important counterpoint to the grind of work. It was so much better to be here, he said, then in Regensburg, where his last job was. There was so much to enjoy in the city, so much to do and see, so much to eat, so many places to visit. "The people in Berlin are more open and they leave you alone more," he told me; "we are much freer here." The anonymity of the big city appealed to his sense of the adventure of working overseas. At the same time, the freedom Mihir evokes is also in comparison with life in India, where parks and public spaces have been plebeianized through "the subtle pleasures of defilement."[32] As Mihir and Bipin discussed one day while watching a Tamil-language movie, these films always evoke the village as an idyllic setting for a "lost" India. "There is always the nostalgia for the village presented in the movies," suggested Bipin, "because we don't live like that anymore in the cities, with the lush greenery and all." While Bipin and Mihir agreed that this world displayed on film was illusory and villages were really not that wonderful, they also agreed that the world depicted in the movies of "rain showers and greenery," as Mihir noted, "would make them feel refreshed."

Parks, greens, and *maidans* (open spaces) in India's urban metropolises were markers of imperial power, located in the British areas and representative of a public European space transplanted to the subcontinent. A perennial site of middle-class Indian self-fashioning, from the anticolonial period through the 1960s, these parks were redrawn as extensions of middle-class neighborhoods, home to staging grounds of national protest, and, after independence, to the rituals of middle-class life such as "morning constitutionals," the play of children and their minders, and after-work socialization, where "middle-class office-goers would take a stroll, sit for a while on the benches, and exchange greetings and gossip."[33] As Sudipta Kaviraj writes, the park, as extension of middle-class sociality, "violated the principle of universal access, [since] underneath the formal publicity was a subtle, unstated hierarchy."[34] Lower-class city dwellers did not think of the public green as their own. Beginning in the 1960s, as political and economic refugees began to move to cities like Calcutta in large numbers, they began to use the pavement and the parks as temporary sleeping quarters and homes that were then sometimes regularized and sometimes demolished. The poor claimed public space in part as a way of asserting membership in a democracy. The state, lacking resources to be responsible to these populations, responded by sometimes treating these settlements as part of the compact between a state and its people.[35] While occupation of public space by the poor was tentative at first, it became one of a congeries of practices that marked public space in India's cities as the rightful domain of the poor. Through noise and filth, the poor "expressed their social insubordination by causing everyday irritation to their social superiors."[36]

Sites of pleasure outside the home are where lines of class antagonism are being drawn in India today.[37] Yet the direction of this conflict is far from predetermined. In urban India, city beautification programs attempt to use the symbolic power of the middle class to monopolize public pleasures. Yet, the insistent use of public space outside India by the middle class points to how middle-class control over public space in India has been successfully contested. There is also good historical reason to believe that the modes of self-discipline and modes of pleasure inaugurated by the middle class and described here will also be appropriated and improvised on by the poor in ways that do not accord with bourgeois sensibility.[38]

It is against this background of occupied space in India's cities that the pursuit of pleasure by Indian programmers in the cities of America and Europe should be understood. The pursuit of leisure time is in a very real sense a fantasy of what bourgeois life should look like. The practices and pleasures of open space no longer available to the middle class in India are available in Europe and the United States, and Indian programmers walk (or jog) the same routes through parks and pursue similar genteel activities that their parents and grandparents once aspired to on the maidans of Kolkata, Hyderabad, Mumbai, and Delhi. The rise of the gated community in India responds to the experience of Indians in diasporic spaces in Europe and the United States—it brings what is experienced outside back into India.

On a Sunday afternoon in the springtime, we decided to go on a picnic in Treptower Park, a green space in East Berlin famous for its Soviet memorial to the fallen soldiers of World War II. The preparations for the picnic were elaborate and began the previous day. Each of us was given a dish to cook and bring, and we arranged to meet at Meenakshi and Rajeshwari's house at noon the next day.

The Soviet War Memorial at Treptower Park is a marvel of Soviet Cold War aesthetics. A giant statue of a Soviet soldier crushing a swastika underfoot with sword drawn and child in arm is flanked by a semicircle of friezes depicting war scenes and phrases by Stalin in both Russian and German. All the hallmarks of the socialist realist style have been used to full effect: the statues tower above neatly manicured lawns, a plaque declares that the homeland will never forget its fallen soldiers (some of whom are buried here), the common man is glorified, the scale is emotional, the limbs embodying the strength of Mother Russia and her heroic fighters appropriately bulky. We toured the site, looking up toward the blue sky as the shadows of the monument raked across the ground. The art of the past dutifully marveled at, we moved on to the main entertainment of the day. Finding a partly sunny, partly shady patch of grass, we spread our picnic blankets on the ground and covered them with dishes and cups, silverware, bottles of water, and multiple containers of food. Someone unpacked a Frisbee, another person a soccer ball.

In the long afternoon of eating, drinking, and playing, everyone was relaxed and joking. Meenakshi and Rajeshwari threw the Frisbee back and forth, warming themselves in the sun, and took a turn at soccer. People traded stories about friends they knew, about work, stories of moving from one job to another. They exchanged strategies for getting visas to the United States and asked each other whether parents could get visas to visit them in Germany. They joked about eating too much and about Indian politicians, they started song games based on a well-known canon of Hindi film music, they played cards.

Over the year and a half I spent in the field, my notebook recorded a similar excursion every weekend in good weather. We visited the Reichstag and the Tiergarten, Sanssouci (a baroque palace in Potsdam), and the rose garden in Humboldthain Park near my house dozens of times. We trekked to Kreuzberg to eat the city's best falafel, and we traveled to Alexanderplatz to marvel at the TV tower and buy spices and vegetables at the Thai grocery store; we walked around lakes and ate ice cream. We shopped at H&M, the high-fashion, low-price clothing retailer, and we went to the Sri Lankan Hindu temple at the other end of Kreuzberg. We watched cricket at the Indian Embassy and sang Jana Gana Mana on Indian Independence Day.[39] These excursions recalled the uses of space Kaviraj described, the strolling and constitutionals, eating and joking, occupying parks, taking the air, and playing across the green grass—enjoying urban life in terms of its pleasures of space, order, and cleanliness. While these pleasures seem barred from enjoyment in India, they are readily available in Europe.

Elaborating leisure activities allows Indian middle-class subjects to "escape without leaving" the demands of a flexible subject.[40] Enjoying the park and the excursion taps into practices of enjoyment that open up a space beyond the uses of pleasure for the sake of work. Taking time in the park, playing games, and trekking to the top of a hill at midnight all expand experience beyond the dictates of producing qualities of a subject that can be marshaled as commodities in the future. These pleasures play out explicitly within the frame of the politics of the middle class in India, where Humboldthain Park, for instance, stands in for the right to pleasure as a means of attaining a middle-class quality of life. These ambivalences in the pursuit of leisure are reflected in the homes of short-term workers, where a kind of freedom is made possible by the very temporariness of these homes, making them a socially useful space for experiments in leisure.[41]

A Hostel in the Home

In the twelve months since I had first met this group of programmers at the embassy on Indian Independence Day, I had come to spend almost every evening at Meenakshi and Rajeshwari's apartment, which was just a few doors down from my own. We would usually meet after work and stay up late in the night chatting. They both had to be up early, by six, to get to their jobs on time. I had been interning for the last few months at a research center focusing on German and European migration politics in order to understand better how the Indian IT phenomenon fit into existing migration legislation. Our working lives were mirroring one another's. We all went off to work in the morning and reconvened afterward to cook, socialize, and talk.

I came to think of Meenakshi and Rajeshwari's apartment and the other nearby apartments programmers shared as a home-hostel space, a hybrid social world that was part home, part dormitory, at once a site for the reconstitution of family and household relations, a place to reflect on the conditions of working as a transnational coder, and a space for experimentation and play.[42] In her study of young people at college in Kerala, Ritty Lukose argued that the hostel or dormitory was a key site for the production of youth politics. In the hostel, women engaged in talk about morals, made fun of each other, mocked both male students and social classes, and revisited burning questions of social change and respectability.[43] As a "liminal space," the hostel is used by Lukose's informants to work through the contradiction of consumption and career that currently take center stage in the lives of young college-going Indians.[44]

Like the hostel, the home of the short-term IT worker is a temporary accommodation. It is a space for reinvention and reconsideration of received ideas and new impressions, places where new "habitations of modernity" can be tried out. Although generally the argument has been that globalization (or in an earlier key, modernization) is changing Indian households and families or that the behavior of transnational migrants can be explained through recourse to the maintenance of family and household structure, this section takes a different tack.[45] I argue instead that in a situation in which the lines between work and leisure are blurred for the sake of generating new productive impulses, homes become a staging ground for both justifying transnational work as maintaining a middle-class quality of life and for inventing new forms of life for the middle class.[46] As Jean Comaroff notes, "Spatial contexts—and one might add, the processes that are played out within them—are themselves major media of socialization, invisibly tuning the minds and bodies of those who people them to their inner logic."[47] I would additionally add that for programmers, spatial processes rather visibly turn minds toward their logics, as programmers comment on and make available for debate the very relationship between the world of work and the home that they are further developing.

The house has long been a hidden source of productivity at the same time that the home and the family have served as symbolic reservoirs of opposition to the market and the public sphere.[48] Both colonial and nationalist actors in South Asia targeted the home to provide evidence for the magnanimity or corruption of British rule. Nationalists used this version of the home to argue for interior cultural identities that were resistant to colonial influence, while colonialists used the example of the backwardness of Indian women in the home to justify continuing colonial dominion. In these maneuvers, the home was consolidated as a sphere of Hindu and Muslim purity, a private space that was represented by religious devotion, female modesty, and modern home economics.[49] But, as attention to late nineteenth-century and early twentieth-century female reformers like Pandita Ramabai and Parvati Athavale attests, the tight association between home, the nation, religion, and female purity did not go uncontested. Such women joined nationalist reform movements for widow remarriage and women's education. By creating communal homes for widows, for instance, such reformers collapsed "home and community" outside the confines of the family, calling into question the ability of the upper-caste Hindu domestic sphere to accommodate gender reform. By arguing for "nationalism as a gender-neutral unity of the various and different regions of India," they thwarted nationalist and colonialist discourses of female protection and male activity.[50] In doing so, they reconstructed the home as a site of contestation and negotiation among nationalist, colonialist, and feminist movements. Contemporary efforts to revisit the meaning of the home bear witness to these earlier moments, relying on the "very materiality" the home "appears to embody" to press claims for a new relationship between domesticity and the public, the self and the economy.[51]

In the current constitution of relations between market and home, the boundaries between the two have been reconfigured, even at the level of ideology, as permeable. In other words, historically the home has been the site of much of the hidden work done to maintain the sphere of the market and capital. Here, the home emerges from its hiding place as a space in which programmers both reflect on the conditions of labor and make themselves into subjects capable of being inserted into these labor regimes.

Meenakshi and Rajeshwari devoted a majority of the space in their home to creating a large sitting room for guests. They have divided their one-room apartment across the middle with a curtain that they could close when guests arrived. Behind the curtain that they drew when guests were there, they had two single beds and two closets on wheels for their clothing. They shared a bedside table with two small lamps on it, and a collection of crime novels and autobiographies is arranged on a shelf above the beds. Before the curtain, white plastic chairs accommodated visitors. Everyone who arrived between five and eight in the evening was given piping hot tea served in flimsy plastic cups. Tea-talking sessions sometimes went on until midnight.

The apartment belonging to Madhu and Bipin, one of two married couples in this group, had a kitchen, separate bedroom, and large sitting room. One side of the sitting room had a dining table, the other a large couch and coffee table with chairs arranged around it. On a low table near the dining table sat a personal computer. Everyone without a desktop computer at home would come over to their apartment to surf the web, send e-mail, and scan online job advertisements.

Mihir lived alone. His one-room apartment had a small kitchen and a room with his bed, a large flat-screen television and DVD player, a low, rectangular coffee table, and a collection of white plastic chairs. On the bedside table, he had a few books and a reading lamp, as well as a portrait of Shirdi Sai Baba. Mihir's house was where everyone assembled when they wanted to watch movies together. Mihir could have gotten a roommate to save money but did not as he hoped his aging parents would be able to visit him for several months at a time. In preparation for their eventual visit, he took care to keep the rooms clean and orderly. He applied contact paper to the floor in the kitchen to cover over what he thought of as an unacceptable amount of ground-in grime from previous occupants. Shyam, from Delhi, lived in the same apartment complex as Mihir, and I am told that he has a similar setup, though I have never seen it. Lacking the television and DVD player, Shyam's apartment afforded little opportunity for socializing. Srinu, Mayur, and another man named Arun, who is a biologist, lived in a two-room apartment. Mayur and Srinu shared a small room with bunk beds. They were both excellent cooks and invited us over from time to time for great feasts where we sat in Arun's room on the floor as there was little space elsewhere, played cards and song games, and gossiped.

In all these homes, space is given over to socializing, and personal space is economized. The apartments formed a network, with Usha and Bipin's home an important site for its space and for its access to the computer. Rajeshwari and Meenakshi's house, with its large "hall" or sitting room, could accommodate a dozen comfortably and was often the go-to destination after work. Mihir's house was important for film-watching parties, and Mayur, Arun, and Srinu's for foodie parties. These homes helped produce "corporate authorship," through which the commensuration of the world of work with the expanding horizons of middle-class Indian life emerged in their collective figuration of a good life. As Matthew Hull has recently pointed out in his study of Pakistani bureaucracy, for spatial artifacts, "it is often less important what they stand for than . . . how they arrange people around themselves."[52]

Homes serve as meeting points for excursions at the same time that their arrangement invites, almost insists on, discussion of the day's events, politics, and explicit comparison of life in Germany with life elsewhere. The home is thus doubly located, first as a temporary space that matches a temporary lifestyle, and second as a "ring" of homes that arrange individual programmers in a network of friends and a cohort of young overseas Indians who can collectively work through the contradictions of being abroad. The chairs in Meenakshi and Rajeshwari's apartment, for instance, are plastic and not very expensive yet bought in a quantity to allow for socializing. They index concomitantly the temporary nature of life in Berlin for short-term programmers, a market economy of cheaply and readily available goods, and the value of socialization as a means of creating forms of enjoyment in excess of that same market efficiency.

One day, Meenakshi and Rajeshwari's home was used in the morning for cooking, as the three of us gathered to make food for an upcoming party at Mayur, Srinu, and Arun's house. As we cooked, we talked. The topic was love and marriage. Rajeshwari had a boyfriend who had moved from Hyderabad to Canada, but he had not told his parents of their relationship as they would not approve of a "love marriage." Rajeshwari was debating trying to find a job in Canada so as to join him. Asking our advice separately, she wanted to know from me if conditions for working in Canada were better than in Germany, and from Meenakshi, whether she should encourage her boyfriend to tell his parents about their relationship. Meenakshi told her to wait, saying that "if the boy's family is truly opposed to the match, then it is better not to interfere." Rajeshwari, however, was not so sure and was getting tired of waiting and questioned her boyfriend's continued need for subterfuge. Such moments of conversation turned the home into an intimate space for figuring out acceptable ways to navigate relationships on one's own but within the bounds of respect for the family and were an example of what Smitha Radhakrishnan called being "appropriately Indian," of negotiating and, in the process, cementing both Indian particularity and global universalism.[53]

Later that day, the home became a forum for discussing differences between the United States, Germany, and India, where some were of the opinion that Germany was better than the United States because at least Germans, in Mihir's words, "left you alone to do your own culture," whereas in the United States, Indians who moved there very quickly forgot their culture. For instance, he continued, friends of his who now lived in the United States "forgot they are supposed to take off their shoes when going into a temple." Still again, the home was a space of play, where charades and card games allowed them to play with being "black ticket" salespeople (a popular role in charades: ticket scalping) and clever card sharks. And still later, the forum turned to a serious discussion of religion and science, reminiscent of Dipesh Chakrabarty's discussion of *adda*, a social form of meandering talk where the vicissitudes of "modernity" are opened up for appropriation.[54]

In the middle of the twentieth century, sociologists and anthropologists examined how industrialization was affecting "the" Indian family, positing that the joint family would disappear into nuclear family units, while arranged marriages would yield to free choice in marriage partner and fraternal unity would lessen as the conjugal couple was emphasized.[55] Although several authors pointed out that the joint family was probably not as widespread in precolonial India as has often been assumed, the trope of "modernization" as reflected in the transition from joint to nuclear family held sway. Opposing this modernist logic, Patricia Uberoi points out that the relationship between family structure and globalization is hardly predictable.[56] The home is a space where divisions are made available for contestation, not simply reproduced.

In the current iteration of market-family relations, the relationship of the home to the market is ever more explicitly charted out as one of interdigitation rather than opposition. The home and the idea of the family are both reenacted and made fluid by IT workers abroad. These fluidities show how the IT workers experiment with ways of living as a key means of commensurating the complicated subjecthood of the fast and cheap coder and the cultural supplement to European reason they are often asked to inhabit at work with the vision they have of themselves as "heroic citizens" of the new India.

Given the interpenetration of home and world, it may be that the homes of IT professionals will continue to have a hostel-like quality, where the conditions of life can be commented on and renegotiated. In an earlier moment, Jane Collier, Michelle Rosaldo, and Sylvia Yanagisako wrote, "What gives shape to much of our concept of the Family is its symbolic opposition to work and business—in other words, to the market relations of capitalism."[57] If the home and family are not quite structurally opposed to capitalism anymore but instead overlap with it as the site of both the production of work culture and the elaboration of a critique of labor, then the hostel stands in for a space of transition that is no longer fixedly opposed to the world of business but must take up that world and try to domesticate it.[58]

In her kitchen, Meenakshi practiced the art of improvisation as a way of developing techniques of the self that distanced her from the computer as stupid, direction-following cook. In her sitting room, at the front door, before she left the house, she practiced the art of motivation through thinking positively, checking her inked phrases and her dolphin jumping out of the water for inspiration before stepping over the threshold of her home. Making these signs herself, she imbued them with her creative energies in a way that repeats, but does not simply conform to, how office culture asks her to invest her creative self in the company. In these instances, the home served as a training ground for work, producing feelings of hope, encouraging hard work and concentration, but at the same time, it produced a heightened sense of play with new ways of doing things.

The Pleasure of Leisure

Pleasure's link to work and leisure, as theorized in the literature on control societies, is often premised on the loss of a space of leisure to the demands of work. Yet, I found that adjacent to these more familiar and well-rehearsed professional intrusions into leisure was the pursuit of pleasure as passing time in the bourgeois pursuits of strolling, picnicking, and eating alfresco. Leisure time no longer stands in direct contrast or opposition to work but has instead become a mottled and dappled field, at once the space in which to develop work-related habits and dispositions and a space dedicated to the pleasure of pursuing everything that is not work. As Karin Knorr Cetina writes in her exploration of the politics of knowledge societies, one of the main consequences of the growing importance of information comes in the form of recognizing that "knowledge" implies different epistemes, what she calls "epistemic framing." Different kinds of knowledge imply different lifeworlds, where the "merging and reconfiguring different orders" are a central activity in social life.[59] Leisure and work have, since the early twentieth century, been opposing lifeworlds, but in the current moment, their relationship is being reconfigured. If leisure is now conceived of as a space and time where workers mobilize and develop the expertise of self-management, this also makes leisure a site for an explicit refusal of this narrative. A specifically Indian middle-class imaginary emerges through an ethic of improvisation that treats leisure not as fully given over to work but puts it in a complementary and contrastive relationship to work. This ethic emerges at once from the limits of work as a site of rewarding labor and from the history of making an urban middle class in India as a public with a right to public enjoyments and public space.

The life of leisure has been infused with pleasures of the nonconstructive variety. Enjoying parks, as programmers do here, is one of these pleasures. Looking around I can see many more. Indeed, just as much as any activity (or, to the point, no activity at all) can be seen as preparation for work, it is also stubbornly constructed as not work. Eating and cooking, for example, can be a mode of work on the self. It can also be made into an elaborate ritual of taking time and expending energies in the opposite direction of work—the popularity of the black ticket seller in charades seems to comment on the many clandestine routes one might take to gain admission to the bourgeoisie pleasures of the city.[60] The skills practiced in leisure time are a dialectic between what is necessary for office culture and what opposes those very structures.

The dual nature of leisure is rather like the dual nature of other aspects of capital I have been discussing in this book. Both flexible, producing future possibilities and diverted toward immediate ends, the world of leisure is a site for the reinvention of subjecthood. While this reinvention is one of the main requirements for cognitive laborers, it neither necessarily emerges out of the culture of the office nor leads back to the workplace. In this chapter, I have argued that Indian programmers both work on themselves in a conscious way to be better at their jobs and be successful at work and explore the pleasures that Berlin offers as a reward for their efforts that cannot be invaded by work. Self-improvement is a response to the global conditions of work that make it necessary to constantly reinvent oneself, especially for those who labor in knowledge economies in which race and difference are used to solidify the Indian programmer's reputation for cheap and fast coding. Likewise, the kinds of urban pleasures that Indian programmers pursue in Berlin are a response to embattled urban space in India. Perhaps the middle classes are reestablishing control over such spaces through multiplexes and shopping malls in the latest instantiation of class politics in space in India. But the story of the plebeianization of the Indian park should warn us against being complacent in the story of middle-class hegemony.

The middle class has made available for reappropriation the practice of self-improvement and pleasure as closely aligned. In this sense, those in the middle class may be innovating on the boundary between self-improvement and pleasure in a much more radical way than has previously been described. That is, they may be blurring the boundary between the unrestrained space of outside and the usual places of self-improvement: the home, the family, and the educational institution. While this blurring may make family life a site of consumption, it also makes the park a place where consumption can be criticized; while it purges the street of hawkers and pavement dwellers, it also sends a powerful message that the pleasures of the city are meant to be a reward for work. This message can be turned toward an argument for a democratization of pleasure, understood as passing time slowly among one's friends.

In his study of formerly "criminal tribe" cultivators in South India, Anand Pandian notes that the discourses of self-improvement simultaneously index the history of state-led reform of such groups through agriculture and an alternate ethic of cultivation that can, at times, valorize ways of life (such as *ganja* growing and petty thieving) that upend the prevailing ideology of agriculture as morally uplifting.[61] In a similar way and for these middle-class subjects, discourses of self-improvement both participate in a neoliberal reform of subjectivity that makes of the individual an always adapting entrepreneur of her qualities and participate in creating a counterweight to this subject by providing a platform from which to argue that chaneling pleasure into work is one-sided. In part I of this book I argued that short-term Indian programmers are able to marshal such a critique because of how they are placed within companies as racialized, replaceable, yet exotic and interesting migrant workers—like computers themselves who cook but cannot write a recipe. This initial critique is elaborated outside of work through practices of pleasure that take their distance from work even while they articulate a desire to succeed in the workplace.

SIX

THE TRAVELING DIAPER BAG

Gifts and Jokes as Materializing Immaterial Labor

In a large and airy sitting room, illuminated by a bright ceiling light giving the walls a warm yellow glow, a young nephew of Mihir's swayed back and forth on a swing, affixed to two sturdy iron hooks in the ceiling of Mihir's parents' house. His cousins, nieces, and nephews populated a nearby couch. Their apartment is in the city of Pune, near Mumbai, in a centrally located neighborhood called Bhavani Peth, which had been inhabited by professional and upper-caste Punekars since at least the 1940s. The family apartment overlooks a courtyard dotted with potted plants and flowers peeking out between the motorcycles, scooters, and small cars that line the interior walls of the building. I unpacked the small packet of photos from his travels across Europe that Mihir had entrusted to me. As we all sat drinking tea and eating snacks from the low glass coffee table in the center of the room, I noticed along another wall a series of shelves with small objects on them—an ostrich egg, a statue of the Eiffel Tower, a porcelain bear from Berlin, and another building I did not recognize, which turned out to be the Kuala Lumpur towers in Malaysia. Mihir's mother picked up each of these small souvenirs in turn, guiding me through their histories. These were gifts picked up on the parents' trips to visit Mihir in his various jobs abroad or gifts he brought back with him on his twice-yearly visits. The lion with the fish's tail was from Singapore, where he had worked for two years, the Eiffel Tower from Paris, the bear from Berlin, and the ostrich egg was from South Africa.

At the time of my visit, Mihir had been working in Germany for over three years. It was the longest time he had spent in any one country outside of India. Mihir had worked on short-term contracts in South Africa, Malaysia, and Germany. At each place, he had brought his parents to visit for a month or more. They always brought back something from Mihir to remember their travels by, proudly displaying these gifts in the showcase in their living room.

The objects displayed in the sitting room of Mihir's parents stand in for an absent son. They materialize his success, the care of his family, and a foreign world of experience and value brought within the confines of the household. An only child, Mihir was especially close with his parents, concerned that as they grew older they would have no one to take care of them. With a regular audience of appreciative kin and neighbors to admire them, such objects concretize a collective nurturing enterprise over which Indian middle classes can both confederate and compete.

At an earlier moment during fieldwork, Rajeshwari and I were on our oft-repeated morning walk in Berlin's Gesundbrunnen Park Rose Garden when, after a heated debate comparing India and the West, she paused the conversation to tell me a joke.[1] "We have a saying," she declared, "Germans are hardworking. Indians are both lazy and hardworking." I asked her how Indians can be both hardworking and lazy at the same time. "Well, it's like with time," she responded. "The Germans are very punctual, and once they come to work, they work until it is time to leave. But they may not necessarily enjoy the work. But Indians, they may come late but will enjoy the work while they are doing it." "And Americans?" I asked. "Americans," she answered, "are cunning."

Within the context of a European office, getting to work late but working hard while there is most often not a sign of a promotable, high-value employee. In the workplace, this characteristic can indicate that the Indian workforce is good at writing code but not good at "front end" operations such as dealing with customers, who demand punctuality. In Rajeshwari's joke, she explicitly brings pleasure into the domain of work.[2] The lazy and hardworking Indian is someone who enjoys software development but does not take everything that surrounds the work too seriously—such as punctuality and constant productivity. Calling Indians, herself included, lazy and hardworking, she draws on the norms of corporate culture and then creates a space between them for an interested but nonprofessional relationship to work. In Rajeshwari's reckoning, the opposition between ordered Germany and unruly India is a mark of distinction, implying a different relationship to labor, one governed by the pleasure of writing source code, fixing bugs, running tests, and figuring out how to translate client demands into workable programs.[3]

Mihir's gifts and Rajeshwari's joke invite me to think about how Indian coders in the diaspora extend—and curtail—the meaning of their work outside the office. This chapter follows the potential subversion of jokes and gifts at the same time that it recognizes how they normalize social relations for the Indian middle class. The way Indian programmers tell jokes and give gifts is a local resolution to the demands a regime of immaterial labor makes of them and is thus a way to rematerialize—that is, make concrete and open up to revision—this work.[4]

Shalini Shankar notes that objects make social meaning available for negotiation by making them visible at the center of collective attention.[5] Giving gifts and telling jokes fine-tune the ability of programmers to open up cognitive labor to questioning and, concomitantly, to innovate ways of inhabiting the world that is a resounding note in building an Indian middle-class sensibility. In other words, telling jokes and giving gifts at once spur critique of a global cognitive economy and consolidate middle-class hegemony.[6]

In chapter 4, I showed that technologies of state produced a cadre of expert technicians who would become the Indian middle class. The middle classes were called on to lead India's technological development in the years leading up to Indian independence. Their identity as moral and developmental leaders has largely been enabled by their association with technological development. Far from diminishing with the rise of neoliberal, open market policies in India, this position coalesced around using private, entrepreneurial high-tech initiatives for the good of the nation. In this chapter, I turn to another side of this relationship. I ask, "How does cognitive labor get materialized by Indian middle classes for consumption at home?"

Many accounts of the Indian IT workers characterize them as tacking back and forth between Western and Indian cultures.[7] Such a characterization correctly identifies the dilemma that Indian programmers face in commensurating global white-collar work and Indian citizenship. Yet it also misses the most interesting thing about how Indian coders move between worlds—they sketch out a blueprint for defining the Indian middle class as they go.[8]

I have been arguing in this book that autonomist Marxism has been at the vanguard of conceptualizing how subjects are constituted under contemporary capitalism. As autonomist Marxists expand the notion of the cognitariat to include a discussion of how contemporary capitalism remakes cooperation, creativity, and improvisation into the formal properties of production, they theorize what has changed in capitalist relations since Marx.[9] Contemporary capitalism stresses flexibility and the open horizon of the future as elements of productivity. But because autonomist Marxists largely posit a universal, unmarked cognitive laborer, they tend to miss the contradictions that emerge as labor is embodied.[10] Focusing on these contradictions reveals, for instance, how leisure time concomitantly serves as an arena in which to build alternatives to the rigors of the office and as confirmation of middle-class status conceived of as the right to enjoyment. Spaces of leisure allow an ethic of denying work's hold on life to emerge precisely because under contemporary capitalism leisure is experienced as threatened and is therefore brought to the center of social attention, as I argued in chapter 5. This ethic of pleasure, or eros, constitutes at the same time an exclusionary bourgeois sensibility for the Indian middle class. In other words, eros neither is completely subsumed within the logics of cognitive work nor provides a liberatory escape from capitalism and its attendant inequalities. Here, I examine how the potential open-endedness of eros is closed off in building a middle-class Indian sensibility. In other words, even while jokes and gifts extend the "life" of programming work beyond the ambit of an individual's experience of labor, they also curtail dissent and set limits on the acceptable extension of these worlds.

Jokes and gifts, although normally considered two very separate kinds of social forms, have formal properties that make them "good" to rematerialize cognitive work. Both jokes and gifts have a part that is social and a part that is individual: a part that depends on someone doing the telling or choosing, and an audience that does the listening, commenting, and passing along. By seeming to embody the delicate calibration of individual initiative and collective obligation, both jokes and gifts invite reflection on how to inhabit the world.[11]

In what follows, I unpack the many different ways that gifts and then jokes extend and curtail eros, from providing care at a distance to marking class distinctions, from shaking off the seriousness of work to ending an argument. In commensurating worlds of work and worlds beyond work, jokes and gifts do what might be called *affective unwork* and *affective work*. They loosen the bind between the worker and the job (they "unwork" it), but also, they reconstitute a bind between the work and other worlds (they "work" it) in such a way as to stop further elaborations of eros. They make possible creative play within and against the dictates of the economy knowledge.[12]

Gifts Connect and Nurture

The fish and ostrich egg, Kuala Lumpur towers, and Berliner Bear extend Mihir's influence even when he is not present at home. Such objects extend the "fame" of programmers to kin and friend networks in India. They create felicitous arguments to those family members who sustain programmers financially and emotionally about the worth of programming overseas and the value of an individual's experience abroad.[13]

An expansive and continually elaborated theory of the gift is one main contribution of anthropology to social theory. In Marcel Mauss's seminal formulation, a theory of the gift is a necessary correlate and corrective to a theory of individualized commodity exchange. Recently, David Graeber has rehabilitated Mauss's theory of the gift to argue for the historical specificity of modern debt.[14] In this work, Graeber points out that even Mauss's morality of the gift is most often understood as a kind of exchange relationship, framing the gift as simply the other side of trade.[15] The consequence of thinking of debt as only an exchange rather than as also reciprocation, according to Graeber, is that the entire world of social obligation, mutuality, and reciprocity has been reduced to a single and singular form of economic transaction built on the principles of formal equality and social distance.[16] Yet, despite remarking on the significance of gifting outside exchange, Graeber builds a largely "economistic" theory of debt forgiveness in the remainder of the text. Although this economic reading of the gift is useful in complicating received notions of debt, it curiously sidesteps the social meanings of gifts, focusing instead on the transactional demands that the law of the gift implies. There is also an erotics of the gift.

While recognizing that gifts answer a demand for reciprocation, there is also a pleasure of sending and choosing small gifts. In this section, I explore eros as counterconduct—a pleasure in gifting that disrupts the logic of a cognitive economy work ethic that transacts work hours for increased remuneration.[17] In the pathways they take, small gifts set down social networks as a hedge against the risks inherent in short-term programming. They lay the groundwork for future moves to other sites within a globalized programming economy. And, in their "unimportant" materiality, they both open up and set limits on the possibilities for life outside of work.

In my field notebook, I wrote the following shortly before a trip I took back to the United States:

I was leaving in a few days and I had promised Aunty to take some photos back with me to give to her daughter, who also happens to live in New Jersey. Aunty proceeded to pull out a rather large package wrapped in a plastic bag from Woolworth's. This was obviously not photos. "You don't mind, do you Sareeta dear?" she asked me. When my husband saw how big it was, he started shouting, "Why are you giving her such a large thing? She won't have room for it!" I told her not to worry, it's not a problem. I could make space in my suitcase. I asked her what it was. As she handed it to me, she said, it's a diaper bag. I peeked inside the bag and saw a small white foam and plastic diaper bag with "Sesamstrasse" written on it and Big Bird, Elmo, and Cookie Monster dancing merrily along its border. I did not have the heart to tell Aunty that "Sesamstrasse" is just the German version of Sesame Street, and her relatives in the United States were surely able to buy similar bags without much trouble. There is a new baby in the family you see, she said, and handed me her daughter's address in New Jersey. I glanced at the address and said, well I may have to mail the diaper bag because your daughter lives about three hours by car ride from my house. She said her daughter knew already and would come to collect the bag. I returned home and dutifully called Aunty's daughter the following day. Preethi told me on the phone that she won't pick up the bag but she is sending her brother, an engineer who works close to where I live. The bag itself isn't for her, even though she just had a baby. Rather, it is going to travel with another Aunty to Cleveland, where she is visiting her daughter. From Cleveland it will then go on to India with this daughter to finally reach Preethi's cousin, who also just had a baby of her own. Preethi, on the other hand, is getting ready to send her one-year-old to India with her in-laws. I asked if it was difficult, to send her baby to India. She told me that yes, it was, but both she and her husband have jobs and it is just becoming too much for them to handle. So, the diaper bag is going to India after all. It is bought in Germany, then travels to New Jersey by plane, then from northern Jersey to southern Jersey by car, then from Jersey to Ohio by plane, where it will finally board another plane to go to its final destination, Bangalore. All this for a bit of plastic costing no more than thirty dollars, and passing through the hands of professional people who earn salaries in euros and dollars, not rupees.

A diaper bag might seem an odd way to materialize cognitive work, since it is a low-worth object similar to those easily acquirable in any Indian city, but only if materialization is conceptualized as producing financial worth as high-price commodities. This diaper bag is a small plastic token of a parent's love. When children are raised by their grandparents while parents work, the effort invested in making a diaper bag move to India helps to lay nurturing blanket of care over distance. The diaper bag constitutes a community, pulling together strands of kin and friendship over the three continents of Europe, North America, and Asia, creating new bonds in the same gesture that it refreshes existing ones. Although the final recipient may not be aware of all the complicated steps of the bag's dance across the oceans, she is cognizant of the time between its purchase and its arrival, of the status marker of a diaper bag for India where diapers and bags to put them in are uncommon, and of the simple fact that it has passed through innumerable hands to get to her. All this makes it not just a diaper bag but an object invested in chains of care that stretch and connect places across the globe.

In diaspora, the giver and receiver roles of gifting are stretched out across space, so that relations of obligation extend in all directions across the network of kin and family through which a present has passed, since "at any given moment any event [of gift giving] is infused with an ambience of potentialities or 'futurity,' as well as the past."[18] The motion of these gifts, passing as they do through multiple hands, constitutes the very network on which they depend, making of scattered groups a diasporic community—linked through webs of allegiance, obligation, memory, and exchange to multiple points of origin.

The futurity crystallized in small gifts such as the traveling diaper bag disrupts the usual way that diasporic economics are considered. Rather than transmitting remittances home, gifts translate cognitive labor into nurture. Often, the way that money is transacted for objects of care reflects a system of value that rests less on the purchase price of objects than on the amount of work invested in them. They make promises of return and of care that imply time spent in regimes of cognitive labor abroad will only be temporary.

In her study of Sri Lankan housemaids working in the Gulf states, Michele Ruth Gamburd shows how family structures are maintained despite long-term separation by means of investing profits into conspicuous items of consumption such as refrigerators, on the one hand, and into emblems of masculinity such as alcohol, on the other. The combination of large electronics and liquor maintains the standing of a family in the village and enhances male potency, associated with the abandonment of intoxication.[19] By comparison, in the current instance, the problem is transforming a surfeit of capital into the goods of affection. What will count as nurturing objects will depend on the care with which gifts are chosen and the work it takes to send them.

Choosing and Sending Gifts: Signaling the New

The rhythm of most programmers' weekends is punctuated by the purchases of concrete items, either to be sent to India or to be used, always with the idea that they are movable objects of consumption, such as a laptop computer or DVD player. On one occasion, several members of the group bought cell phones that were on sale in a local supermarket to send to India with someone who was soon to travel there. These cell phones had a particularly sleek black look and were spade shaped with a slide-out keyboard—a design that they said their relatives in India would appreciate and that was not available there. Another time, I went with Madhu, Bipin, Meenakshi, and Rajeshwari to the clothing store H&M to pick out T-shirts to send home. The four spent almost an hour going through racks of shirts, rejecting all those that they thought could be easily purchased in India. Now that Indians have access to similar consumer goods as those abroad, they told me, it has become harder to choose gifts that family will value. They first rejected all T-shirts with sayings or graphics on them. These were too commonplace in Indian metropolises today. Next, they thought about color choices. They tried to find colors that were not so readily available in India, like pale yellows for men or unusual shades of blue. Finally, they settled on plain polo shirts in a variety of colors, which they thought would be something different from what could be gotten at home.

The taste that programmers enact when deciding among colors and styles of T-shirts and among cell phone aesthetics may be understood as creating a pattern of consumption that marks class membership.[20] Yet, from the perspective of gifting, it is independent, individual, and chosen activity that distinguishes IT workers and other professionals from the mass of Indians at home and, increasingly, those abroad working in lower-paid service industries. These gifts are understood at home as a marker of this choice, signifying the worth of having traveled abroad, and acting as a material stand-in for absent sons, daughters, spouses, and parents. Gifts bring with them a world that people at home cannot yet access. Being part of the Indian middle class is not only about access to consumer goods but about access to the broad and open-ended worldly possibilities that these goods can index, since "these goods communicate a desire to belong to the same wider world to which both the inhabitants of the global metropoles and the affluent . . . belong."[21] Small gifts then simultaneously divert cognitive labor into chains of care and consolidate an Indian middle-class position as being part of establishing ways of living for Indian subjects more broadly. Picking just the right T-shirt can open up a conversation by proxy about what could be a good life and how it is best lived, as design, price, color, and quality become indexes of affection and of material well-being. In other words, perhaps what is most important in the materialization of immaterial work for middle-class Indians abroad is the opportunity to try out, argue over, and negotiate the "ends" of work.

Many cell phones, T-shirts, and photos make their way into Adi and Maya's suitcases as they move back to London. On a sunny day in May in their Kreuzberg apartment, friends and well-wishers come and go, many bearing small packages. While a Tamil film plays in the background, in the bedroom, three suitcases sit on the bed with their guts spilling out. Programmers approach Maya and Adi with parcels to be delivered to family in the United States, in England, and in India. They have each figured out a person in London who will pick up the package and send it on or take it in their suitcases further on this journey. Maya and Adi find room for most of the packages they are given. While the couple fits the parcels together with their clothes in their suitcase like a complex, three-dimensional puzzle, in the front room the talk turns to the film. A familiar debate begins on the quotidian scene of family life flickering on screen, as the audience weighs the material well-being of life abroad with the emotional attachments such images evoke. The debates frame gifting as an act that is both economic and extraeconomic, transferring wealth and innovating ways of inhabiting regimes of cognitive migrant labor.

Gifts materialize cognitive work by commensurating the world of work with the demands of family and friends.[22] They help make convincing arguments for the value of work overseas and extend care at a distance, even as they produce a feeling of ownership over a cosmopolitan world of goods and ideas by signaling the new. In these ways, gifts both disrupt and reaffirm the logic of cognitive labor—they slow down the pace of work through care taken in choosing and sending low-worth things, and they performatively enunciate the worth of the global IT industry to making middle-class lives in India.

The joy of converting money into gifts is one way to make cognitive labor material. Telling jokes which bend and warp the conventions of cognitive work is another. As I recount below, jokes also diffuse and limit the extent to which the norms of labor can be subverted.

Joking as Undermining the Office

Anthropologists seem to be rediscovering humor as a site of social analysis.[23] Taking exception to earlier structural analyses of jokes that treated humor as a means of reasserting social order, more recent analyses strive to understand how jokes work in situations of uncertainty and how they "may unsettle the status quo and destabilize the social order."[24] Like some earlier cultural analyses, these new efforts nevertheless see jokes as providing a counterdiscourse or alternative frame to accepted norms. In this way, they follow from Mary Douglas's argument that jokes "connect widely differing fields" in a way that "destroys hierarchy and order."[25] When viewed from within cognitive economies, jokes do something else. They help translate the labor of coding into the delight of juxtaposing different possible social orders and the opportunity juxtaposition affords for imagining new worlds.[26]

In corporate work, this enjoyment faces off against what Gabriella Coleman calls "the question of sovereignty" or the ability to shape and pursue projects in acts of individual expression and technical creation."[27] In

Coleman's account of hacker wit, jokes simultaneously build a common platform of insider knowledge and elevate a single coder above his peers by reminding "the user that behind these highly systematized genres, there is a discriminating and creative individual."[28] Like Coleman's hackers, the Indian programmer emerges as a thinking and desiring presence in the office, where others are governed only by the rule of the clock or the rule of profit. This kind of focus on the embodied pleasures of coding does not strictly oppose immaterial labor but is rather a counterconduct, a practice that emerges when affect is constructed as something essential to the workplace.[29] It can "unwork" programming, moving it toward "pleasure in the now" rather than ends-oriented labor as it is constructed through the examples of the hardworking German and the cunning American.

Lee Siegel's study of humor in India argues that as an alternative to Greek-derived traditions, where tragedy and comedy are two opposing sides of theatricality, in Sanskritic theories of humor, jokes are a flavor (*rasa*) that can be added to any emotional tone—from romantic love to heroism—as intentional parody. "The comic rasa," writes Siegel, "is experienced when something tastes funny, when representations of the emotions of love or courage or sadness fail to produce the corresponding and expected" emotions.[30] Comedy is used to point out that "the depictions of the emotions which correspond to the aesthetic sentiments—courage, fear, sorrow, love, and the others—are not real or appropriate."[31] In other words, when drawing on this tradition of humor, the turn to a joke can be used to remind oneself or others not to take themselves too seriously or, in a more piquant vein, to point out the hypocrisy of those who should know better—the lecherous holy man, the venal man of the people, the criminal police officer. The lazy programmer as a contradictory trope brought to light the comic rasa of corporate culture where adherence to coming and going on time often masks the nonperformance of work. Being lazy but hardworking, in Rajeshwari's joke, is both a source of pride and an admission of a shared flaw. It also mocked the programmers themselves—those who should be professionally ambitious but find themselves to be more lazy than the hardworking Germans around them. This ironical attitude toward the self has been a pillar of middle-class identity in South Asia since the colonial period, where "irony provided a center to" both the large-scale adjustments to new political realities and "the almost invisible readjustments of behavior in the everyday."[32] The current conjuncture that resituates middle-class Indians as essential to, yet often marginalized within global coding economies, marks another moment of increased social tension in which "laughter and insight go hand and hand."[33]

I often noticed that jokes of the kind Rajeshwari told me came after moments of intense, unresolvable discussion and disagreement. She told me her joke after we had been walking in the park and talking for some time. We turned in our conversation to the topic of why, in her terms, India is "so behind" the West. I dutifully recited my history of colonialism and the theory of the drain of wealth from India by the British Raj, and Rajeshwari countered with the impatience of time. She responded that the British Raj was, after all, history and that little progress had really been made since then. I wanted in part to reply to her with an account of how those structures of governance carried over into Indian governing ideologies after independence, but I stopped myself, aware that her whole life and experience in India had led her to this question and to her assessment of the current situation. We had reached a sort of impasse in the conversation at this point, and into this breach Rajeshwari came with her joke.[34]

I do not wish to pin down a single meaning or function to Rajeshwari's comic intervention in the eddy of our conversation. Perhaps she was finding through the joke a way to resolve the dilemma of India's "backwardness" by pointing out the two disparate ideas of civilized life submerged in this narrative—one measured in work finished, the other measured in work enjoyed. Perhaps, too, she was poking fun at me, the cunning American, who argues a question about India's present state of development in terms of a narrative of past colonial events. Maybe the joke was a reminder not to take the discourse of progress too seriously. But the joke also made me uneasy in that it provided an answer to Rajeshwari's question—"Why is India so behind the West"—in the varying capacities of Indians, Germans, and Americans. Indians simply did not have the work ethic, according to this other possible reading of the joke.

One day in early spring as we were sitting around drinking hot cups of tea in Meenakshi and Rajeshwari's sitting room, as the conversations had meandered yet again from the advancement of Europe over India and the impending rise of India nonetheless, Mihir stopped everything with a cutting joke. Mihir had a friend and his wife visiting from Switzerland where they were both doing postdocs in microbiology. This friend, an old classmate from Mumbai, explained how the lab facilities over there were so much better than in India and the scientists so much more dedicated to their work. His wife, though, was of the opinion that the vanguard of science was moving squarely away from Europe. It was already located in the United States. "And," she continued, "it would soon be moving to India and China completely." We all nodded sagely in agreement. If IT technologies could move to India and China, was it not only a matter of time before other sciences moved there as well? Mihir broke out into a grin.

Pausing for dramatic effect, he looked around at all of us seated on the floor and began. Three archaeologists, Mihir reported, "are digging in the distant future. The first is Russian. He digs 50,000 feet down, finds copper wires, and says, look, we had telephones! The second is American. The American digs 60,000 feet down, finds cables, and says, look, we had fiber optics. The third is Indian. He digs 100,000 feet, finds nothing, and says, look, we had cellular phones!"

The room roared with laughter, thighs were slapped to shouts of "Too good, too good." And I asked Mihir later what made the joke so funny. He answered, "Everyone is going so crazy over this technology thing. This is just taking it to the extreme." Mihir thought that "everyone, absolutely everyone, these bosses, the politicians, whomever," were touting the prospects of IT labor to ridiculous extents.

The joke came after an afternoon-long meandering conversation among a dozen or so programmers that ranged from science and religion to national development. The discussion was quite heated at times, with one faction arguing for the inevitable rise of India in the world and another asserting that almost anywhere was better than India. The evidence presented for the former were historical figures such as Ashoka (the third-century BCE Hindu-Buddhist emperor), whereas evidence for the latter was modern-day comparisons of working conditions for scientists in the United States, Germany, and especially Switzerland. Talk had once again reached an impasse. There was no simple way to resolve what was better for Indians, waiting for India to rise or seemingly abandoning India and searching out the conditions in which their work could be done elsewhere. Mihir's joke is again quite ambiguous. It could be poking fun at those who cling to the idea of a once and again resplendent India, including Hindu nationalist idealogues who claim the primacy of Hindu science. Or it could be saying, with an ounce of pride, that Indians will, no matter what, even in the face of all evidence to the contrary, never really give up on India and will make something out of nothing, a trait of tenacity and improvisation, often called *jugaad*, of which they can be proud.

What the joke did do was to defuse the argument and make an opening in this impasse. Everyone laughed, or at least smiled appreciatively, and the talk could move on to other things. Here, the timing of the joke provided its comedic flavor; it was again an exhortation not to take the dominant mode of the discourse (patriotic, heroic) too seriously. And it was a way to defuse the tension within the group around intractable problems, like international development and the unknown future, and the necessity of being a patriotic Indian. By allowing rigorous discussion while also drawing a line around the limits of discussion, these conversations and the jokes that end them reinforce "the middle class's claim of being an enlightened representative of public opinion while also needing to distinguish itself" from how other groups might expand the materialization of labor.[35]

Distance from the World of Work (and Migration)

Another mode of joking I came across loosens personal attachment to the politics of global IT work. While I was sitting with Adi talking to him about visa laws in various countries, he quite unexpectedly pulled from his worktable a letter he had received from the German visa office. I reproduce it here in full because what he gave me after showing me this letter was a joke that seemed to mirror, if even in a different register, the form of the letter. It read, in German (and excerpted for length):

Dear Mr. Srinivas:
According to the documents provided here, you last entered the Federal Republic of Germany on 05.06.2002 with a visa that allowed you to take up employment as an IT-Specialist.

The first resident permit was issued you for this purpose on 07.07.2003 through 30.06.2004.

In the meantime, you moved into my area of responsibility and applied for an extension of your residence permit on 25.06.2004. At the same time you stated in your interview of 05.08.2004 that you have been unemployed since 01.10.2003.

According to the Ordinance on Employment of 01.08.2002, as IT-labor [IT Fachkraft], you have the right to unemployment benefits for six months after having been employed for a period of one year. This time limit is expired and new employment has obviously not been obtained.

According to § 10 AuslG I.V.m. *IT AV* [the Immigration Law], a residence permit can be issued.

Foreigners are allowed to reside in the Federal Republic of Germany only for special purposes. Such a special residence purpose is, for example, an activity or apprenticeship according to the *AAV*. This also means, however, that it lies in the interest of the Federal Republic of Germany for the foreigner to leave immediately on completion of the purpose of residence.

Because of the high population density and the duties of the Federal Republic of Germany towards members of the states of the European Union as well as members of other foreign states that have taken up permanent residence on federal territory, there is an official interest in controlling the immigration and residence of members of foreign states. For this reason, following the prescriptions of the foreigners' laws is particularly important.

This means that it lies in the interests of the Federal Republic of Germany for foreigners as a rule to emigrate again immediately on the completion of the purpose of residence.

Because of the factual and legal situation described I intend to reject your application for an extension of the residence permit.

I further intend to issue you an emigration deadline of 3 months after receiving my final decision and in the case of an involuntary emigration to threaten you with extradition to India according to § 50 para. 2 AuslG.

At the same time I notify you here that you can be extradited to another country to which you are allowed to immigrate or that is bound to accept you.

Your Sincerely,
On behalf of [*Im Auftrag*]

After we parsed the bureaucratic language, we talked for a while about the claims of this particular bureaucrat. Adi was particularly irked by the power that this individual had over his case. It was clear from the language that the bureaucrat could have decided to extend his visa. In fact, the reason to deny a visa had to be made in terms of whether "the residence of the foreigner for any other reason restricts or places in danger the interests of the Federal Republic of Germany." We focused on the reasons she had given, "the high population density and the duties of the Federal Republic of Germany towards members of the states of the European Union as well as members of other foreign states that have taken up permanent residence on federal territory." There was no population density problem in Germany. Newspapers had been reporting for years that the birth rate in Germany was sinking, to the detriment of the country. Unless, of course, as Adi pointed out, she had meant that the "immigrant" population was too high in Germany. This was clearly a political issue, thought Adi. He further opined that it revealed the anti-immigrant attitude of most Germans—this was already known to him. He was perplexed and bothered by the seemingly arbitrary decision-making process. It was the power of the state as embodied in the deciding bureaucrat that troubled Adi.[36] He thought that well-qualified technological experts like himself should be subject to a different, more logical decision-making process and not lumped together with all other immigrants.

After we finished talking about his letter, he thought for a while and with a grin rushed back over to his desk. He told me he wanted to show me something and printed out an e-mail he had received earlier in the week. It was a joke about outsourcing, and it read (excerpted for length):

OUTSOURCING ANNOUNCEMENT, Washington, D.C.—Congress today announced that the Office of the President of the United States will be outsourced to overseas as of August 30. The move is being made to save $400K a year in salary, a record $521 billion in deficit expenditures and related overhead.

"The cost of savings will be quite significant," says Congressman Adam Smith (R-Wash), who, with the aid of Congress's research arm, the General Accounting Office, has studied outsourcing of American jobs extensively. "We simply can no longer afford this level of outlay and remain competitive on the world stage," Congressman Smith said. Exporting American jobs has been a popular trend lately, ironically at the urging of President Bush.

Mr. Bush was informed by e-mail this morning of the termination of his position. He will receive health coverage, expenses and salary until his final day of employment. After that, with a two week waiting period, he will then be eligible for $240 a week from unemployment insurance for 13 weeks.

Unfortunately he will not be able to receive state Medicaid health insurance coverage as his unemployment benefits are over the required limit. "I'm in shock," Mr. Bush stated, "I thought for sure I'd have some job security around here. I have no idea what I'll do now," he further lamented.

Preparations have been under way for some time for the job move.

Sanji Gurvinder Singh of Indus Teleservices, Mumbai, India, will be assuming the Office of President of the United States as of September 1. Mr. Singh was born in the United States while his parents were here on student visas, thus making him eligible for the position. He will receive a salary of $320 USD a month but with no health coverage or other benefits.

Congress stressed patience when calling Mr. Singh as he may not be fully aware of all the issues involved with his new position. A Congressional Spokesman noted that Mr. Singh has been given a script tree to follow which will allow him to respond to most topics of concern. The Spokesperson further noted that "additional savings will be realized as these scripting tools have already been used previously by Mr. Bush here in the US. Such scripts will enable Mr. Singh to provide an answer without having to fully understand the issue itself."

Congress continues to explore other outsourcing possibilities, including that of Vice-President and most Cabinet positions.

This kind of humor is not quite about refusing to take oneself seriously; it is instead about refusing to take the world the programmers operate in too seriously. As Mihir explained, "Outsourcing is hype." At the same time, because it is hype, Adi will get another job in London. And again, at the same time, because of the hype about the political costs of outsourcing, Adi was refused a visa extension. This was how Adi sketched out the humor of this joke to me: it poked fun at all these bureaucratic nation-states and their obsession with the Indian IT worker.

The formalism of the joke mimics the formal tone of the bureaucratic letter. Using the genre of a newspaper article, the joke circulates like a piece of authentic news, using the writerly conventions of an article to produce tension between the reality of the news report and its unbelievable content.[37] The unknown author interlaces the story with "knowing winks" to the audience that heighten the comedic tension in the text. The name of the congressman, for instance, is Adam Smith, a nod to the author of the *Wealth of Nations* and one of the founding fathers, as it were, of capitalism. The joke also pays loving fidelity to the legal rules and regulations that affect non-national workers and have become a staple of the experience of migrant coders. It points out why, for instance, the Indian worker is eligible to be president (he was born in the United States while his parents were there on a student visa) and reveals when President Bush's health care and unemployment benefits will expire (thirteen weeks). The joke makes the theme of cost saving present throughout, highlighting the small salary ($320) the Indian "president" will make.

For Adi, this joke cancels out the sting of the letter from the Foreigner's Office. He is reassured that it is all just farce, the life of the IT worker is a tale, told by an idiot, and all the world's a stage. Adi not only tells jokes to regain his perspective but also meditates regularly and attends, when in India, local meetings with others who meditate. He often tries to convince others to meditate too, with varying success. Like meditation, the joke helps him let go of his anger about the visa letter. In his interpretation, the ultimate message of the joke is that nation-states act in ways that are arbitrary yet unassailable. The only solution is to detach from the very idea that the nation-state might be a rational actor, make new opportunities for oneself when able, and laugh, whenever possible.

Dominic Boyer and Alexei Yurchak analyze an emergent mode of parody in the United States they call "American stiob," after a late-socialist version of parody "typified by a parodic overidentification with the predictable and repeatable forms of authoritative discourse."[38] This overidentification with authoritative discourse is effective as a means of dissent precisely because of its ability to resist being slotted, and therefore dismissed, as political.[39] In other words, by hewing closely to forms of political speech but changing the content, such hyperrealistic parody can unearth and make available for critique the status quo and the rhetorical tropes that undergird it that would otherwise be difficult to combat.

The fake news announcement about outsourcing the U.S. presidency uses this mode of parodic overidentification, which is heightened when Adi puts the joke side by side with, in his opinion, the equally ridiculous letter from the German Foreigner's Office. The strict adherence to the form of an article allows for the content of the joke—the replacement of President Bush with an Indian worker in Mumbai—to appear credible and, in the process, reveals petty injustices (lack of benefits, race toward the lowest wage) of the actual, everyday workings of the software outsourcing industry. At the same time, unlike the public addresses that Boyer and Yurchak analyze, this joke circulates in a more limited public sphere, where its ability to rupture the perceived way of doing things confronts the need to accept and find ways to thrive within the status quo. Because Indian programmers parody from the racialized margins of European-American life, their critique is almost exclusively made available for private consumption. These kinds of jokes do not point in one unambiguous direction but work instead on multiple fronts to reconcile the uneven politics of the multiple worlds IT workers traverse.

The jokes that Indian professionals tell can create an opening toward imagining things otherwise; they can also be an invitation to accept the unchangeable and work around it, as they do for instance, when they refuse to add comments to their coding projects as a way to make them indispensible in their jobs. Jokes can create closure around seemingly intractable problems, inaugurating agreement in a situation where opinions cannot be resolved.[40] Rituals of telling stop dissent and bring about temporary conversational closure by pointing out the shared, intimate, and contractual nature of diaspora. They build group voice but also undercut that voice from assuming a homogeneous form by refusing to make definitive pronouncements on the future. Jokes can both provide an artificial support presuming agreement in the diasporic community of programmers and remove this prop allowing contradictions to emerge.[41] They arrange, like the chairs do in Meenakshi's sitting room, the group in a circle around one another.

The ways that such jokes work, I will argue in the last section, are key to understanding the middle class as formed through identification with existing frames of sociality but also critiquing the demands that others (family, friends) can make of them. Being a middle-class Indian requires continual assessments that sort what can be individualized from what "confirms and commands long-term commitments."[42] The habitation of being Indian, diasporic, and a programmer partakes of the pleasures of aligning personal goals with social roles but also moving away from them.

Middle-Class Eros

The times and places of a joke's telling and a gift's giving, how each is chosen, and how each draws an audience of participants around it help programmers bend work toward pleasure. Eros, expressed through enjoyment of jokes and appreciation of gifts, does not conform to value as measured financially but produces for Indian middle classes something just as valuable—it materializes the access to different ways of life that working abroad provides, and it provides a means of adjudicating among these ways of inhabiting the world. In doing so, the joke and the gift create spaces of experimentation and negotiation within their experience of diaspora.

A few days after visiting Mihir's parents in their apartment in Bhavani Peth, I was at my uncle and aunt's house when their daughter-in-law's brother and his wife come to visit. They had with them a suitcase full of stuff they had brought back with them from the United States, where they live, for family and extended kin in Pune. The contents of the suitcase tumbled out onto the living room floor, prompting the brother-in-law to tell us a joke. This gifting, he revealed, "goes too far sometimes." "You know," he continued, "parents sometimes ask people to take big things in their suitcases, like kitchen utensils." And this is not even the worst of it: "Some families send a weekly package of food to their kids in the U.S., by plane!" He laughed, as he told me that these parents think their poor kids will starve in the United States without their care packages. I asked how this could be legal, and he allowed, they pay bribes at the airport to get these packages on the planes.

A programmer named Mayur Reddy was baptized during our late-spring visit to Berlin's Treptower Park with a moniker he would never be able to shed. His phone kept ringing. He was on call with his support team that Sunday and had to be available to answer questions about his company's product and to come into the office if necessary. Each time his phone chirped, he picked it up and walked a few feet away. By the third time, someone shouted out, "Hey, 'Mobile Ready,' what are you answering the phone all the time for?" "Mobile ready" is a pun on "Reddy," and it became his nickname. The joke temporarily punctured the pressure of work, which is real, but at these moments of pleasure, work must not be taken too seriously—a demand for leaving work behind that his fellow programmers are ready to support.

Middle-class erotics are not boundless. Developing a middle-class imaginary also requires setting limits to pleasure and to critique. Even while they are commensurating worlds of work and of family and friends, joking and gifting are mobilized to curtail dissent. "Mobile Ready" was teased because he was too focused on work—ready with his mobile phone attached to his ear, even when we were off duty and in the park. He seemed to fully embrace the demand of the cognitive economy to fully surrender the "soul" to capitalism, making him unable to turn off his cognitive economy self to focus on the pleasures of daily life. This joke pokes fun at Mayur's cognitive economy work ethic, devaluing the world of work and revaluing his family and friends who demand his time and attention. Parents who FedEx food go overboard too, from the opposite direction. They express their care in daily fussing, expressing at once their inability to let their children be on their own and their ignorance about how life is lived overseas.

The traveling diaper bag extended care for a child across the distance of overseas jobs. As it moved from Europe to the United States and then India, it picked up value as it knit people together and gained in significance as care was taken to transport such a little bag over so many seas. These expeditions transformed cognitive labor into materially affective intimacy. One wonders whether a joke could be made out of this kind of gifting or whether such a small object might remain a testament both to the virtue of hard work and to the pressing need to slow the rush of capitalist labor.

A SPECULATIVE CONCLUSION

Secrets and Lives

Had I heard about Meenakshi? It was Rajeswhari calling me from their apartment about six weeks after I had left Berlin. Meena was gone. She had returned to Hyderabad without telling anyone. Meenakshi had lost her job after the end of her last contract. Failing to find another position afterward, she was compelled to leave the country when her visa ran out. While all this was going on, she pretended to go to work every day as if nothing were wrong. Thinking back over the previous year, it seemed that throughout this period of joblessness, Meenakshi appeared to be happy about her office and her work, telling me often about how much fun it was to interact with her international colleagues. After Meena was forced out of Berlin, she returned to India, and she cut off all contact with everyone she had known in Germany. Wanting to hear more of her story, I asked Rajeshwari a few weeks later if she had heard anything or if she knew how I might get in contact with her again. Rajeshwari told me she had had no contact with her, and she doubted anyone else would either. "After what she did," intoned Rajeshwari, "I don't think anyone would want to talk to her."

Meenakshi's story highlights the risks undertaken by Indian programmers as they cycle through visa-backed programming jobs in Europe. To improve their economic and social position in India, they take short-term positions abroad, knowing and hoping these will catapult them into permanent careers. Conditions of labor in the IT industry, which are based on a vision of seemingly limitless and flexible achievement, often mask the costs of taking these jobs—even for industry insiders. For many short-term programmers, promise of future success creates blind spots vis-à-vis current conditions of work. Tracing stories such as Meenakshi's reveals the provisional status of their labor and its implicit trade-off of temporary instability for future permanence. This slender promise is one way that Indian programmers are bound to short-term, precarious jobs.

Meenakshi's story is, in another sense, an ethnographic lapse. Despite the countless meals and evenings of gossip I had shared with her, Meenakshi disappeared fully when she went. My failure to find her and ask her about her departure might reveal a flaw in method. As an ethnographer, after all, I was meant to develop a close rapport with informants and share intimate, even secret, knowledge with them. Yet, over the course of writing this book, I began to think of her silence itself as telling. Like the partial access to offices that informs part I, Meenakshi's disappearance—and the reactions to it from friends and colleagues—tells its own story of risk and possibility in cognitive work.

In initial attempts to write this ethnography, Meenakshi's story led me to focus on the kinds of ideological double binds that keep short-term programmers in jobs that are unfulfilling to them. In this framing, Meenakshi is another victim of a "capitalist metabolism that harvests vitality and deposits it into privileged life worlds."[1] Although this aspect remains important to my understanding of race, class, and code in short-term corporate programming, I now also want to take Meenakshi's departure as a potential opening. Respecting her silence, I do not want to make it speak definitively for one story or another, but I want to treat the silence itself as meaningful as a possible "outside" to the politics of work and affect as normally understood.

This concluding chapter unfolds in three parts. I initially discuss the circumstances that may have led Meenakshi to her double life. Then, I turn to two ways to understand the aftermath of her deception: I explore how her story exemplifies what Lauren Berlant calls "cruel optimism."[2] And I read her departure in another way, using Kathi Weeks's exposition of "critical utopia."[3] I explore these two possibilities (and recognize there may be several more) so as not to read the secret life as the true, real life behind the façade. Instead, I emphasize the multiple and shifting forms of life that are invoked in this story.

To understand why Meenakshi carried on "working" and did not turn to her circle of friends, it helps to explore the competing versions of what the computer and the Indian programmer should be that have wended their way through this book. When Rajeshwari assures me that no one would want to talk to Meenakshi after what she did, she is telling me that Meena had gone beyond the actions that could be deemed appropriate in pursuing status abroad. Shutting out Meenakshi in this way suggests one version of the Indian programmer that she failed to live up to: a reliable link in a professional diaspora. Hiding her termination and pretending to go to work every day perhaps indicated that she was a figure who could not be trusted. In the Indian programming diaspora, new and better jobs often depended on getting information and sometimes a place to stay from friends and relations outside India. As described in chapter 6, the networks of diasporic Indian households that help provide support and connections for migrant programmers in the United States, Europe, Australia, and elsewhere are forged through chains of gifting that do the affective work of binding work and family life together—gifts help make convincing arguments for why loved ones should take jobs overseas and stand in for the care an absent son or daughter, father or mother would otherwise provide. Meenakshi lost value in these networks in two ways. Unable to marshal her own connections to get a new job, she could not be expected to help others. And her actions branded her as an inherently untrustworthy partner in a venture—like going overseas for work—that was already quite risky.

Another way of accounting for Meenakshi's disappearance would be to read it through a cultural understanding of shame. According to cultural psychologists, shame is a primary moral and social motivator in India, China, Japan, and other Asian countries, whereas guilt serves a similar function in the West. These scholars understand shame to be an emotion that aligns individual action with collective moral sanctions. According to such a theory, Meenakshi hid her firing because of the shame of having one's actions judged negatively by a group of friends and family.[4] While there may be some sense of shame (though it is unclear what kind of shame is at work) driving her actions, I do not take the analysis in this direction.[5] While the analysis of shame can usefully lead a discussion of emotions "away from an ethics of autonomy" and toward "an ethics of community," it remains a calcified analytic as long as it is reducible to the logic of how things work "over there" and "over here."[6] If nothing else, diasporic, middle-class, and transnational Indian coders can certainly not simply fall into the category of an emotional "over there" marked by the East. Rather than argue that they represent an in-between or liminal form of morality somewhere between autonomy and collectivity, I think a better approach begins with the action produced by Meenakshi's departure and then traces how this act calls on and inaugurates new structures of interpretation.[7] In that sense, Rajeshwari's commentary cites her disappearance as an example of negative action and thus works to fortify a narrative of success that remains untroubled by Meenakshi's tale.

Meenakshi's story held up an unwelcome mirror to the instability in programmers' lives. Indeed, many programmers refused to entertain the possibility that what befell Meenakshi could also befall them. Srinu and Mayur told me they were very surprised when they found out that Meenakshi had been pretending to go to work. They too had made no attempt to contact her. Bipin and Madhu said they had no contact with her and did not expect to hear from her again. Mihir simply shrugged and said, "Who knows if she would dare show her face to us again?" When I asked Adi why he thought Meenakshi did what she did, he told me he did not know but that it was really a scandal when everyone found out. He found it unbelievable that she could tell everyone so many lies, and like Rajeshwari, he roundly condemned her for it and echoed the sentiment that he doubted whether anyone would see her again. Asked what he would do if he suddenly lost his job and whether he might be tempted to hide it, he promptly responded, "That would never happen to me because I am always exploring other options. And I make sure I have an untroubled mind so that I won't get caught up in these things and take the wrong road." Adi referred simultaneously to his continuous searching for better opportunities, increasing his skill set, and to his daily meditating, which he deemed crucial to withstanding the stresses of the work he did. His answer suggests yet another view of what the Indian programmer should be—entrepreneurial, calm, and guaranteed successful.

In Adi's response lies one possible reason Meenakshi led a double life. Meenakshi was excommunicated from her group of programmers because they felt she had crossed a moral boundary in lying to them about her job and pretending to go to work every day as usual. Yet her actions conform rather well to a general pattern of risk taking in the short term in the hope of long-term reward. Indeed, many Indian programmers described going abroad or working extra hours at the office in those terms. By taking short-term work, they hoped that a permanent contract would be forthcoming; by working longer hours, they might see a new project in the offing.[8] Within what we might call an ecology of success, Meenakshi chose to remain outwardly successful until she might convert her job loss into a better position. Given enough time, she might have done so.

Meenakshi's double life illuminates the strategies of deferral that Indian IT workers continually practice. Mihir, for instance, took me aside one spring afternoon when we were taking a group trip to the Reichstag. He showed me a visa in his passport for the United States. It had his picture in grainy black and white and a duration of eighteen months on it. To my surprised look, he responded, "Don't tell the others, I don't want them to feel bad that I might be leaving." When I asked him if he planned to move to America, he told me, "Only as a last resort." This visa, procured for him by a friend who was currently in the United States on a similar visa, would allow him to enter the country in the service of a contractor—or body shopper—who would keep him on hand to work on a job-specific basis for a larger U.S. firm. For Mihir, such a move would only begin to look attractive if he had no other options in Germany, because working for a body shop might mean sitting unemployed for months on end (being benched), all the while racking up debt to the contractor who provided the visa.[9] Mihir's strategy of chasing multiple possibilities in a situation of precarious labor coupled with hiding these strategies for the sake of maintaining group solidarity was not very different from Meenakshi's. Conceiving of this strategy as one that will always maximize their potential for success obscures the ever-present risk of failure.[10]

Another ideal of the Indian programmer Meenakshi failed to live up to might be encapsulated in a "respectable femininity" where "the practices within IT firms reflect a particular Indian middle-class culture," which allows for women's agency to the extent that it is "in support of an Indian family life." Respectable femininity complements "a professional, highly competent persona."[11] Both Meenakshi and Rajeshwari were particularly concerned with producing respectable femininity while being young, unmarried, and abroad. They often discussed their ultimate goal as being *of* the family, but not constrained *by* the family. They told me that their role among their circle of friends was to be the ones who made sure all the holidays were celebrated and people met up with and supported one another by hosting pujas in their home, cooking, and holding special prayer sessions. Importantly, they added that they could not be seen to do these kinds of activities too much, since, in Rajeshwari's terms, they would "end up like their grandmothers." Their ability to succeed as career women depended on their walking a careful line between supporting the family and not being reduced to being only a homemaker with limited rights and freedoms. As Smitha Radhakrishnan similarly notes, "Through a discourse of balance, restraint, and 'knowing the limit,' IT women embody the 'right amount' of freedom, distinguishing themselves both from the promiscuous West, as well as from other Indian women of previous generations and of different class positions."[12]

Meenakshi's actions responded to the problem of gender norms even as they were judged by the same rubric. She believed that to be independent yet family oriented, she would have to make a name and career for herself outside India and only then return home. When I sat down with her one day for a formal interview, she explained her reasons for coming to Berlin as the next logical stage in her career and also as a delay tactic. Because her parents wanted someone to take over their aquaculture businesses and her older sister was unwell, they wanted her to marry right away. She was not ready for that and did not think it would be fair to lay the responsibility for the business at the feet of a new husband. To delay her marriage and perhaps change the terms under which she married, she decided to go abroad and have her own career first, before settling down. As Meenakshi constructed it, her freedom to remain unmarried for a time depended on being successful abroad. She was able to delay what she saw as the normal course for her as a young woman through her IT labor. Continuing to pretend to go to work after being terminated while looking for another job may have been her way of keeping that structure of delay alive.

In doing so, Meenakshi's subterfuge crossed the limit of respectable femininity. She and other programmers construed their cohort of young Indian programmers as a para-family, a substitute family in diaspora. This argument was often put forth as important to surviving life abroad. Mihir suggested to me that because they were like a family and maintaining that feeling was important, slights and oversights that normally would cause offense were routinely overlooked. He gave me the example of a younger person in the group asking an older person to run to the store and get sugar right before a party. When this happened, no one complained, although, according to Mihir, it should be the younger one who runs the errand. For the sake of maintaining group solidarity, such slights were in the main brushed aside.

Against this backdrop of maintaining para-family cohesion, Meenakshi's double life may have been read as putting her own career first while jeopardizing the family. This feeling may have been exacerbated by the sense that she was putting the reputation of Indian programmers at risk by lying. Though there was often vociferous disagreement about all aspects of life, on the question of Meenakshi's actions, agreement that she had acted beyond the limit of the respectable was reached quickly, as if to foreclose her breach lending itself to a more significant reevaluation of the meaning of success in this cognitive economy.

Each framing of the ideal Indian IT worker posed above offers a way of understanding why Meenakshi hid her dismissal. One ideal is that of the networked, diasporic Indian professional. Another is that of the Indian programmer as an entrepreneurial subject, eliding failure by being always in search of new and better opportunities. Yet a third is of the Indian woman software developer as liberated but family oriented. Meenakshi failed to live up to each of these in the moment that her strategy of betting on finding a new job before she faced extradition began to crumble. It was likely in the name of these very same ideals or ones very much like them that Meenakshi hid her dismissal in the first place. In doing so, she walled herself off from the very diasporic networks that could have helped her move elsewhere in the global software economy. Perhaps she feared that, as a young woman, these networks would turn against her and urge her to go home and marry instead of going onward.

Two Lives: After Precarity

The previous section was a necessarily speculative account of why Meenakshi may have chosen to hide her dismissal. This section reads her vanishing as meaningful as well. But, rather than taking her disappearance as proof of the wretchedness of her double life, I treat it as an invitation to think through the meaning of work and its alternatives. One possible way to understand Meenakshi's disappearance is as a symptom of—and answer to—the pressures of being flexible and entrepreneurial. According to theorists of the effect of immaterial labor on working populations, neoliberal demands for flexible workers and footloose capital have produced what they term a *new precarity* for working subjects:

In industrial production, abstract labor time was impersonated by a physical and juridical bearer, embodied in a worker in flesh and bone, with a certified and political identity. . . . [I]f capital wanted to dispose of the necessary time for its valorization, it was indispensable to hire a human being, to buy all of its time, and therefore needed to face up to the material needs and trade union and political demands of which the human was a bearer. When we move into the sphere of info-labor there is no longer a need to have bought a person for eight hours a day indefinitely. Capital no longer recruits people, but buys packets of time, separated from their interchangeable and occasional bearers.[13]

For those who work as cognitive laborers, the separation between personal identity and work time means that while their time is bought by the company, the status of their person is both formally "free" and outside the domain of corporate responsibility. In other words, while white-collar corporate IT workers are free to pursue their own interests and bring their own personalities to work, and indeed, the diversity of cultures is considered a value added from the perspective of management, because what is bought by the company are packets of time rather than the whole person, the company is divested of responsibility for the embodied, emotional, and psychic life of the worker as human being. For Berardi, the ultimate, indeed inevitable outcome of the bifurcation of person and a person's time is a kind of psychic collapse of the system as a whole. The global financial collapse of 2008, on the one hand, and the mass use of antidepressants, on the other, concretized this collapse.

Much of the argument about this new precarity seems to take Fordism as a baseline from which to think through change and, in so doing, perhaps unwittingly produces a certain nostalgia for the worker protections that Fordism may have provided.[14] The description of precarity is often a structure of feeling that emanates from the European and American middle classes. Too often, the Euro-American bourgeois affective stance becomes a de facto normative position. In spite of the intention to project marginalization to the center, the experience of the center continues to define the presumed common ground. The rote naming of other precarious subjects (the migrant, the homeless) without exploration of the varieties of precarity and differences in the demand on neoliberal subjectivity made of them ignores what Angela Mitropoulos calls "the reallocation of risk or its valorisation, [and] the displacement and redistribution of uncertainty" that is managed through new types of contractual arrangements.[15]

For many precarious subjects, the dream of a good life that is the original condition for precarity was not available in the same way as it was to working- and upper-class white men. What would it mean to take these other histories into account in theorizing the emergence of precarity as a structure of feeling and as a structure of work? And how would we frame the relationship be- tween neoliberalism and the expectation of subjects across these differences?

The quick summing up of Meenakshi as a boundary-crossing outsider by her peers paints a different picture. In this picture, workers stay attached to the promise of self-fulfilling work and personal expression even when faced with the evidence of the impossibility of this vision of the good life. Lauren Berlant has called this attachment a "cruel optimism," occurring when "a person or world finds itself bound to a situation of profound threat that is, at the same time, profoundly confirming."[16] In addition to being attached to a dream of the good life even in the face of a continual failure to achieve it, such optimism is cruel for the fact that being attached is itself a structure that has become comfortable and therefore in some way an affirmation of life. The failure to take Meenakshi's story as a cautionary tale is an example of this attachment. Her story is generalized as a case of immoral and un- ethical behavior, allowing for a return to the pleasures of impermanency and to upholding the future as a secure one.

In Berlant's discussion of the attachment to precarity, she dissects *Time Out*, a film by Laurent Cantet, in which a middle manager named Vincent loses his job and pretends to go to work each day, meanwhile support- ing himself and his family through gray market transactions. When in the movie he is finally found out by his family, he is returned to the world of white-collar, temporary labor. His father finds him another job, without security or benefits, where the primary work, according to Berlant, is to produce neutral or mildly positive facial expressions as an outward and communicative sign of satisfaction. Berlant writes, "His incapacity to lose everything, to go genuinely off the grid towards the horizon of his negativ- ity, is not surprising, for there is nothing else for him in the impasse, no anarchist energy, no dramatic refusal, no gun and no gasoline for the road. In place of being happy, he gets one more chance at making faces in the social."[17] *Time Out* is a document that attests to the mortgaging of future happiness for the simulated happiness of the present.

Berlant reads the structure of the film as a guide to the way that affect is tethered to the false promise of a future of stability. Similarly, the conclusion becomes a signpost for the emptiness of the impasse; the way out that Vincent cannot take is the path toward "off the grid" dramatic refusal. That is what it would take, writes Berlant, to reach for happiness. Without "an imaginary for the terms and the register in which new claims on social resources of reciprocity could be made,"[18] Meenakshi, it seems, like the protagonist, Vincent, can stand only as a monument to the viciousness of hoping for a risky future.

And yet, Meenakshi has gone off the grid, but she did not pursue an "anarchist energy" to get herself there. Is there no other way to read the impasse except as either a continuity of simulated happiness or as a moment before leaping into the freedom of a new social compact? Can one go off the grid without either being constrained to the exceptional case of personal failure or liberated after the fact as an alternative, anarchist hero?

In Kathi Weeks's salvaging of the idea of utopia, she argues that a critical utopian project would refigure utopia "as a process and a project rather than an end or goal, and open utopia . . . to multiple insights and directions."[19] Arguing for a politics of hope that is grounded in the past and reaches toward possible futures that are as yet unimaginable, Weeks finds in science fiction and the manifesto traces of this fragmentary training of political desire—what she calls the "less is more" advantages of an open and partial critical utopia.[20] Another way to understand Meenakshi's vanishing quite apart from the binary of rebellion and acceptance of cruel optimism is to think of her disappearance as a demand. That the content of this demand remains inarticulate makes it a partial and fragmentary gesture at best, but one that nevertheless moves the discourse of what can be desired in a new direction.

Rather than running along the lines of the networked, successful diasporic Indian middle-class life that has been so clearly articulated by her peers, perhaps her silence is also a statement of another desire—the desire to be left alone. I do not wish to overstate the positive content of this desire. She has also, inevitably, been silenced by those same sets of desirable persons who shun her as outside their fold. And, as she remains in silence, it is a legitimate question as to whether this act can be construed as an act of social resistance much less rebellion.

A close colleague of mine who heard Meenakshi's story urged me to hold to the possibility that Meenakshi's disappearance means that she has killed herself. Her story, according to this reading, would be proof of the ultimate inhumanity of short-term labor that promises so much and delivers only to the few. This line of thinking recalls another moment of silencing and suicide discussed by Gayatri Spivak in her essay "Can the Subaltern Speak?" Bhubaneshwari Bhaduri, the protagonist of that narrative, spoke eloquently of her political convictions through the language of choosing death but nevertheless failed to be "heard" as a political subject and was instead sequestered behind the walls of female delirium and within the language of illicit love. While not denying the psychic and social suffering of failure, I hold the possibility of suicide as one among many possible outcomes for Meenakshi. I argue that these possibilities should not be collapsed into one overdetermining, scandalous reality.[21] Meenakshi's silence might be set in opposition to Bhubaneshwari's lack of amplification.[22] Though her story may very well be carried on as only a story of a woman's failure to succeed, her lack of findability in an era where everyone is purposefully accessible gestures toward an alternative that rejects—without necessarily directly opposing—the strictures and binds of the entrepreneurial classes.

A return to the double meaning of the root of precarity—the *precarium*—can allow for these multiple readings of Meenakshi's story to hold equal weight in analysis. The precarium, as defined in Roman law, was "the use and enjoyment of an object given to another, but it could be revoked at any time."[23] The institution of the precarium was a primary facet of medieval European land rights, where small grants were often ceded to the church and then returned to the landholder as a precarium in exchange for a monthly rent.[24] On the one hand, the power to revoke the right of the precarium tracks with neoliberal conditions of work in which employment in general is destabilized and steady work begins to feel like something granted to the worker that may be revoked at any time. On the other, the precarium was a right of use and enjoyment of something, which suggests precarity as not only or primarily an impoverishment but also as a ground on which to pursue a right to pleasure, however temporarily. These moments of pleasure, when read through Weeks's analysis of critical utopias, are times when we can "flex our desiring muscles" and learn to make wider and more life-affirming demands of the work we do.[25]

In thinking about Meenakshi's positioning vis-à-vis precarity, I want to emphasize a doubling of the meaning of precarity—a form of ownership for enjoyment that can be revoked without warning. Juxtaposing the critical utopia espoused by Kathi Weeks and the cruel optimism put forth by Lauren Berlant inclines toward a reading of these as two simultaneously held positions, rather than as two exclusive alternatives. Meenakshi's disappearance contains both the story of the impossible revoking of a dream and the story of a kind of ownership over her own entrepreneurial self-management that extends a trajectory begun by the move toward eros catalyzed by the restrictions placed on the Indian IT worker as racialized high-skilled subject.

Thinking Race and Class Together at the Scene of Precarity

In Karen-Sue Taussig's account of genetic science in the Netherlands, she argues that Dutch ideas of tolerance inform the way that genetic science is undertaken. In the Netherlands, difference has been managed through what Taussig identifies as pillarization—the assembling of people into identifiable social groups that are internally homogeneous—and through an ethic of "ordinariness" that defines Dutch culture as occupying a normal middle ground between extremes. Taussig suggests that this national framework for managing multiculturalism is reflected in genetic scientists' desire to manage genetic material into recognizable social groups.[26] In Part I, *Encoding Race*, I argue along similar lines that the presence of Indian IT workers in Germany replays German approaches to multiculturalism, which manage difference through an ethic of liberal tolerance—defined as the ability to find in others a recognizable difference that can then be accepted and positively valued. Using the comparative cases of Afrodeutsch and Turkish German populations, I show that Indian programmers offered an acceptable narrative of difference based on assumed religious identity (Hinduism rather than Islam) and temporary status (not permanent migrants who need to be assimilated).[27] Yet, I also contend that these assessments interlace with understandings of race produced in part through a folk genomics that maps genetic variability onto world cultures. This impacted on the way that the qualities of these Indian subjects were formulated, especially as they related to work. Indeed, one way that genomic research seems to be filtering into common-sense understandings of race is precisely through the lens of new work regimes, where the qualities of individual workers are at once naturalized and cultivated. What I call an "indecidability" in the meaning of race lends variety to the way Indian programmers are fit into an office environment, at once underscoring the correctness of sequestering them in limited, short-time jobs and creating the expectation that their difference would lend an unexpected frisson to office culture.

As I argue in part II, *Encoding Class*, pursuing a good life through overseas IT work puts primacy on eros as the pursuit of life "in lasting and expanding relations."[28] The elaboration of this vision of the good life is at once a response to the restrictions placed on back-office Indian programmers in European companies and a means by which a middle-class Indian imaginary is reconstructed, through a dialectic of training the body and the mind for knowledge work and the pursuit of non-work-directed pleasure.

In the deployment of eros to resist the colonization of life by work, these programmers concomitantly produce a middle-class imaginary that is made to stand in for national character. The famous consumerism of the new Indian middle class, then, needs to be understood not only in opposition to Nehruvian austerity but also in conjunction with the global politics of establishing a class identity that converts the politics of racialized labor into those of national identity. By focusing on the good life and not on labor, these diasporic programmers differentiate themselves as a middle class that is neither to be confused with the profligate Indian elite nor with the Indian poor, nor with the global black and brown workforce laboring on the lower rungs of European, U.S., and Australian economies. The consolidation of Indian middle-class identity through eros is at once a critique of work and a way of silencing the multiple extensions of eros and the solidarities they might allow.[29] The transposition between race and class happens there through the mediation of an Indian national imaginary, where, for instance, the purported laziness of the Indian programmer converts to a badge of honor through which the dedication to work rather than to punctuality can be asserted as a particularly *Indian* trait.

Having traced how middle-class eros can be a counterconduct to the emplotment of the Indian IT worker through a racial imaginary that figures "him" as a threat to European job stability, on the one hand, or as a promise of future productivity for Europe, on the other, I now turn to some of the unintended pathways that this counterconduct may open up. To illustrate these possibilities—and how they are foreclosed in most readings of the precarious—I return to Berardi's *Precarious Rhapsody*. "It's a strange word," Berardi writes, in sarcasm tipped with hyperbole, "with which we identify the ideology prevalent in the post-human transition to digital slavery: liberalism. Liberty is its foundational myth, but the liberty of whom? The liberty of capital, certainly. . . . But liberalism also predicates the liberty of the person. The juridical person is free to express itself, to choose its representatives, to be entrepreneurial at the level of politics and the economy. Very interesting. Only the person has disappeared. What is left is like an inert object, irrelevant and useless. The person is free, sure. But his time is enslaved."[30]

Berardi's critique of liberalism in this passage suggests that only the liberty of capital is ensured, while the liberty of the person is a false one, true only formally but not in fact. But what Berardi overlooks is the importance of this formal freedom as the site of the elaboration of practices against the enslavement of time. The "false," de jure, freedom of the juridical person nevertheless makes possible critical utopian pathways that demand that this promise of freedom be kept. By dismissing free expression as a capitalist trick, Berardi fails to recognize the doubling of liberalism as both promise and limit.[31]

As Marx recognized, liberal freedom was surely false in that it allowed the capitalist to buy not the labor of the worker but the labor power, that is, the productivity of the worker as a whole from which surplus labor could be extracted as a gift.[32] At the same time, Marx also allowed that the juridical pretense of fair labor traded on the market yielded class struggle over, for instance, the length of the working day, since the worker as freely transacting citizen could legitimately protect a right to social and bodily reproduction.[33]

The protagonists of this story likewise both recognize and disavow an Indian citizenship that is necessarily imagined through their success in the global market. In doing so, they carve out multiple forms of authority for themselves—both individual and collective. Far from only being enslaved to cognitive economies, programmers work within the formal freedoms and affiliations they provide. In a different context, Matthew Hull discusses how civil servants in Islamabad's Capital Development Authority both deny and assert individual agency, by creating paper records that transfer responsibility to the collective "bureaucracy," on the one hand, and by asserting individual agency by going outside the bureaucracy's normal documented chain of command, on the other.[34] Although Indian programmers do not belong to an identifiable institution like a state bureaucracy, their distancing practices—accomplished through jokes, fierce discussion of the future of India, and criticism of government power writ large—might do a similar sort of mediating work between collective and individual agency. By affirming national identity through collective understandings of Indian-ness that nevertheless are not simply positive, they create a space for their own action that is not always already swallowed up by the trope of dia-sporic programmer as nation. Into these openings comes both a critique of the Indian government and an exploration of a good life not directly tethered to the demands of work and success. Thus, while it is certainly useful to suggest diasporic middle-class Indians, like these programmers, are trying to be Indian and Western at the same time, this description does not go far enough in specifying the relationship between this achievement and either the microprocesses of making agency or the larger structural entailments signaled by the global reorganization of work.

One of Hull's objectives in his book is "to understand collectivization and individualization as simultaneous functions of the same bureaucratic processes, taking neither the agency of the individual nor the organization as given."[35] A similar method can be used to think through the politics of the middle class. That is, I ask, how is a collective authority for this class produced, at the same time that the individual is produced as part of and standing apart from any such collective authority? This model of authority is especially key, since much of the hegemonic power of this class lies in being able to model what comes to look like an inherent collective individualism. Importantly, these constructions produce fissures and contradictions that extend beyond the borders of class as it is usually conceptualized. By in-novating a politics of enjoyment beyond work, Indian programmers both elaborate a vision of Indian middle classness that is inflected through con-sumption and work discipline and produce an alternate vision of the good life that departs from this class identity.[36]

Perhaps most interesting, middle-class eros as a trace of an alternative to the organization of life as work will not stay within the bounds of this collectivity. It remains a possibility—like the possibilities encompassed by the term *liberal freedom*—that may be taken up in other locations and hi-jacked to vastly different ends.

Hari Kunzru's *Transmission*, a novel about a short-term Indian IT worker on the U.S. West Coast, ends with a disappearance.[37] Arjun Mehta, Indian programmer, fired from his job, hiding his dismissal from his family in India, releases a supervirus in the hopes of being reinstated as the only one who can figure out how to defeat it. When this plan fails and he ends up on the FBI's most wanted list, he disappears from a hotel room in San Ysidro, California. Although many "Mehtologists" try to track his movements, the closest they get is rumored sightings of him from time to time with the former Bollywood star Leela (after whom his virus was named) at spots on the Pacific Rim. Arjun Mehta has been claimed by autonomist groups as an anticapitalist hacktivist hero and by the right-wing press as an enemy of America. As the book ends, the main character has passed, in Kunzru's terms, from information to noise, across "the border between the known and the unknown."[38]

Transmission is a fabulist tale of the Indian IT worker as matter out of place. Arjun is someone caught between worlds and misunderstood, his bourgeois aspirations ultimately defeated by a combination of immigration law and capitalist exploitation in the form of unfair hiring practices and racialized biases. In the end, Kunzru posits an escape from the system that is also a (temporary) disruption, while the stable identity Arjun was trying so hard to create was sacrificed to the freedom of moving outside the transmission of information into the unknown. Meenakshi's disappearance, while more pedestrian, similarly comes after a defeat in the march toward middle-class respectability and remains similarly undecidable.[39]

Meenakshi is allied with the fictional Arjun, both mapping out a terrain on which, despite the claims for a definite message, they see a way forward in simply disappearing without leaving behind manifesto or mea culpa.[40] Their disappearances are a critique of current conditions of work without predetermined anarchist, autonomist, or anticapitalist content. Am I being too hopeful in my reading of disappearance as possibility? Perhaps, but my hope is not so much for this group of middle-class programmers, who seem so certain they know what Meenakshi's story requires of them, but for the present they help create and the unknowable futures they might inaugurate.

Coding Past and Future

The offices that I feature in this book broadly use a human capital theory of productivity. That is, most managers considered the individual talents of their workforce and strove to make the best use of these that they could. This way of imagining life fits with a model of power that Deleuze called a "society of control," according to which power is in the management of the given and the calculation of risk, not in the creation of particular kinds of (disciplined) subjects in institutions, or what Deleuze termed "enclosures." Indeed, for Deleuze, it was the computer that best exemplified this form of society. "The societies of control operate with . . . computers," he wrote, "whose passive danger is jamming and whose active one is piracy and the introduction of viruses." In this conceptualization of control, computers produce and reflect a capitalism that is "essentially dispersive . . . deformable and transformable."[41] Do those who put these machines in the service of capital—like the protagonists of this story—embody the dispersed, deformable, and transformable mode of capitalism Deleuze describes? It would be better, I think, not to read Deleuze's essay too literally. The computer as device of control, like the panopticon as device of discipline, is a map of power, not a description of its historical workings.

Encoded in the world of corporate programming is at once the mandate to be flexible and the limit of what can be transgressed. In the first half of this book, the boundary was first set by a politics of race that naturalized what were produced differences among workers as congenital to particular kinds of marked bodies, even while what remained deformable was what the true meaning and stability of these differences would be. In the second half, the lack of fit between this racialization and the imaginary of a transnational working class led to a reconsideration of the very notion of a flexible boundary between work and life, even while it reaffirmed the logic of (now nationally coded) difference. Programmers could also engage in what could be called affective unwork, or the breaking down of the biopolitical imperative to manage life to maximize productivity that is made possible precisely because life has been presented as something that may be managed. Foreshadowing Foucault's work on biopolitics and counterconduct, Herbert Marcuse wrote in 1966 that "in the administered society, the biological necessity does not immediately issue in action; organization demands counterorganization."[42] Affective unwork might be the trace of such a counterorganization.

One final point seems relevant to thinking about the relationship of programming work and cognitive labor. Office programming culture passes through the "oikos," or household. Angela Mitropoulous writes that "human capital theory presents individuation in the context of oikonomic inheritance, whether by way of the transmission of putatively naturalized properties (including that of 'talent,' predisposition, upbringing, and so on) or inherited property in its legal and economic senses. It should also be emphasized that the category of the household is not only a place-holder for questions of the transmission of wealth along the lines of class, but also the scene of the reproduction of the demarcations of race, gender, sexuality and nation."[43]

Although most analyses of coding confine themselves to places where coding is done, that is, to offices, hacker conferences, coffee shops, and the like, the permeable boundary between code and areas of life not associated with programming is equally important. In this book, the boundary between home and work was in many senses redrawn over and again in attempts by various actors to come to terms with and engender proper alignments between personhood and labor. That is, by paying attention to the world of the oikos, it becomes clear that the constitution of Indian IT workers as particular kinds of subjects in a coding economy (and also the constitution of European, German, American, Chinese, and other workers) passes through the way the world of work is made to fit with sites of social reproduction. Too often, ethnographic studies of coding worlds, by confining themselves methodologically to sites of work, fail to make these connections.

In the end, it was this group's failure to extend to Meenakshi the credit of time that ultimately foreclosed the possibility of turning the world of corporate coding into a way to sustain eros. Falling back on a language of moral rectitude, they turned away from extending solidarity with the gamble against time in which they all participated past a certain limit. This limit was marked at once by Germany's migration law and by the conclusion that pretending was morally bankrupt. Here, perhaps, is the key to understanding how some kinds of programming encode the oikos. By setting a limit to what may be risked, tried, and pretended, such coding labor sequesters the pursuit of the good life into predictably deformable cages.[44] Yet here, too, might be a clue to understanding how that same encoding of class and race forges life as a project to be worked on, and unworked, in multiple ways. By vanishing beyond the limit of work, Meenakshi lights for us unexplored pathways for such a project of life.

Introduction: Cognitive Work, Cognitive Bodies

1. For discussions of each of these terms, see Castells, *The Rise of the Network Society*; Hardt, "The Global Society of Control"; Hardt and Negri, *Multitude*; Berardi, *The Soul at Work*; Virno, *Grammar of the Multitude*; and Terranova, *Network Culture*.

2. It may also obscure the relationship of cognitive economies to actually existing factory work. Although such an analysis does not fall within the parameters of this book, it would include both a treatment of how factory work is changed by the valuation of cognitive work and an analysis of the relationship of factory work to office work. The poetry of Foxconn worker Xu Lizhi might be a place to start such a project: https://libcom.org/blog/xulizhi-foxconn-suicide-poetry.

3. This idea that capital can create workers according to its own needs is called the real subsumption of labor to capital. It is often glossed as one of the defining characteristics of post-Fordist capitalism. But this analysis usually does not ask what capital is creating this worker out of—what are the forms of embodiment that serve as both raw material for and as a stubborn impediment to real subsumption? On real subsumption, see Marx, *Capital*, 1019–38; Postone, *Time, Labor, and Social Domination*; Negri, *Marx beyond Marx*; Hardt, "The Withering of Civil Society"; and End Notes, "The History of Subsumption."

4. See Adorno, "The Fetish Character in Music and Regression in Listening," 272.

5. Memmi, *Racism*, gives a reasoned account of the different ways race operates in Europe; see also Ameeriar, "The Sanitized Sensorium."

6. See Cooper, *Life as Surplus*, 24.

7. This changed landscape of work includes increased flexibilization of capital and the accompanying demand that workers be flexible; the development of an "entrepreneurial subject" of work who is always bettering herself and looking for new opportunities; the extension of the working day past the boundaries of the office; and the decrease of social safety nets provided by the state in much of Europe and the United States. These shifts, often analyzed through the rubric of globalization and neoliberalism, are admirably discussed in Weeks, *The Problem with Work*; Berardi, *The Soul at Work*; Virno, *Grammar of the Multitude*; Hardt and Negri, *Empire*; Harvey, *A Brief History of Neoliberalism*; and Brown, *Regulating Aversion*.

8. Nadeem, *Dead Ringers*.

9. Radhakrishnan, *Appropriately Indian*.

10. I explicitly address these two positions in the conclusion. See Berlant, *Cruel Optimism*, and Weeks, *The Problem with Work*.

11. For studies of racialization in factories, see, for example, Ong, *Spirits of Resistance and Capitalist Discipline*; Salzinger, *Genders in Production*; and Thompson, *The Making of the English Working Class*. For resistance to the same, see, for example, Bourdieu, *Language and Symbolic Power*.

12. Even more generally, middle classes have tended to be studied for the way they uphold and benefit from capitalist organizations of labor, not for the ways they at the same time trouble some of these forms of organization. The essays collected in Heiman, Freeman, and Liechty, *The Global Middle Classes*, try to counteract this unfortunate tendency.

13. Berardi takes the notion of eros from Marcuse, who in *Eros and Civilization* argued that "instrumental reason had so saturated all of civilized culture—not just work but also leisure, not just production but also consumption—that a nonrepression of primal sexuality . . . is an indispensable precondition of human liberation." Floyd, "Rethinking Reification," 104. While, for Marcuse, eros is life-affirming sexuality, Berardi reworks this notion away from the idea that primal sexuality is being repressed. He suggests that in the current economic climate, hyperexpressivity rather than repression is a mode of domination. Yet, this expressivity is directed toward particular ends. Accounts of the relationship of Marcuse's and Foucault's approaches to sexuality begin with Marcuse, *Eros and Civilization*; Foucault, *The History of Sexuality*, vol. 1; Berardi, *The Soul at Work*; and Renaud, "Rethinking the Repressive Hypothesis."

14. I choose to use eros rather than desire to emphasize that this relationship to the world is not motivated by a Lacanian lack—which then must be bridged—but rather to connect the uses of pleasure to the elaboration of different modes of being in the world. Likewise, although the concept of eros connects to Foucault's readings of pleasure, sexuality, and morality discussed in the second volume of *The History of Sexuality*, I am interested in eros as a way to understand how hyperexpressivity as a demand of contemporary neolib-

eral regimes can be resisted and rechanneled through the elaboration of a good life.

15. I am thinking here of Trouillot, "Anthropology and the Savage Slot."

16. See chapter 3 for a fuller treatment of this point.

17. The definition of the Indian *middle class* is much debated. Some scholars suggest differentiating the Indian middle class into layers (dominant, subordinate, etc.). Others suggest pluralizing the term. As Baviskar and Ray point out, the sociological definition of middle class, which estimates its numbers (taking income, education, and purchasing power together) as, at most, 26 percent of the Indian population, must also be supplemented with studies that investigate its symbolic power (*Elite and Everyman*, 2). In this text, I stress the processural qualities of middle classness, asking what it means to feel and become middle class.

18. It is ironic that this temporary visa program was called a "green card," since the U.S. green card is for permanent residency.

19. Kolb, "Pragmatische Routine und Symbolische Inszenierung"; Kolb, "The German 'Green Card' "; Oberkircher, "Die deutsche Greencard aus der Sicht Indischer IT-Experten." A comparison of U.S. and German visa programs for high-tech labor can be found in Hutzschenreuter, Lewin, and Ressler, "The Growth of White-Collar Offshoring."

20. Marx wrote in the first lines of the *Communist Manifesto*, "A specter is haunting Europe—the specter of communism." If there is a "new" specter haunting Europe, then it may be the specter of late liberal, "immaterial" capitalism, which is accompanied by nostalgia for Fordist labor organization (see Berlant, *Cruel Optimism*). If so, then the ethical opening Marx makes to class as an analytic needs to be carefully reopened. As I will argue in this book, attempts to do so to date—the precariat (Standing, *The Precariat*), the cognitariat (Berardi, *The Soul at Work*)—move in this direction but so far cannot ground their analyses in relation to existing social and historical relations. They therefore unintentionally subsume within them the critical differences that are the subject of this book. Starting instead with social and historical process may yield a more adequate account of how new kinds of work and working bodings emerge from the lived practices of contemporary capitalism. For more on class as an ethical category, see Foucault, *Security, Territory, Population*, 77. I use the term *third world* to indicate the long history of its usage, and to make clear the way it "lay[s] . . . claim on us prior to our full knowing" (Butler, *Bodies That Matter*, 229). The way such terms are deployed here is, following Butler, part of their necessary "work[ing] and rework[ing] in political discourse" (229).

21. The immigrant population of Germany is about 8.8 percent of the total population, and 6 percent (1.55 million) of those immigrants are from Turkey. By contrast, estimates show that there are approximately 50,000 Indian citizens and people of Indian descent living in Germany, less than 1 percent of the

total population. See Gottschlich, *Developing a Knowledge Base for Policymaking on India-EU Migration*, 3.

22. The German green card program expired in 2004 and was not renewed. Today, a German firm wanting to hire programmers from abroad must agree to pay a salary of 66,000 euros—about 30 percent higher than what programming jobs pay on average in Europe—while a foreign resident wanting to set up a business in Germany must invest 250,000 euros and hire five people to gain residence rights. As of this writing, the German parliament has passed an EU directive authorizing a "blue card" for professional migrant workers which is set to lower the salary requirements to as low as 35,000 euros and remove investment requirements for business owners. See "German 'Blue Card' to Simplify Immigration," http://www.dw.de/dw/article/0,,15915424,00 .html, accessed June 9, 2012. These vacillations suggest that migration law too is following the same trend that describes reconstitution of work, with a kind of "just in time" migration law proposed that will be responsive to the needs of the moment. These practices dovetail with the outsourcing of work to India and elsewhere to create a flexible and global technoeconomy around software and software services.

23. Collier, *Post-Soviet Social*, 3. Lisa Rofel's account of Chinese cosmopolitanism in *Desiring China* as exhibiting varied textures of neoliberalism is kindred with the kind of desires I explore for Indian IT workers in this book.

24. For an excellent account of research methods—and barriers to ethnography—in corporate coding, see Upadhya, "Ethnographies of the Global Information Economy," where she argues that access to corporate IT culture for ethnographers is often highly restrictive, as are the things that programmers are willing to discuss in the office. Hannerz, "Other Transnationals," provides insights on how to "study sideways," while Nader, "Up the Anthropologist," remains the seminal text on studying "up."

25. These practices are perhaps grounded in the notions of timepass and *adda*, the first connoting the practice of spending time in deliberately doing nothing, the latter connoting spending time in leisurely, meandering conversation. For timepass, see Jeffrey, *Timepass*. For adda, see Chakrabarty, *Provincializing Europe*.

26. Fabian, "Presence and Representation," 762.

27. Marx, *Capital*, chap. 6.

28. I take as my inspiration here Keith Hart's meditation on cosmopolitan anthropology, "'Anthropology' and the New Human Universal."

29. Rana, *Terrifying Muslims*, 11.

30. Their strategies here are heir to the late-colonial middle-class manipulations of time and narrative that Partha Chatterjee traces in *The Nation and Its Fragments*, where middle-class Bengalis operated with both the grid of linear time and the returning narration of time outside these confines (54–55).

31. On the relationship between Indian nation and diaspora, see Amrute, "Living and Praying in the Code"; Gopinath, *Impossible Desires*; Shukla, *India Abroad*; Shankar, *Desi Land*; and Mankekar, *Unsettling India*.

32. There are many moments in fieldwork when an anthropologist is recognized and named as a particular kind of person. Some of these become emblematic of the discipline's relationship to the field, for instance, Geertz's narration of his presence in Bali as discussed by Clifford in "On Ethnographic Allegory." In retrospect, these moments help set the tone for the kind of person the ethnographer is taken to be—though, of course, this is affirmed, overturned, undone, and questioned in interaction.

33. The title of this self-published humorous poem with twenty-odd verses plays on homophones: *Internet* and *Inder nett* (nice Indian), which sound the same in German. Wallace, "Germany's New Recruits," presents a rosy picture of the welcome Indian IT workers receive in Germany.

34. For a discussion of the differences between ethnicity and race, see Omi and Winant, *Racial Formation in the United States*.

35. Fanon, *Black Skin, White Masks*, xv.

36. Postracial formations deny the salience of race—arguing that racism has been transcended through affirmative action and through the deconstruction of the biological grounds of race—even while they use race as a marker of internal qualities and characteristics. See Bonilla-Silva, *Racism without Racists*. I bring this insight together with post–genomic understandings of race, which argue that race describes probabilities that are likely to inhere in populations, such as when it is argued that South Asians are genetically predisposed to heart disease because of a tendency to store belly fat. This latter, probabilistic idea of race is woven into racial exclusion in complex ways, one of which is to give renewed energy to racial thinking because it seems to map onto the new flexibility of formerly distinct categories demanded by a similarly flexible capitalist system.

37. "Qualities and capacities inherent in vitality have become a potential source for the production of value," remarks Nikolas Rose, a process that he calls the production of "biovalue." Rose suggests that the commodification of research in population genetics such that biopolitics (power over life itself) becomes bioeconomics (capitalization of life). This idea may be properly applied more broadly, outside of the strict domain of the biotech industries. Rose, "The Value of Life," 42.

38. Cooper, *Life as Surplus*.

39. To take the position that virtual labor has eclipsed manual labor is to take the dream of corporate capital for reality. But it is equally problematic to insist that real workers and real labor only take place in the factory. To do this is in a certain way to sequester manual workers within their work, ignoring the connections that link them to the circulation of capital in its most esoteric forms. It also turns a blind eye to the very real forms of expropriation and

control that take place *within* the office buildings where symbols for consumption are produced. Curiously, like the position of universal virtual labor that it critiques, the valorization of a working underclass assumes that there is an identifiable real laborer; it simply locates this laborer on the other side of the divide between intellectual and manual work. And it valorizes labor as the source of all value without recognizing the particularly capitalist historical context of the development of the idea of labor as context-free. See Postone, *Time, Labor, and Social Domination*, for a useful critique of this position.

40. Gilman, "Thilo Sarrazin and the Politics of Race in the Twenty-First Century." A wide-ranging discussion of race and the Nazi legacy in Germany can be found in Linke, *German Bodies*.

41. For recent accounts of this shift, see LiPuma and Lee, *Financial Derivatives and the Liquidation of Risk*; Ho, *Liquidated*; Hardt and Negri, *Empire*; Lazzarato, "From Capital-Labour to Capital-Life" and "Immaterial Labor"; and Deleuze, "Postscript on the Societies of Control."

42. Virno, *Grammar of the Multitude*, 61.

43. Berardi, *The Soul at Work*, 90.

44. Berardi, *The Soul at Work*, 105.

45. This path unseats divisions between mental and physical, brain and body, matter and thought, all in a thoroughly "modern" environment. For debates within anthropology on this issue, see Bond and Bessire, "The Ontological Spin."

46. I follow here Karen Barad's elaboration of embodiment, which begins with action and then shows how bodies and objects are precipitated out of moments of repeated actions. Barad, "Posthumanist Performativity."

47. Recent literature on the new South Asian middle class includes Fernandes, *India's New Middle Class*; Deshpande, *Contemporary India*; Heller and Fernandes, "Hegemonic Aspirations"; Varma, *The Great Indian Middle Class*; Baviskar and Ray, *Elite and Everyman*; Liechty, *Suitably Modern*; and Nisbett, "Friendship, Consumption, Morality"; for a historical overview and the relationship to colonialism, see Joshi, *The Middle Class in Colonial India*.

48. Fernandes, "The Politics of Forgetting," 2415.

49. Satish Deshpande points out the antimonies in defining *a* middle class in his *Contemporary India*. One way to address this problem is to further divide the middle class into "layers" that are more or less elite or hegemonic. While this has great sociological value, it is not the route I follow here, because it does not yield much in the way of how classes of whatever layer are formed and how individuals come to see themselves as members of a class.

50. Edwards, *The Practice of Diaspora*, 14.

51. Marx, *Capital*, 547.

52. Marx, *Capital*, 532.

53. As literary critic Katherine Hayles writes, "Computers are no longer merely tools (if they ever were) but are complex systems that increasingly produce the conditions, ideologies, assumptions, and practices that help constitute what

we call reality" (*My Mother Was a Computer*, 60). The literature on the social meaning of technology is large and growing. Work that has been seminal to the ideas presented here includes Fuller, *Behind the Blip* and *Software Studies*; Chun, *Programmed Visions*; Marino, "Critical Code Studies"; Mackenzie, *Cutting Code* and *Transductions*; and Raley, "Code.surface || Code.depth."

54. Berardi, *The Soul at Work*, 13.

55. See Amrute, "Where the World Ceases to Be Flat," for a review of some of these works. The sociological study of corporate software work was pioneered by Kunda, *Engineering Culture*, and Kunda and Barley, *Gurus, Hired Guns and Warm Bodies*.

56. Winner, "Technology Today," 1010–11.

57. Though the term is Agamben's, it has of late come into much more widespread circulation to connote a life that is valued only as living substance and not as political substance. See Agamben, *Homo Sacer*. Important elaborations on this theme are found in Mbembe, "Necropolitan," and Puar, "The Right to Maim."

Part I: Encoding Race

1. Ahearn, "Commentary," 11.

2. There is an ongoing literature that tries to bring race back into the study of technology to which I am indebted, including Chun, *Programmed Visions*; Nelson, Tu, and Hines, *Technicolor*; Nakamura, *Digitizing Race*; Kolko, Nakamura, and Rodman, *Race in Cyberspace*; and Eglash, *African Fractals*. My approach tries to think through the question of embodiment in terms of how it fits in post-Fordist capitalism.

3. Haraway, *Primate Visions*, 3.

4. I am using *milieu* in the sense implied by Foucault in his *Security, Territory, Population*, as an ensemble of givens, both natural and social, through which the given characteristics of a population are managed.

Chapter 1: Imagining the Indian IT Body

1. The title of this section is a play on Benjamin's essay "Paris—Capital of the Nineteenth Century." Borneman, *Belonging in the Two Berlins*, gives an excellent account of the different temporalities, ways of life, and cityscapes of East and West Berlin before and after the fall of the Berlin Wall.

2. Though page views are unavailable for this website, it currently has 1,031 "likes" on Facebook, which may provide some indication of its circulation.

3. Tina Campt's discussion of kinetic images and race in Germany and Kajri Jain's treatment of images as socially dense have been seminal to the evolution of my thought here. See Campt, *Image Matters*, and Jain, *Gods in the Bazaar*.

4. For an engaging discussion of metaphor in computing, see Chun, *Programmed Visions*, 55–95.

5. For an excellent discussion of the transparency of state in Berlin, see Sperling, *Reasons of Conscience*.

6. Sperling, *Reasons of Conscience*, 10–11.

7. Ewing, *Stolen Honor*. El-Tayeb's, "'Blood Is a Very Special Juice'" and "The Birth of a European Public" provide a compelling analysis of race and citizenship in contemporary Europe.

8. Partridge, *Hypersexuality and Headscarves*.

9. A perspective on Turkish German youth can be found in Otyakmaz, *Auf allen Stühlen*. The history of some extraordinary Afrodeutsch subjects is told in Campt, *Image Matters*.

10. Thinking through the multiple ways images of the Indian IT worker circulate can offer a striated and complex understanding of how race is taken up and pinned down in technoeconomies—by using marks on bodies. Reading these images in terms of their qualities of abduction and in terms of a visual language that points not toward underlying structures of meaning but toward other sign structures (which Peirce developed as a tripartite relationship among objects, signs, and interpretants) uncovers multiple futures and histories of associations between race and technology. See Peirce, "A Syllabus of Certain Topics of Logic"; Helmreich, "An Anthropologist Underwater"; and Gell, *Art and Agency*.

11. Huyssen, "Voids of Berlin," and Ladd, *Ghosts of Berlin*, discuss the visual practices in newly unified Berlin.

12. Trouillot, "Anthropology and the Savage Slot."

13. See Herder, *Ideen zu einer Philosophie der Geschichte der Menschheit* [Ideas for the philosophy of the history of humanity], 1784–91. Schlegel, who studied Sanskrit in Paris beginning in 1802, formed his interest in India through a rejection of Paris and French culture, which he understood as thoroughly capitalist, materialist, modern, and hegemonic in Europe. See his *Über die Sprache und Weisheit der Inder* [On the language and wisdom of the Indians]. Schlegel sought to posit a German protonational identity based on its difference from the rest of Europe. Dusche, "Friedrich Schlegel's Writings on India," 45.

14. Kontje, "Germany's Local Orientalisms," 67; Barua, Gerhard, and Kossler, *Understanding Schopenhauer through the Prism of Indian Culture*, discusses the influence of Indian philosophy in German intellectual traditions.

15. Zöller, "Philosophizing under the Influence—Schopenhauer's Indian Thought," 15.

16. For a discussion of Germany's colonial ambitions and their grounding in ideas of the East, see Zantop, *Colonial Fantasies*.

17. Mazumdar, "The Jew, the Turk, and the Indian."

18. Marx, "The British Rule in India."

19. See Weber, *The Protestant Ethic and the Spirit of Capitalism* and *The Religion of India*. For the case against Weber's evaluation of anticapitalist India, see Singer, *When a Great Tradition Modernizes*, and Lockwood, *The Indian Bourgeoisie*.

20. Cho, Kurlander, and McGetchin, *Transcultural Encounters between Germany and India*, 139–85.

21. Scholarship on colonialism and postcolonialism in South Asia has shown how the tropes of stability in South Asia have rested on the twin pillars of community (often thought of as religious community) and caste, with the floating signifier of the Indian woman serving to produce both as convincing models of Indian difference (see Appadurai, "Is Homo Hierarchicus?"; Dirks, *Castes of Mind*; Rao, *The Caste Question*; Sinha, *Specters of Mother India*; and Spivak, "Can the Subaltern Speak?"). For accounts of the general shape of European Orientalism vis-à-vis India, see Inden, *Imagining India*; Trautmann, *Aryans and British India*; Figueira, *Aryans, Jews, Brahmins*; Hodkinson and Walker, *Deploying Orientalism in Culture and History*; and Murti, *India*.

22. See Kapur, *Diaspora, Development, and Democracy*, and Saxenian, *Silicon Valley's New Immigrant Entrepreneurs*.

23. Called the *Anwerbestoppverordenung*, this measure had the unintended consequence of increasing migration as children and spouses of workers who previously traveled between Germany and Turkey rushed to join their working fathers and husbands in Germany before passage between the two countries was effectively closed for them. Chin, *The Guest Worker Question in Postwar Germany*, analyzes these measures.

24. See Brubaker, *Citizenship and Nationhood in France and Germany*; and Linke, *Blood and Nation*.

25. Although German law and popular culture continually treat migrants as foreigners, Afro-German and Turkish-German populations develop ways of belonging to and pushing at the exclusionary practices of the nation-state. For a detailed analysis of the relationship of the German green card program and migration law reform in Germany, see Amrute, "Producing Mobility." See also Kymlicka, *Politics in the Vernacular*, and Joppke, "Multiculturalism and Immigration."

26. As the name suggests, the idea behind the *Gastarbeiter* (guest worker) program was for workers to come to work in Germany and then return home. Many guest workers engaged in circular forms of migration, working seasonally in Germany, with migrant families doing the same. Few provisions were provided Turkish guest workers living in Germany, even as it became apparent that workers had begun to live where they worked and to raise families in Germany. In 1977, the German government responded to the existence of a Turkish minority population in the country by calling a halt to the recruitment of foreign guest workers. Currently, the population of Germany is about 3 percent Turkish and Turkish German.

27. See, for instance, https://www.bild.bundesarchiv.de/cross-search/search /_1452212928/?search[view]=detail&search[focus]=1, accessed September 14, 2013.

28. Sebaly, "The Assistance of Four Nations in the Establishment of the Indian Institutes of Technology, 1945–1970."

29. For more on these incidents, see Eckert, "Xenophobia and Violence in Germany 1990 to 2000," and Koopmans, "Rechtsextremismus und Fremden-feindlichkeit in Deutschland: Probleme von heute—Diagnosen von gestern." The current uptake of Syrian refugees in Germany develops against the background of this earlier history.

30. Greser and Lenz were the subject of an exhibition in 2012 at the German Historical Institute London called "Germans and Fun?" In an interview with journalist Daniel Zylbersztajn, Lenz described their work as "caricature" rather than "cartoon," concerned with socially and politically relevant events in addition to comedy, which he described as a dying art due to the lack of adequate training in drawing and to the twenty-four-hour news cycle, through which important events were promptly forgotten. See http://www.ghil.ac.uk/events_and_conferences/special_events/special_events_2012/exhibition_germans_and_fun.html.

31. Berardi, *The Soul at Work*; LiPuma and Lee, *Financial Derivatives and the Globalization of Risk*; and Harvey, *A Brief History of Neoliberalism*.

32. Rose, "The Value of Life," 39.

33. Trouillot, "Anthropology and the Savage Slot."

34. Abu El-Haj, "The Genetic Reinscription of Race."

35. Comaroff and Comaroff, *Ethnicity, Inc.*, 51.

36. Abu El-Haj, "The Genetic Reinscription of Race"; Nelson, "Bio Science"; Rabinow, "Artificiality and Enlightenment"; Reardon, "The Human Genome Diversity Project."

37. Weinbaum, "Racial Aura," 217; Fanon, *Black Skin, White Masks*.

38. Deleuze, "Postscript on the Societies of Control."

39. A fascinating discussion of Indian sexuality as enhancement of European sexuality is found in Arondekar, *For the Record*.

40. bell hooks rather appropriately calls this process "eating the other." See hooks, "Eating the Other."

41. hooks, "Eating the Other," 368–69.

42. For the general contours of European thought on India, see Inden, *Imagining India*. For a detailed analysis of German Orientalism as a scholarly discipline, see Marchand, *German Orientalism in the Age of Empire*; Cowan, *The Indo-German Identification*; and McGetchin, Park, and SarDesai, *Sanskrit and "Orientalism."* Manjapra, *Age of Entanglement*, provides an account of scholarly rapprochement between Indian and German intellectuals.

43. hooks, "Eating the Other," 367.

44. For a similar colonial case, see Bhabha, *The Location of Culture*.

45. Haraway, "A Cyborg Manifesto." I use the term here to indicate ways that the flesh of the Indian programmer is enmeshed with the technology of the computer.

46. See, for comparison, Lilia Moritz Schwarcz's penetrating analysis of Brazilian imperial cartoon culture, where she notes that "caricature reworked

and revolutionized hitherto consensual and naturalized public positions and images" and gave form to "major impasses and contradictions" ("The Banana Emperor," 316–17).

47. As Achille Mbembe writes in his discussion of Cameroonian political cartoons, "What is special about an image is its likeness—that is, its ability to annex and mime what it represents, while, in the very act of representation, masking the power of its own arbitrariness, its own potential for opacity, simulacrum, and distortion" (*On the Postcolony*, 142).

48. Beth Coleman, "Race as Technology," 184. For an allied reading of race and human potentiality, see Cooper, *Life as Surplus*.

Chapter 2: The Postracial Office

1. In the office setting, she spoke standard German (*Hochdeutsch*). I many times witnessed colleagues who spoke standard German within the office and then switched to East German, and especially Berliner, dialects when on smoke breaks. Boyer, "The Corporeality of Expertise," provides a useful discussion of the evaluation of expertise across the East-West German divide.

2. Chun, *Programmed Visions*, 139.

3. The literature on the blurring of work and leisure is vast. Some of the key works include Virno, *Grammar of the Multitude*; Berardi, *The Soul at Work*; and Stephens and Weston, "Free Time." The genealogy of this literature owes a debt to the work of the Frankfurt School, whose writers took on the task of examining processes of power and subjugation under late capitalism. White-collar office work was especially fruitfully discussed in Kracauer, *The Salaried Masses*.

4. There have been many names coined for this kind of economy. Among them are *post-Fordist* (see the work of David Harvey); *finance capital* (see LiPuma and Lee, *Financial Derivatives and the Globalization of Risk*); *the attention economy* (see Beller, *The Cinematic Mode of Production*); *the immaterial economy* (Hardt and Negri, *Empire*) and *promissory finance* (see Appadurai, *Banking on Words*). Each term focuses on different aspects of this shift away from factory-based production. I use *cognitive labor* here to emphasize a particular relationship to work in IT offices.

5. Manual labor has not disappeared in this scenario, but the conditions under which it takes place have, changing also its relationship to the production of surplus value. A useful attempt to rethink the worker in contemporary capitalism is found in Dyer-Witherford, "Empire, Immaterial Labor, the New Combinations, and the Global Worker." Pang, "The Labor Factor in the Creative Economy," investigates factory-style labor in cognitive economies but stops short of analyzing how an understanding of such work contributes to a more complex picture of cognitive economies as such.

6. Berardi, *The Soul at Work*, 90.

7. Rana, *Terrifying Muslims*, 117.

8. Vora, *Life Support*, 67.

9. On postrace theories, see Bonilla-Silva, *Racism without Racists*; Joseph, *Transcending Blackness*; Ibrahim, *Troubling the Family*; and Nishime, *Undercover Asian*. Foundational texts on the relationship between race and computing include Eglash, *African Fractals*, and Nelson and Tu, *Technicolor*; Nakamura, *Digitizing Race*; and Kolko, Nakamura, and Rodman, *Race in Cyberspace*.

10. See, for instance, Janis, "Obama, Africa, and the Post-Racial."

11. Manz, "Constructing a Normative National Identity," 481–82. A starting point for a discussion of the postwar German reaction to the Holocaust is in Santner, *Stranded Objects*, and Postone, "Anti-Semitism and National Socialism."

12. Partridge, *Hypersexuality and Headscarves*, 152.

13. Bunzl, *Anti-Semitism and Islamophobia*.

14. I like the way "inhere" in its Latin root suggests a kind of stickiness or the way that social process yields some substance that appears to stick to the racially marked worker (*inhaerere*, "stick to," OED).

15. See, for instance, Haraway, "A Cyborg Manifesto"; Latour, *Science in Action*; Downey and Dumit, *Cyborgs and Citadels*; Gray, *The Cyborg Handbook*; and Smith and Morra, *The Prosthetic Impulse*.

16. This chapter's approach to human-nonhuman infra-action is inspired in particular by Barad, "Posthumanist Performativity," and Ingold, "Toward an Ecology of Materials." Ingold who writes of things and bodies as "a gathering together of materials in movement" and of materials as "matter considered in respect of its occurrence in processes of flow and transformation" (438).

17. Muehlebach, *The Moral Neoliberal*.

18. For critiques of liberal tolerance, see Markell, *Bound by Recognition*, and Povinelli, *The Cunning of Recognition*.

19. Bhabha, *The Location of Culture*, 86.

20. Bhabha, *The Location of Culture*, 87.

21. Marx, *Capital*, chap. 7, sec. 1.

22. Marx, *Capital*, chap. 7, sec. 1.

23. Adam Smith discusses divisions of labor in pin factories and the lack of the same among greyhounds in *The Wealth of Nations*.

24. Schaffer, "Babbage's Dancer."

25. The political history of the split between Hindi and Urdu and their ties to religion and the nation-states of Pakistan and India is told in Faruqi, *Early Urdu Literary Culture and History*, and King, *One Language, Two Scripts*.

26. On the framing abilities of such uses of language, see Goffman, *Frame Analysis*. On the relationship of metapragmatic functions—codes about how the unspoken aspects of language-use should be interpreted—see Silverstein, "Metapragmatic Discourse and Metapragmatic Function."

27. Povinelli, *Economies of Abandonment*.

28. On the framing of Turkish and Muslim immigrants in Germany, see Ewing, *Stolen Honor*; Bunzl, *Anti-Semitism and Islamophobia*; and Partridge, *Hypersexuality and Headscarves*.

29. I paraphrase this conversation from fieldwork notes that I took down during the meeting and include some direct quotations I was able to note down.

30. The connection between being Turkish, male, and prone to violence is a key trope in what Katherine Ewing calls the "stigmatization" of Muslim men in Germany. Ewing, *Stolen Honor*.

31. http://www.xing.com/net/beraternet/woran-arbeite-ich-gerade -46444/arbeiten-mit-offshore-programmierern-indien-3904670, accessed December 7, 2015.

32. Partridge, *Hypersexuality and Headscarves*, 151.

33. This aspiration is one of the anchors for a transnational, neoliberal ideology of individual self-development and responsibility that suppresses and sidelines the material and social entanglements that allow such an individual to be produced. A useful attempt to revisit the materiality of race as such an entanglement is found in Weinbaum, *Wayward Reproductions*.

34. Virno, *Grammar of the Multitude*, 103.

35. Average annual salary, not including benefits, for project managers in Berlin is about 50,000 euros ($69,000); for software developers it is about 40,000 ($55,000); and for technical support it is about 30,000 ($41,000). See http://www.salaryexplorer.com/salary-survey.php?loc=81&loctype=1&jobtype =2&job=1, accessed December 7, 2015.

36. The language ideology of international office English is a fascinating topic of its own that deserves separate treatment. For sense-reference predication, see Silverstein, "Metapragmatic Discourse and Metapragmatic Function."

37. Berardi, *The Soul at Work*, 74.

38. Berardi, *The Soul at Work*, 86.

39. Deleuze, "Postscript on the Societies of Control."

40. On the effects of night work in the Indian IT industry, see Poster, "Saying 'Good Morning' in the Night," and Aneesh, *Neutral Accent*.

41. Office titles varied from site to site, but in general, the term *developer* was used for those who were writing source code. *Engineer* (including the titles "head engineer" and "engineer") usually referred to those doing advanced technical support work.

42. Miller and Rose, "Production, Identity, and Democracy," 430.

43. Radhakrishnan, *Appropriately Indian*. See also Ameeriar, "The Sanitized Sensorium."

44. Usha Amrit, "Indian Workforce in Cross Cultural Environment," December 17, 2011, http://theindernet.blogspot.com/2011/12/indian-workforce-in -cross-cultural.html, accessed June 21, 2013.

45. LiPuma and Lee, *Financial Derivatives and the Globalization of Risk*.

46. Marchand, *German Orientalism in the Age of Empire*.

47. Aihwa Ong cites a similar instance of what she calls "self-orientalism in *Flexible Citizenship*. What is happening here is a little different, since it is not self-orientalism as a kind of strategic essentialism that is at play. Rather, this essentialism represents an attempt to smooth over, harmonize, and blend sets of seemingly opposed practices. The Art of Living Foundation has come under fire in India due to environmental destruction in the Yamuna floodplain after one of its large-scale gatherings.
48. Latour, *An Inquiry into Modes of Existence*; Barad, "Posthumanist Performativity."

Chapter 3: Proprietary Freedoms in an IT Office

1. Virno, *Grammar of the Multitude*, 106.
2. Critical code studies, inaugurated by Mark Marino in 2006, asks what it means to analyze source code as a semiotic system—in terms of its own logic, languages, and representations. See Marino, "Critical Code Studies." While my project does not "read" code in the way Marino suggests, it is in sympathy with digital humanities scholars who want to contextualize coding practices. While critical code studies (CCS) begins with snippets of code, I begin from the other side, with the practices of coders both in and outside the office. A very instructive instance of CCS work is Stephen Ramsay's "Algorithms Are Thoughts, Chainsaws Are Tools," March 2010, http://vimeo.com/9790850, accessed June 20, 2014. For a useful description of the significance of CCS, see https://www.hastac.org/initiatives/hastac-scholars/scholars-forums/critical-code-studies, accessed June 20, 2014.
3. Aneesh, "Global Labor."
4. Kelty, *Two Bits*.
5. Coleman, *Coding Freedom*.
6. For a discussion of deontics in anthropology, see Kockelman, "From Status to Contract Revisited."
7. Røyrvik and Brodersen, "Real Virtuality," 647.
8. Ross, *No Collar*.
9. Deleuze, "Postscripts on the Societies of Control," 4.
10. Eros is found in and inflected through sites of work, while the sites of pleasure can become training grounds for the office. I differ from Berardi's account of eros in *The Soul at Work* in seeing eros in the everyday practices of coders, rather than an impulse that would have to be brought in from the outside, or after the veil of ideology was lifted. See also Postone's critique of the singular and totalizing capitalism proposed by Marcuse and others in his *Time, Labor, and Social Domination*.
11. Marcuse, *Eros and Civilization*, xiv.
12. Berardi, *Precarious Rhapsody*, 108.
13. Berardi follows Foucault's critique of Marcuse when he writes that Marcuse "give[s] the notion of repression an exaggerated role" because

power is productive rather than simply repressive. Foucault, "Body/ Power," 59.

14. Ramello, "Access to vs. Exclusion from Knowledge," 78.

15. Boyle, "The Second Enclosure Movement and the Construction of the Public Domain"; Gosseries, "How (Un)fair Is Intellectual Property?," 3; Woodmansee and Jaszi, *The Construction of Authorship*, 29–56.

16. Ramello, "Access to vs. Exclusion from Knowledge"; see also Gosseries, Marciano, and Strowel, *Intellectual Property and Theories of Justice*.

17. Quotation is from Jaszi, "On the Author Effect," 55; See also: Ghosh, *CODE*; Kelty, *Two Bits*; Galloway, *Protocol*, 170.

18. Graeber, *Debt*, 101.

19. Galloway, *Protocol*, 166.

20. Kant, "Perpetual Peace," 99; Hart, "'Anthropology' and the New Human Universal."

21. A function, or method, is a piece of code that is chunked together because it does something in particular by means of an algorithm.

22. Knorr Cetina, "Sociality with Objects," 12.

23. Knorr Cetina, "Sociality with Objects," 10, 18.

24. Terranova, *Network Culture*, 118.

25. Virno, *Grammar of the Multitude*, 68, 76.

26. Jackson, "Gentrification, Globalization, and Georaciality," 204.

27. Foucault, *Security, Territory, Population*, 355.

28. Thank you to Timothy Emmanuel Brown for pointing out this connection to me.

29. Coleman, *Coding Freedom*, 97.

30. The "scrum" is a regular meeting designed to keep track of smaller segments of a large project. It is part of what is called an "agile" software development process, where regular check-ins with teams on their progress should lead to meeting more deadlines and heading off problems earlier in a development process. The term *scrum* is adapted from rugby, where players lock arms at the beginning of play.

31. O'Carroll, "Fuzzy Holes and Intangible Time," 188.

32. O'Carroll, "Fuzzy Holes and Intangible Time," 180.

33. Coleman, *Coding Freedom*, 106. Berry, *The Philosophy of Software*, provides an overview of multiple theories of code and its social extensions.

34. Radhakrishnan, *Appropriately Indian*, 90.

35. Lessig, *Code and Other Laws of Cyberspace*, 4–5. An insightful ethnographic treatment of legal norms around code as speech is found in Coleman, "Code Is Speech."

36. Weeks, *The Problem with Work*, 210–13.

37. Lawrence Liang as quoted in Philip, "What Is a Technological Author?," 213.

38. Philip, "What Is a Technological Author?," 213.

39. The "standing reserve" enunciated by Heidegger is thus simultaneously turned inward and opened up to social action. Rather than human potential becoming a resource to be consumed by technological production—pace Heidegger—the body in reserve here is an ability to make code stand still and be diverted to new deployments. Heidegger, "Questioning concerning Technology."
40. Philip, "What Is a Technological Author?," 216.
41. Alleyne, "Challenging Code"; Söderberg, *Hacking Capitalism*.

Chapter 4: The Stroke of Midnight and the Spirit of Entrepreneurship
Epigraph: Chanana, *Computers in Asia*, 34.

1. Nehru, "Tryst with Destiny."
2. The title of this chapter is a play on Weber, *The Protestant Ethic and the Spirit of Capitalism*. Had Weber witnessed the rise of postcolonial nationalism, he would not have been surprised at the particular welding of patriotism and entrepreneurial spirit at work here.
3. These narrative maneuvers speak to the affect of capital projects, how they depend not only on evaluations of utilitarian interest but also on the persuasiveness of rhetoric. For a good discussion of capitalist affect, see Mazzarella, *Shoveling Smoke* and "Affect: What Is It Good For?" "Some Elements of a Sociology of Translation," by Michael Callon, uses the notions of enrollment, representatives, and mobilizations to show how various (human and nonhuman) actors use intermediaries to work together in a particular set of circumstances.
4. By income and family background definitions, Adi is certainly an upper-class Indian. Yet, because the definition of middle class is so capacious, on the one hand, and is laminated on the IT industries, on the other, he considers himself to be a middle-class Indian, at least during this period of his life. For the capaciousness of the middle class, see Heller and Fernandes, "Hegemonic Aspirations"; for the middle-class position as tied to IT, see Upadhya, "Employment, Exclusion and 'Merit' in the Indian IT Industry."
5. The modernization and development discourses that marked the period after India's independence through the 1990s often compared developed and underdeveloped countries as if they were individuals. Countries were said to mature, to be in a role relative to one another, to be behind or ahead on the road to modernity. The measures of development varied significantly over time, with India's progress sometimes measured in literacy, sometimes in modernist architecture and large infrastructural building projects, at times in poverty reduction, and at others in weapons technology. See Gupta, *Postcolonial Developments*; Sinha, *Specters of Mother India*; and Abraham, *The Making of the Indian Atomic Bomb*.
6. Corbridge and Harriss, *Reinventing India*, is a thoughtful primer on liberalization in India.

7. Romila Thapar's essay, "Cyclic and Linear Time in Early India," provides a useful starting point for a discussion of time in South Asia.

8. Hardt, "The Whithering of Civil Society," 36.

9. Aziz Premji is the chairman of the IT firm Wipro. Nandan Nilekani is the cofounder of Infosys, another large Indian IT firm, and is now chairman of the UIDAI (Unique Identification Authority of India) program.

10. Radhakrishnan, *Appropriately Indian*.

11. See Pal, "The Machine to Aspire To."

12. Knorr Cetina, "Sociality with Objects," 13.

13. Programmers are thus working in the hyphenated space between the "nation" and the "state." Khilnani, *The Idea of India*, and Appadurai, *Modernity at Large*, analyze the way the Indian nation is both served by and divorced from the Indian state.

14. Trouillot, *Silencing the Past*, 20.

15. Trouillot, *Silencing the Past*, 27.

16. The power of globalization as an analytic derives from the meaning and practices it takes on as it moves across locations. Anna Tsing supports this view, writing "the key is to situate" powerful global perspectives "in relation to the political economies that make them possible and the struggles over meaning in which they participate" ("The Global Situation"). Lowe, "Metaphors of Globalization," provides another useful approach to teasing out histories of the global North and South.

17. See Patibandla, Kapur, and Petersen, "Import Substitution with Free Trade."

18. Prakash, *Another Reason*, 100, 102.

19. Chatterjee, *The Nation and Its Fragments*, narrates the relationship between Indian elites and nationalist discourse in the late colonial period. Sartori, "The Categorical Logic of a Colonial Nationalism," gives an alternative account of Indian nationalism and British colonial categories.

20. Chatterjee, *The Nation and Its Fragments*, 178.

21. Roy, *Beyond Belief*, 111.

22. Roy, *Beyond Belief*, 123–25.

23. Roy, *Beyond Belief*.

24. Sharma, *The Long Revolution*, 5.

25. This was done in the National Sample Survey, begun in 1950.

26. Sharma, *The Long Revolution*, 30–31.

27. Sundaram, *Pirate Modernity*.

28. Kapur, *Diaspora, Development, and Democracy*, 186.

29. See Chakravartty, "Weak Winners of Globalization."

30. Sebaly, "The Assistance of Four Nations in the Establishment of the Indian Institutes of Technology, 1945–1970," 132.

31. Leslie and Kargon, *Exporting MIT*, 112.

32. Sebaly, "The Assistance of Four Nations in the Establishment of the Indian Institutes of Technology, 1945–1970," 135.

33. Bassett, "Aligning India in the Cold War Era," 790.

34. Sarkar Committee, "Development of Higher Technical Institutions in India," 1.

35. Leslie and Kargon, *Exporting MIT*, discusses the relationship between MIT and the IITs. The "four directions" for the IITs maps onto a religious topography of India, where there are the four primary directions or *disa*, in Vedic cosmology.

36. Sarkar Committee, "Development of Higher Technical Institutions in India," 2.

37. Sarkar Committee, "Development of Higher Technical Institutions in India," 13.

38. Sarkar Committee, "Development of Higher Technical Institutions in India," 15.

39. Sarkar Committee, "Development of Higher Technical Institutions in India."

40. See Abraham, *The Making of the Indian Atomic Bomb*.

41. See Gupta, *Postcolonial Developments*, and Roy, *Beyond Belief*.

42. Prakash, *Another Reason*.

43. In his review of Nehruvian science, "Nehruvian Science and Postcolonial India," David Arnold argues that Nehru's approach exemplifies the dilemma in postcolonial science more broadly of how to reconcile universal ambitions and local needs.

44. Nehru, "Speech at the Administrative Staff College of India, Hyderabad," 170.

45. Nehru, "Scientists and an Integrated View of Life," 211, 216.

46. Mehta, "Indian Constitutionalism," 26.

47. Sebaly, "The Assistance of Four Nations in the Establishment of the Indian Institutes of Technology, 1945–1970."

48. The IBM 1401 was first bought by Esso to be used for accounting and inventory. It was soon followed by IBM's manufacture of other models, including the 1620, used for scientific calculations at Delhi University, Rookee Engineering College, Bombay University, the Physical Research Laboratory, Ahmedabad Textile Industry Research Association, and IIT Kanpur. Sharma, *The Long Revolution*, 77–78.

49. Sharma, *The Long Revolution*, 81.

50. Sharma, *The Long Revolution*, 81.

51. For a popular account of protectionism and its aftermath as it impacts the computer industry, see Nilekani, *Imagining India*. For a scholarly treatment, see Grieco, *Between Dependency and Autonomy*.

52. Amrute, "Living and Praying in the Code."

53. Sharma, *The Long Revolution*, 96. In the face of the FERA provisions, IBM offered to split the company into a low-tech Indian sector and a high-tech 100 percent IBM-owned export-oriented manufacturing sector. Finally

unable to come to an agreement with the government on these terms, IBM pulled out of the Indian market in 1977.

54. Nilekani, *Imagining India*.

55. Gupta, *Postcolonial Developments*; Corbridge and Harriss, *Reinventing India*.

56. Sharma, *The Long Revolution*, 310–11.

57. Chanana, *Computers in Asia*, 3.

58. Panti Computer Systems, started by MIT graduate Narendra Patni with Poonam Patni as Data Conversion Inc., for example, began as a data conversion company that had accounts with LexisNexis and the American Film Institute to digitize large quantities of information at much lower prices than could happen in the United States. Sharma, *The Long Revolution*, 258–59.

59. I am thinking here of the way Foucault linked conduct with self-discipline and governance. See Foucault, *Security, Territory, Population*.

60. Guha, *India after Gandhi*, 687.

61. Patibandla, Kapur, and Petersen, "Import Substitution with Free Trade."

62. Fuller and Narasimhan, "Information Technology Professionals and the New-Rich Middle Class in Chennai (Madras)," 144.

63. Weiner, "Inalienable Wealth."

64. Srivastava, *Entangled Urbanism*.

65. Karin Knorr Cetina uses the idea of epistemic cultures to highlight "the content of the different knowledge-oriented lifeworlds, the different meanings of the empirical, specific constructions of the referent (the objects of knowledge), particular ontologies of instruments, specific models of epistemic subjects." Following on her analysis of the specificity of epistemes, we can ask a related question: how do those who are the subjects of such epistemes understand, evaluate, and move between "knowledge-oriented lifeworlds"? Knorr Cetina, "Culture in Global Knowledge Societies," 364.

66. See, for instance, Tharoor, *India*.

67. Nandan Nilekani's *aadhaar* program—providing a unique identification number for Indian citizens—is an example of this.

Chapter 5: Computers Are Very Stupid Cooks

1. Barad, "Posthumanist Performativity." Meenakshi's relationship to the computer as stupid cook might be a kind of materialist ontology that creates a specific, oppositional reality. Though much work on materiality stresses the ways technologies and human bodies work together to produce realities, sometimes it is the opposition between a human and a machine that is productive of a particular ontology. On materialist ontologies, see in particular the work of Anne Marie Mol, Tim Ingold, Bruno Latour, John Law, and Donna Haraway. For debates on the ontological turn, see David Graeber, "Radical Alterity Is Just Another Way of Saying 'Reality.'"

2. Knorr Cetina, "Sociality with Objects," 16.

3. For an account of how leisure-time activities now produce laboring subjects, which are called "entrepreneurial" or self-managing, see, in particular, Brown, *Regulating Aversion*. Ulrich Bröckling usefully defines this subjecthood as a "parallelization of individual and enterprise" requiring the "invocation of autonomy, creativity and self-initiative, the . . . exhortation to continuous improvement and the . . . virtually unbounded belief in the power of believing in oneself" ("Gendering the Enterprising Self," 14–16). Michel de Certeau's distinction between strategies and tactics, which he particularly develops in an analysis of conditions of living where work and leisure are blurred, is apposite here.
4. Bröckling, "Gendering the Enterprising Self," 12.
5. Ramamurthy, "Material Consumers, Fabricating Subjects," 541.
6. Thus, leisure emerges as a problem in a particular way in the current moment, making it available for social action. I follow here Foucault's concept of problematizations in "Polemics, Politics and Problematizations."
7. Though I take issue with the idea that tactics were ever formally bonded to (and therefore might reference the possibility of pure) communities, the kinds of activities I describe can also be described as Certeauian "tactics," that "select fragments taken from the vast ensembles of production in order to compose new stories with them" (*The Practice of Everyday Life*, 35). Thanks to Christian Novetzke for pointing me toward this passage in Michel de Certeau's work.
8. Amrute, "Where the World Ceases to Be Flat."
9. Nadeem, *Dead Ringers*, 46.
10. See, in particular, the work of Leela Fernandes, especially *India's New Middle Class*.
11. For a discussion of the right to pleasure and the politics of class and violence in urban India, see Amrute, "Moving Rape."
12. Guyer, "Prophecy and the Near Future."
13. Virno, *Grammar of the Multitude*, 84–85.
14. Virno writes, "Now, these requirements are not the fruit of industrial discipline, rather, they are the result of a socialization that has its center of gravity outside the workplace" (*Grammar of the Multitude*, 84).
15. Rojek, *Decentering Leisure* and *The Labor of Leisure*.
16. Kracauer, *The Salaried Masses*.
17. Veblen, *The Theory of the Leisure Class*.
18. I play here on Dipesh Chakrabarty's term for the way Indian colonial middle-class subjects inhabited colonial categories. See Chakrabarty, *Habitations of Modernity*.
19. Berardi, *The Soul at Work*, 83.
20. Deleuze, "Postscript on the Societies of Control," 4.
21. Besnier and Brownell, "Sport, Modernity, and the Body," 450.
22. Berardi, *The Soul at Work*, 105.

23. Kracauer, *The Salaried Masses*, 77.

24. Farquhar and Zang, "Biopolitical Beijing," 303.

25. Berardi, *Precarious Rhapsody*, 108–9.

26. Green, "Breathing in India, c. 1890."

27. Alter, "Somatic Nationalism."

28. Alter, "The Body of One Color," 64.

29. Amrute, "Living and Praying in the Code."

30. Alter, "The Body of One Color," 66.

31. Ramamurthy, "Material Consumers, Fabricating Subjects," 525.

32. Kaviraj, "Filth and the Public Sphere," 110.

33. Kaviraj, "Filth and the Public Sphere," 102.

34. Kaviraj, "Filth and the Public Sphere," 101.

35. Chatterjee, *The Politics of the Governed*.

36. Kaviraj, "Filth and the Public Sphere," 110.

37. Amrute, "Proprietary Freedoms in an IT Office."

38. See, for instance, Ramamurthy's discussion of consumption practices among cotton pickers in "Material Consumers, Fabricating Subjects."

39. See Amrute, "Living and Praying in the Code," for a more thorough treatment of these trips.

40. Farquhar and Zang, "Biopolitical Beijing," 321.

41. A classic and highly nuanced account of the relationship between time-discipline, work, and dissent is Thompson, "Time, Work-Discipline, and Industrial Capitalism." Crary, *24/7*, attempts to chart a similar territory for the more current moment.

42. Thanks go to Amita Baviskar for encouraging me to think more about these homes as hostels. Meijering and van Hoven, "Imagining Difference," similarly reports frequent socializing among Indian IT workers in Germany, yet they frame this tendency purely within the question of assimilation to a "host" society, thereby missing the creative and processual aspects of these spaces.

43. Lukose, *Liberalization's Children*, 114. Ray and Qayum, *Cultures of Servitude*, tracks the way the house is being reimagined through relations of caste, class, and domestic labor. Safri and Graham, "The Global Household," investigates how households respond to transnational labor movements. Here, and in the case Lukose discusses, an early moment of reimagining domestic space is unfolding as a precursor to establishing a fixed household.

44. Lukose, *Liberalization's Children*, 96–131.

45. Carol Upadhya, for instance, argues that "unlike in the colonial context where the inner world of tradition and spirituality was shielded (largely through the medium of the patriarchal family) from corruption and west-ernization . . . [in] the contemporary era the private sphere of the family (and even the self) is increasingly being penetrated by public discourses and external interests, such that the boundary between public and private life is becoming fuzzy" ("Rewriting the Code," 69–70). Rather than posit an increasing

penetration, I would argue that the line was always fuzzy and has been subject to acts of policing and renegotiation over time.

46. The way that houses are used by programmers points toward a different kind of relationship between work and home, labor and leisure, that is not covered by the idea of a disciplinary society. If Deleuze and others who have been elaborating this idea are correct, rather than being worlds neatly divided by person, material form, and function, our worlds increasingly overlap. I understand jogging here as a sign of these overlapping worlds, where leisure time becomes a training ground for what might be required of the programmer at work. What interests me is the fluidity with which programmers move across these shared spaces, treating them at once as a household, a hostel, and a home and thinking of their residents at once as friends, colleagues, and family. Of course, these categories only ever existed separately in the imagination of researchers who dreamed they could find households that were distinct from families and homes that were distinct from houses in their case studies. What I am pointing out is that from the point of view of the people in them, the relationship between home and household, for instance, is no longer congruent, nested, or even supporting. That is, previously the relationship of family to household and home was often thought of as mutually reinforcing if not containing one another. Now, however, no such simple symmetry exists at the level of what people think about the homes to which they belong.

47. Comaroff, *Body of Power, Spirit of Resistance*, 54.

48. Collier, Rosaldo, and Yanagisako, "Is There a Family?" See also the essays collected in Gary and Hansen, *At the Heart of Work and Family*.

49. The classic arguments on this relationship are to be found in Chatterjee, "The Nationalist Resolution of the Women's Question"; Chakrabarty, *Provincializing Europe*; and Sinha, *Specters of Mother India*. For an account of Bengali upper-caste womanhood, see Sarkar, *Words to Win*. For a discussion of Tarabai Shinde's critique of male colonial patriarchy, see O'Hanlon, *A Comparison between Women and Men*, where O'Hanlon shows how gender became a weapon in the consolidation of caste privilege, leading, for example, to middle-caste groups adopting *purdah* in the nineteenth century as markers of social status.

50. Grewal, *Home and Harem*, 207; 221.

51. Burton, *Dwelling in the Archive*, 32. A similar argument is made forcefully for queer domestic spaces in Gopinath, *Impossible Desires*, while foundational analyses of the protean nature of the home in postcolonial worlds can be found in George, *The Politics of Home*, and Mohanty, *Feminism without Borders*. For a review of everyday acts of women's resistance to colonial modernity, see the essays collected in Ghosh, *Behind the Veil*.

52. Hull, *Government of Paper*, 134.

53. Radhakrishnan, *Appropriately Indian*.

54. Chakrabarty, *Provincializing Europe*. For an analysis of this discussion of science and religious belief, see Amrute, "Living and Praying in the Code."

55. Uberoi, *Freedom and Destiny*. See Majumdar, *Marriage and Modernity*, for an account of the historical place of the conjugal couple in Bengal marriages.

56. Uberoi, *Freedom and Destiny*.

57. Collier, Rosaldo, and Yanagisako, "Is There a Family?," 77.

58. Helen Thompson reminds us that the economy is a late addition to the public/private split that was initially a split between the public and the oikos (the family and the economy of the household). Thompson, "The Personal Is Political."

59. Knorr Cetina, "Culture in Global Knowledge Societies," 365.

60. This is reminiscent of *jugaad*, a work-around.

61. Pandian, *Crooked Stalks*. *Ganja*, a term for marijuana, is used in Hindi and possibly came to the Caribbean by way of indentured Indian laborers, and is derived from the Sanskrit *ganjya*, meaning "of hemp." Thanks to Richard Solomon for this reference.

Chapter 6: The Traveling Diaper Bag

1. Moritz Schwarcz similarly points out how humor can "help create solidarity and shared universes" in "The Banana Emperor," 310.

2. I define pleasure not as a response to a lack but as pursuit of varied ways of life.

3. Herzfeld, *Cultural Intimacy*, discusses jokes and insults as a means for creating ethnic and national solidarities.

4. There are many ways to conceptualize material and immaterial relationships. Among the most fruitful are those that begin with action in the world and then show how material and immaterial things precipitate out from this action. This approach is at the basis of, for instance, Karen Barad's exploration of material performativity in *Meeting the Universe Halfway*, Annemarie Mol's understanding of enactments in *The Body Multiple*, and Tim Ingold's reading of things and bodies as leaking into one another in "Toward an Ecology of Materials." Also noteworthy are the essays collected in Guins, *The Object Reader*.

5. Shankar, *Desi Land*, 92. Shankar follows Myers's discussion of objectification in *The Empire of Things*.

6. By hegemony, commentators on India's middle class mean the ability of this class to set normative patterns of behavior for other, lower-class and subaltern groups, to which these latter groups at least partially accede. See, for example, Baviskar and Ray, *Elite and Everyman*. While hegemony usefully indicates the way that middle classes can produce ideologies that both include and dominate lower classes, in less careful hands it can lead to a static picture of class relations that only always move in one direction, from the top down. To counteract this tendency, it is important to analyze both class relations and class as relational. See Negri, *Marx beyond Marx*. Cooper, "Marx beyond Marx, Marx before Marx," is also helpful on this point.

7. Radhakrishnan, for instance, describes their struggle as trying to be appropriately Indian, while Nadeem suggests that they are latter-day mimic

men, aping American customs to be influential in India. See Radhakrishnan, *Appropriately Indian*, and Nadeem, *Dead Ringers*.

8. As Baviskar and Ray write, "More fluid processes of change and more complex social relations and cultural identities . . . [are involved in] being and becoming middle-class" (*Elite and Everyman*, 9).

9. Virno calls the office a "loquacious" factory where ideas and desires are constantly fostered and communicated with other white-collar workers for the sake of future production (*Grammar of the Multitude*, 107).

10. Autonomist Marxism highlights the productive capacities of workers' movements to generate capitalist social organization. This insight is most useful in that it opens up to historical analysis what counts as a worker; see Weeks, *The Problem with Work*. Yet, by being focused on the worker vanguard and its ability to generate capitalist forms, this literature seeks utopian possibilities outside current conditions of work and only in the future, creating an artificial distinction between the politics of the office and the politics of resistance to capital.

11. See Dave, *Queer Activism in India*, for an inspired discussion of the pleasures of incommensurability. I argue here that working through this pleasure is formative of middle-class Indian identity. A contextually informed discussion of commensuration is found in Povinelli, "Radical Worlds," and Grossberg, *Cultural Studies in the Future Tense*.

12. Hardt, "Affective Labor," is a useful starting point for a discussion of affect in the workplace. What the term *affective unwork* is meant to signal is how affect can also be used to loosen the binds tying workers to the capitalist organization of their labor.

13. For a complex discussion of how gifts extend the personality of the giver, see Appadurai, *The Social Life of Things*; Munn, *The Fame of Gawa*; and Strathern, *The Gender of the Gift*.

14. It was the ability to "give, receive and repay," represented by gifts, that would allow "people, classes, families and individuals" to "sit down like knights around their common riches . . . [and] achieve happiness." Mauss, *The Gift*, 80–81.

15. Without a return, according to Mauss, to the contracts and obligations of gifts, mankind would be left to "the mere pursuit of individual ends" (*The Gift*, 75).

16. "Debt," writes Graeber, "is strictly a creature of reciprocity and has little to do with other sorts of morality (communism, with its needs and abilities; hierarchy, with its customs and qualities). . . . Exchange implies equality, but it also implies separation. It's precisely when the money changes hands, when the debt is cancelled, that equality is restored and both parties can walk away and have nothing further to do with each other" (*Debt*, 121–22).

17. Visa-dependent contract workers particularly are interested in these small disruptions because of the way that their "formally free" labor is not

only tied to wage but also to residence—their loss of job also means possible deportation. This is a feature of the global economy more generally, where labor migration allows capital freedom of movement but restricts the free movement of labor on the market. Thanks to Christian Novetzke for raising this important distinction.

18. Munn, "Constructing Regional Worlds in Experience," 5. For a discussion of diaspora as linking past and future, see Ho, *The Graves of Tarim*.

19. Gamburd, *The Kitchen Spoon's Handle*.

20. In Bourdieu's terms, such consumer practices are practices of distinction. See Bourdieu, *Distinction*. According to this understanding, unmarked T-shirts and slim phones become markers of being a middle-class Indian because they create meaningful separations. They set apart those who have been abroad or with connections abroad from those who cannot mobilize these same resources. While the Bourdieuian approach provides significant explanatory power, it can only partially account for the time and effort spent in choosing and sending these gifts. That is, it accounts for the development of taste only as a means of effecting class membership.

21. Schielke, "Living in the Future Tense," 45.

22. Commensuration is a process by which things are valued and compared against and through one another, often through the attempt to find a common metric (or convention) by which to do so. See Povinelli, "Radical Worlds," and Grossberg, *Cultural Studies in the Future Tense*.

23. See, for example, the special issue of *American Ethnologist* on jokes and humor, May 2013; *Anthropological Forum* 18, no. 3 (2008), devoted to jokes, edited by John Carty and Yasmine Musharbash; and Rutherford, *Laughing at Leviathan*. A classic study of jokes and social roles is Radcliffe-Brown, "On Joking Relationships."

24. Bernal, "Please Forget Democracy and Justice," 300. See also Vienne, "Make Yourself Uncomfortable."

25. Douglas, *Implicit Meanings*, 155.

26. Dave, *Queer Activism in India*.

27. Coleman, *Coding Freedom*, 103.

28. Coleman, *Coding Freedom*, 103.

29. The term *counterconduct* is taken from Foucault, *Security, Territory, Population*.

30. Siegel, *Laughing Matters*, 8.

31. Siegel, *Laughing Matters*, 9.

32. Kaviraj, "Laughter and Subjectivity," 222.

33. Rutherford, *Laughing at Leviathan*, 40.

34. Contrary to Sanjay Srivastava's finding that a postnational imaginary has replaced a postcolonial one, which "marks the emergence of a confident cosmopolitanism among the middle classes and a confidence about the place of 'Indian Culture' within transnational flows and ideas," I found that there was

still a great deal of precarity for these middle-class Indians. This difference may be a result of both the different footing Indians have when migrating and when at home and the differences within this class formation between those who are still striving for elite status and those who have arrived. See Srivastava, "National Identity, Bedrooms, and Kitchens," 83.

35. Baviskar and Ray, *Elite and Everyman*, 6–7.
36. Kenneth McGill points out that in Germany, such decisions fall under the category of *Ermessung*, or personal discretion that hinges on a bureaucrat's ability to represent the needs of state through individual decision making. McGill, personal e-mail communication, January 28, 2014. On bureaucratic imaginaries, see Sperling, *Reasons of Conscience*.
37. For another instance of newspaper parody, see Bernal, "Please Forget Democracy and Justice."
38. Boyer and Yurchak, "American Stiob," 191.
39. Boyer and Yurchak, "American Stiob," 212.
40. A joke is a gift in the sense of an offer to do things differently, but as a gift it implies indebtedness, chains of relations that cannot easily be undone. For the poison of the gift, see Derrida, *Given Time*. For an excellent reading of the gift in French social theory and philosophy, see Roitman, *Fiscal Disobedience*.
41. Edwards, *The Practice of Diaspora*.
42. Tsing, "Sorting Out Commodities," 37. A more standard account of Indian middle-class commodity cultures can be found in Brosius, *India's Middle Class*.

Conclusion

1. Vora, *Life Support*, 102.
2. Berlant, *Cruel Optimism*.
3. Weeks, *The Problem with Work*.
4. See, for example, Wong and Tsai, "Cultural Models of Shame and Guilt," 210.
5. The difficulty in deriving which specific South Asian notions of shame might be at work here is neatly captured in two thinkers' elaboration of the concepts of *sharam* (by Salman Rushdie in his novel *Shame*) and *lajya* (by Richard Shweder in "Toward a Deep Cultural Psychology of Shame"), both of which are glossed by the English "shame."
6. Shweder, "Toward a Deep Cultural Psychology of Shame," 1121.
7. I call this approach, following Butler, *Bodies That Matter*, and Barad, "Posthumanist Performativity" and *Meeting the Universe Halfway*, a performative one. For the founding discussion of performativity in language, see Austin, *How to Do Things with Words*.
8. The phrase they use to describe these decisions, *going for foreign*, indicates the daring required to just pull up stakes and "go for it" in this way.
9. For detailed accounts of this labor practice, see Aneesh, *Virtual Migration*, and Biao, *Global Bodyshopping*.

10. While going back to India and then later getting another temporary job abroad may not be a complete failure, programmers did not see this path as a successful one to take. It would be considered a rather unfortunate detour.

11. Radhakrishnan, "Professional Women, Good Families," 211.

12. Radhakrishnan, "Professional Women, Good Families," 211.

13. Berardi, *Precarious Rhapsody*, 32.

14. The following discussion is greatly indebted to talks with Marina Peterson, Anne-Maria Makhulu, and Catherine Fennell.

15. Mitropoulos, *Contract and Contagion*, 29.

16. Berlant, *Cruel Optimism*, 2.

17. Berlant, *Cruel Optimism*, 221.

18. Berlant, *Cruel Optimism*, 221.

19. Weeks, *The Problem with Work*, 225.

20. Weeks, *The Problem with Work*, 175–225.

21. For more on the relationship between the hidden and the public and how the former (especially hidden lives) stands in for the real beneath the latter, see Shelton, "My Secret Life."

22. Spivak, "Can the Subaltern Speak?"

23. Du Plessis: Borkowski's Textbook on Roman Law 4e, Glossary, http://global.oup.com/uk/orc/law/roman/borkowski4e/resources/glossary/#P, accessed September 14, 2013.

24. For a detailed bibliography of the precarity literature as well as further definitions of the term, see Berlant, *Cruel Optimism*, 293–94nn1,7.

25. Weeks, *The Problem with Work*, writes that utopian demands can "inspire the political imagination, encourage us to stretch that neglected faculty, and expand our sense of what might be possible in our social and political relations" (206).

26. Taussig, *Ordinary Genomes*.

27. For a reading of Islam in Germany in light of the Nazi legacy and anti-Semitism, see Bunzl, *Anti-Semitism and Islamophobia*. Needless to say, the construction of India as Hindu is erroneous.

28. Marcuse, *Eros and Civilization*, 222. As discussed previously, I use Marcuse's formulation of eros but detach it from the repressive hypothesis, which no longer holds given that, as Foucault taught us, it is not repression but expressivity through which sexuality is put to use.

29. For more on the relationship between South Asian diasporas and the politics of race, the model minority, and assimilation in the U.S. context, see Prashad, *The Karma of Brown Folk* and *Uncle Swami*.

30. Berardi, *Precarious Rhapsody*, 33.

31. In previous, early liberal formulations of freedom, for instance, the juridical freedom of the individual was tied to the political institution of the citizen, but citizenship was not extended equally for all (for instance, to women, slaves, and colonial subjects). Of course, also underlying this kind of

freedom was the freedom of the market—and the "freedom" of workers to sell their labor on the market at a price that labor could command.

32. For an excellent delineation of labor and labor power, see Postone, *Time, Labor, and Social Domination*.

33. For Marx's arguments on the working day, see *Capital*, chap. 10. See also *The Critique of the Gotha Program* for Marx's explanation of the necessary limitations of bourgeois right in *The Marx-Engels Reader*.

34. Hull, *Government of Paper*.

35. Hull, *Government of Paper*, 129–30.

36. This approach to class aligns with what Lauren Bear, Karen Ho, Anna Tsing, and Sylvia Yanagisako describe as the way "inequality emerges from heterogeneous processes through which people, labor, sentiments, plants, animals, and life-ways are converted into resources for various projects of production," in "Gens: A Feminist Manifesto for the Study of Capitalism," http://www.culanth.org/fieldsights/652-gens-a-feminist-manifesto-for-the -study-of-capitalism.

37. For a different take on this novel, see Vora, *Life Support*.

38. Kunzru, *Transmission*, 256.

39. Kunzru encodes a hidden transcript of circulating objects of class and race in knowledge economies. I use a similar method of juxtaposition to understand how the Indian programmer as migrant expert links together stories of capital flow, economic change, and subjectivities.

40. For a similar dynamic of resistance and recuperation in late liberalism, see Povinelli, *Economies of Abandonment*, and Stewart, *Ordinary Affects*.

41. Deleuze, "Postscript on the Societies of Control," 6.

42. Marcuse, *Eros and Civilization*, xxv.

43. Mitropoulos, *Contract and Contagion*, 200.

44. The reference is to "the iron cage" in Weber, *The Protestant Ethic*.

Abraham, Itty. *The Making of the Indian Atomic Bomb: Science, Secrecy, and the Indian State*. London: Zed Books, 1998.

Abu El-Haj, Nadia. "The Genetic Reinscription of Race." *Annual Review of Anthropology* 36 (2007): 283–300.

Adorno, Theodor W. "The Fetish Character in Music and Regression in Listening." In *Essays on Music*, edited by Richard Leppert, 288–317. Translated by Susan H. Gillespie. Berkeley: University of California Press, 2002.

Agamben, Giorgio. *Homo Sacer*. Stanford, CA: Stanford University Press, 1998.

Ahearn, Laura. "Commentary: Keywords as a Literacy Practice in the History of Anthropological Theory." *American Ethnologist* 40, no. 1 (2013): 6–12.

Alleyne, Brian. "Challenging Code: A Sociological Reading of the KDE Free Software Project." *Sociology* 45 (2011): 495–511.

Alter, Joseph S. "The Body of One Color: Indian Wrestling, the Indian State, and Utopian Somatics." *Cultural Anthropology* 8, no. 1 (1993): 49–72.

Alter, Joseph S. "Somatic Nationalism: Indian Wrestling and Militant Hinduism." *Modern Asian Studies* 28, no. 3 (1994): 557–88.

Ameeriar, Lalaie. "The Sanitized Sensorium." *American Anthropologist* 114, no. 3 (2012): 509–20.

Amin, Ash, ed. *Post-Fordism: A Reader*. London: Wiley-Blackwell, 1995.

Amrute, Sareeta. "Living and Praying in the Code: The Flexibility and Discipline of Indian Information Technology Workers (ITers) in a Global Economy." *Anthropology Quarterly* 3, no. 23 (2010): 519–50.

Amrute, Sareeta. "Moving Rape: Trafficking in the Violence of Postliberalization." *Public Culture* 17, no. 2 (2015): 331–59.

Amrute, Sareeta. "Producing Mobility." PhD diss., University of Chicago, 2008.

Amrute, Sareeta. "Proprietary Freedoms in an IT Office: How Indian IT Workers Negotiate Code and Cultural Branding." *Social Anthropology* 22, no. 1 (2014): 101–17.

Amrute, Sareeta. "Where the World Ceases to Be Flat." *India Review* 10, no. 3 (2011): 329–40.

Aneesh, Aneesh. "Global Labor: Algocratic Modes of Organization." *Sociological Theory* 27, no. 4 (2009): 347–70.

Aneesh, Aneesh. *Neutral Accent: How Language, Labor, and Life Become Global.* Durham, NC: Duke University Press, 2015.

Aneesh, Aneesh. *Virtual Migration: The Programming of Globalization.* Durham, NC: Duke University Press, 2006.

Appadurai, Arjun. *Banking on Words: The Failure of Language in the Age of Derivative Finance.* Chicago: University of Chicago Press, 2015.

Appadurai, Arjun. "Is Homo Hierarchicus?" *American Ethnologist* 13, no. 4 (1986): 745–61.

Appadurai, Arjun. *Modernity at Large.* Minneapolis: University of Minnesota Press, 1993.

Appadurai, Arjun. *The Social Life of Things.* Cambridge: Cambridge University Press, 1988.

Aristotle. *Nicomachean Ethics.* Translated by Terence Irwin. Indianapolis: Hackett, 1999.

Arnold, David. "Nehruvian Science and Postcolonial India." *Isis* 104, no. 2 (2013): 360–70.

Arondekar, Anjali R. *For the Record: On Sexuality and the Colonial Archive in India.* Durham, NC: Duke University Press, 2009.

Austin, J. L. *How to Do Things with Words.* Cambridge, MA: Harvard University Press, 1962.

Barad, Karen. *Meeting the Universe Halfway: Quantum Physics and the Entanglement of Matter and Meaning.* Durham, NC: Duke University Press, 2007.

Barad, Karen. "Posthumanist Performativity: Towards an Understanding of How Matter Comes to Matter." *Signs* 28, no. 3 (2003): 801–31.

Barua, Arati, Michael Gerhard, and Matthias Koßler, eds. *Understanding Schopenhauer through the Prism of Indian Culture: Philosophy, Religion, and Sanskrit Literature.* Berlin: De Gruyter, 2012.

Bassett, Ross. "Aligning India in the Cold War Era: Indian Technical Elites, the Indian Institutes of Technology at Kanpur, and Computing in India and the United States." *Technology and Culture* 50, no. 4 (2009): 783–810.

Baudrillard, Jean. *Simulacra and Simulation.* Ann Arbor: University of Michigan Press, 1994.

Baviskar, Amita, and Raka Ray. *Elite and Everyman: The Cultural Politics of the Indian Middle Classes.* New Delhi: Routledge, 2011.

Bear, Laura, Karen Ho, Anna Tsing, and Sylvia Yanagisako. "Gens: A Manifesto for the Study of Capitalism: Theorizing the Contemporary." *Cultural Anthro-*

pology, March 30, 2015. Accessed January 8, 2016. http://www.culanth.org
/fieldsights/652-gens-a-feminist-manifesto-for-the-study-of-capitalism.

Beller, Jonathan. *The Cinematic Mode of Production: Attention Economy and the Society of the Spectacle*. Hanover, NH: Dartmouth College Press, 2006.

Benjamin, Walter. "Paris—Capital of the Nineteenth Century." In *The Arcades Project*, edited by Rolf Tiedemann, 77–88. Cambridge, MA: Belknap Press of Harvard University Press, 2002.

Berardi, Franco "Bifo." "Cognitarian Subjectivation." *e-flux*, 2010. Accessed July 10, 2014. http://www.e-flux.com/journal/cognitarian-subjectivation/.

Berardi, Franco "Bifo." *Precarious Rhapsody: Semiocapitalism and the Pathologies of the Post-alpha Generation*. Boston: Semiotext(e), 2009.

Berardi, Franco "Bifo." *The Soul at Work: From Alienation to Autonomy*. Los Angeles: Semiotext(e), 2009.

Berlant, Lauren. *Cruel Optimism*. Durham, NC: Duke University Press, 2009.

Bernal, Victoria. "Please Forget Democracy and Justice: Eritrean Politics and the Powers of Humor." *American Ethnologist* 40, no. 2 (2013): 300–309.

Berry, David M. *The Philosophy of Software: Code and Mediation in the Digital Age*. London: Palgrave Macmillan, 2011.

Besnier, Niko, and Susan Brownell. "Sport, Modernity, and the Body." *Annual Review of Anthropology* 41, no. 1 (2012): 443–59.

Bhabha, Homi. *The Location of Culture*. London: Routledge, 2004.

Biao, Xiang. *Global Bodyshopping*. Princeton, NJ: Princeton University Press, 2006.

Bond, David, and Luc Bessire. "The Ontological Spin" Commentary. *Cultural Anthropology*, February 28, 2014. Accessed January 7, 2016. http://culanth.org /fieldsights/494-the-ontological-spin.

Bonilla-Silva, Eduardo. *Racism without Racists: Color-Blind Racism and the Persistence of Racial Inequality in America*. 3d ed. Lanham, MD: Rowman and Littlefield, 2009.

Borneman, John. *Belonging in the Two Berlins: Kin, State, Nation*. Princeton, NJ: Princeton University Press, 1992.

Bourdieu, Pierre. *Distinction: A Social Critique of the Judgment of Taste*. Cambridge, MA: Harvard University Press, 1984.

Bourdieu, Pierre. *Language and Symbolic Power*. Edited by John B. Thompson. Cambridge, MA: Harvard University Press, 1991.

Boyer, Dominic. "The Corporeality of Expertise." *Ethnos* 70, no. 2 (2005): 141–48.

Boyer, Dominic. "Thinking through the Anthropology of Experts." *Anthropology in Action* 15, no. 2 (2008): 38–46.

Boyer, Dominic, and Alexei Yurchak. "American Stiob: Or, What Late-Socialist Aesthetics of Parody Reveal about Contemporary Political Culture in the West." *Cultural Anthropology* 25, no. 2 (2010): 179–221.

Boyle, James. "The Second Enclosure Movement and the Construction of the Public Domain." *Law and Contemporary Problems* 66 (2003): 33–74.

Bröckling, Ulrich. "Gendering the Enterprising Self: Subjectification Programs and Gender Differences in Guides to Success." *Distinktion* 11 (2005): 7–23.

Brosius, Christiane. *India's Middle Class: New Forms of Urban Leisure, Consumption and Prosperity*. London: Routledge, 2010.

Brown, Wendy. *Regulating Aversion: Tolerance in the Age of Identity and Empire*. Princeton, NJ: Princeton University Press, 2008.

Brubaker, Rogers. *Citizenship and Nationhood in France and Germany*. Cambridge, MA: Harvard University Press, 1994.

Bunzl, Matti. *Anti-Semitism and Islamophobia: Hatreds Old and New in Europe*. Chicago: Prickly Paradigm Press, 2007.

Burawoy, Michael, ed. *Global Ethnography: Forces, Connections, and Imaginations in a Postmodern World*. Berkeley: University of California Press, 2000.

Burton, Antoinette. *Dwelling in the Archive: Women Writing House, Home, and History in Late Colonial India*. Oxford: Oxford University Press, 2003.

Butler, Judith. *Bodies That Matter: On the Discursive Limits of "Sex."* New York: Routledge, 1993.

Callon, Michael. "Some Elements of a Sociology of Translation: Domestication of the Scallops and the Fishermen of St. Brieuc Bay." In *Power, Action and Belief: A New Sociology of Knowledge?*, ed. John Law, 196–223. London: Routledge, 1986.

Campt, Tina. *Image Matters: Archive, Photography, and the African Diaspora*. Ann Arbor: University of Michigan Press, 2012.

Castells, Manuel. *The Rise of the Network Society*. Malden, MA: Blackwell, 1996.

Chakrabarty, Dipesh. *Habitations of Modernity: Essays in the Wake of Subaltern Studies*. Chicago: University of Chicago Press, 2002.

Chakrabarty, Dipesh. *Provincializing Europe: Postcolonial Thought and Historical Difference*. Princeton, NJ: Princeton University Press, 2000.

Chakravartty, Paula. "Weak Winners of Globalization: Indian H-1B Workers in the American Information Economy." *aapi nexus* 3, no. 2 (2005): 1–25.

Chanana, Charanjit. *Computers in Asia*. New Delhi: Marketing and Economic Research Bureau, 1973.

Chatterjee, Partha. "The Nationalist Resolution of the Women's Question." In *Recasting Women: Essays in Colonial History*, edited by Kumkum Sangari and Sudesh Vaid, 233–53. Delhi: Kali for Women, 1989.

Chatterjee, Partha. *The Nation and Its Fragments*. Princeton, NJ: Princeton University Press, 1993.

Chatterjee, Partha. *The Politics of the Governed: Reflections on Popular Politics*. New York: Columbia University Press, 2006.

Chin, Rita. *The Guest Worker Question in Postwar Germany*. Cambridge: Cambridge University Press, 2007.

Cho, Joanne Miyang, Eric Kurlander, and Douglas T. McGetchin, eds. *Transcultural Encounters between Germany and India: Kindred Spirits in the Nineteenth and Twentieth Centuries*. London: Routledge, 2014.

Chun, Wendy Hui Kyong. *Programmed Visions: Software and Memory*. Cambridge, MA: MIT Press, 2013.

Clifford, James. "On Ethnographic Allegory." In *Writing Culture: The Poetics and Politics of Ethnography*, edited by James Clifford and George E. Marcus, 98–121. Santa Fe, NM: SAR Press.

Coleman, Beth. "Race as Technology." *Camera Obscura* 24, no. 1 (2009): 177–207.

Coleman, Gabriella. "Code Is Speech: Legal Tinkering, Expertise, and Protest among Free and Open Source Software Developers." *Cultural Anthropology* 24, no. 3 (2009): 420–54.

Coleman, Gabriella. *Coding Freedom: The Ethics and Aesthetics of Hacking*. Princeton, NJ: Princeton University Press, 2013.

Coleman, Gabriella. "Ethnographic Approaches to Digital Media." *Annual Review of Anthropology* 39 (2010): 1–16.

Collier, Jane, Michelle Z. Rosaldo, and Sylvia Yanagisako. "Is There a Family?" In *The Gender/Sexuality Reader*, edited by R. Lancaster and M. di Leonardo, 71–81. London: Routledge, 1997.

Collier, Stephen J. *Post-Soviet Social: Neoliberalism, Social Modernity, Biopolitics*. Princeton, NJ: Princeton University Press, 2011.

Comaroff, Jean. *Body of Power, Spirit of Resistance: The Culture and History of a South African People*. Chicago: University of Chicago Press, 1985.

Comaroff, John L., and Jean Comaroff. *Ethnicity, Inc.* Chicago: University of Chicago Press, 2009.

Cooper, Melinda E. *Life as Surplus: Biotechnology and Capitalism in the Neoliberal Era*. Seattle: University of Washington Press, 2008.

Cooper, Melinda E. "Marx beyond Marx, Marx before Marx: Negri's Lucretian Critique of the Hegelian Marx." In *Reading Negri: Marxism in the Age of Empire*, edited by Pierre Lamarche, Max Rosenkrantz, and David Sherman, 127–48. Chicago: Open Court, 2011.

Corbridge, Stuart, and John Harriss. *Reinventing India: Liberalization, Hindu Nationalism, and Popular Democracy*. Cambridge: Polity, 2000.

Cowan, Robert. *The Indo-German Identification: Reconciling South Asian Origins and European Destinies, 1765–1885*. Rochester, NY: Camden House, 2010.

Crary, Jonathan. *24/7: Late Capitalism and the Ends of Sleep*. New York: Verso, 2014.

Dave, Naisagiri. *Queer Activism in India: A Story in the Anthropology of Ethics*. Durham, NC: Duke University Press, 2012.

de Certeau, Michel. *The Practice of Everyday Life*. Translated by Steven Rendall. Berkeley: University of California Press, 1984.

Deleuze, Gilles. "Postscript on the Societies of Control." *October* 59 (1992): 3–7.

Derrida, Jacques. *Given Time: 1. Counterfeit Money*. Chicago: University of Chicago Press, 1992.

Deshpande, Satish. *Contemporary India: A Sociological View*. New Delhi: Viking, 2003.

Dirks, Nicholas B. *Castes of Mind: Colonialism and the Making of Modern India.* Princeton, NJ: Princeton University Press, 2001.

Douglas, Mary. *Implicit Meanings: Essays in Anthropology.* London: Routledge and Kegan Paul, 1975.

Downey, Gary Lee, and Joseph Dumit. *Cyborgs and Citadels: Anthropological Interventions in Emerging Sciences and Technologies.* Santa Fe, NM: SAR Press, 1997.

Du Plessis, Paul. *Borkowski's Textbook on Roman Law 4e.* Accessed September 14, 2013. http://global.oup.com/uk/orc/law/roman/borkowski4e/resources /glossary/#P.

Dusche, Michael. "Friedrich Schlegel's Writings on India." In *Deploying Orientalism in Culture and History: From Germany to Central and Eastern Europe,* edited by James Hodkinson and John Walker, with Shaswati Mazumdar and Johannes Feichtinger, 31–54. Rochester, NY: Camden House, 2013.

Dyer-Witheford, Nick. "Empire, Immaterial Labor, the New Combinations, and the Global Worker." *Rethinking Marxism* 13, nos. 3–4 (2001): 70–80.

Eckert, Roland. "Xenophobia and Violence in Germany 1990 to 2000." *International Journal of Comparative and Applied Criminal Justice* 26, no. 2 (2002): 231–46.

Edwards, Brent. *The Practice of Diaspora: Literature, Translation, and the Rise of Black Internationalism.* Cambridge, MA: Harvard University Press, 2003.

Eglash, Ron. *African Fractals: Modern Computing and Indigenous Design.* New Brunswick, NJ: Rutgers University Press, 1999.

El-Tayeb, Fatima. "The Birth of a European Public: Migration, Postnationality, and Race in the Uniting of Europe." *American Quarterly* 60, no. 3 (2008): 649–70.

El-Tayeb, Fatima. " 'Blood Is a Very Special Juice': Racialized Bodies and Citizenship in Twentieth-Century Germany." *International Review of Social History* 44, no. 7 (2008): 149–69.

End Notes. "The History of Subsumption." 2 (April 2010). Accessed January 10, 2014. http://endnotes.org.uk/en/endnotes-the-history-of-subsumption.

Ewing, Katherine Pratt. *Stolen Honor: Stigmatizing Muslim Men in Berlin.* Stanford, CA: Stanford University Press, 2008.

Fabian, Johannes. "Presence and Representation: The Other and Anthropological Writing." *Critical Inquiry* 16, no. 4 (1990): 753–72.

Fabian, Johannes. *Time and the Other: How Anthropology Makes Its Object.* New York: Columbia University Press, 1983.

Fanon, Frantz. *Black Skin, White Masks.* New York: Grove Press, 2008.

Farquhar, Judith, and Qicheng Zang. "Biopolitical Beijing: Pleasure, Sovereignty, and Self-Cultivation in China's Capital." *Cultural Anthropology* 20, no. 3 (2005): 303–27.

Faruqi, Shamsur Rahman. *Early Urdu Literary Culture and History.* Oxford: Oxford University Press, 2001.

Fernandes, Leela. *India's New Middle Class: Democratic Politics in an Era of Economic Reform.* Minneapolis: University of Minnesota Press, 2006.

Fernandes, Leela. "The Politics of Forgetting: Class Politics, State Power and the Restructuring of Urban Space in India." *Urban Studies* 41, no. 12 (2004): 2415–30.

Figueira, Dorothy Matilda. *Aryans, Jews, Brahmins: Theorizing Authority through Myths of Identity*. Albany: State University of New York Press, 2002.

Floyd, Kevin. "Rethinking Reification." *Social Text* 19, no. 1 (2001): 103–28.

Foucault, Michel. "Body/Power." In *Power/Knowledge: Selected Interviews and Other Writings*, edited by Colin Gordon, 55–62. New York: Pantheon, 1980.

Foucault, Michel. *The History of Sexuality*. Vol. 1, *An Introduction*. New York: Vintage, 1990.

Foucault, Michel. *The History of Sexuality*. Vol. 2, *The Use of Pleasure*. New York: Vintage, 1990.

Foucault, Michel. "Polemics, Politics and Problematizations." In *Essential Works of Foucault*, edited by Paul Rabinow, 1998. Accessed December 7, 2015. http://foucault.info/foucault/interview.html.

Foucault, Michel. *Security, Territory, Population: Lectures at the Collège de France, 1977–1978*. New York: Picador, 2007.

Fuller, Chris, and Haripriya Narasimhan. "Information Technology Professionals and the New-Rich Middle Class in Chennai (Madras)." *Modern Asian Studies* 41, no. 1 (2007): 121–50.

Fuller, Matthew. *Behind the Blip: Essays on the Culture of Software*. Brooklyn, NY: Autonomedia, 2003.

Fuller, Matthew. *Software Studies: A Lexicon*. Cambridge, MA: MIT Press, 2008.

Galloway, Alexander. "Networks." In *Critical Terms for Media Studies*, edited by W. J. T. Mitchell and B. N. Hansen, 280–96. Chicago: University of Chicago Press, 2010.

Galloway, Alexander. *Protocol: How Control Exists after Decentralization*. Cambridge, MA: MIT Press, 2004.

Gamburd, Michele Ruth. *The Kitchen Spoon's Handle: Transnationalism and Sri Lanka's Migrant Housemaids*. Ithaca, NY: Cornell University Press, 2000.

Garwood, Ian. "Shifting Pitch: The Bollywood Song Sequence in the Anglo-American Market." In *Asian Cinemas: A Reader and Guide*, edited by D. Eleftheriotis and G. Needham, 346–57. Honolulu: University of Hawai'i Press, 2006.

Gary, Anita, and Karen V. Hansen, eds. *At the Heart of Work and Family: Engaging the Ideas of Arlie Hochschild*. New Brunswick, NJ: Rutgers University Press, 2011.

Gell, Alfred. *Art and Agency: An Anthropological Theory*. Oxford: Oxford University Press, 1998.

George, Rosemary Marangoly. *The Politics of Home: Postcolonial Relocations and Twentieth-Century Fiction*. Berkeley: University of California Press, 1999.

Ghosh, Anindita, ed. *Behind the Veil: Resistance, Women and the Everyday in Colonial South Asia*. London: Palgrave Macmillan, 2008.

Ghosh, Rishab, ed. CODE: *Collaborative Ownership and the Digital Economy*. Cambridge, MA: MIT Press, 2005.

Gilman, Sander. "Thilo Sarrazin and the Politics of Race in the Twenty-First Century." *New German Critique* 117, 39, no. 3 (2012): 47–59.

Goffman, Erving. *Frame Analysis: An Essay on the Organization of Experience.* Edited by Bennett Berger. Boston: Northeastern University Press, 1986.

Gopinath, Gayatri. *Impossible Desires: Queer Diasporas and South Asian Public Cultures.* Durham, NC: Duke University Press, 2005.

Gosseries, Axel. "How (Un)fair Is Intellectual Property?" In *Intellectual Property and Theories of Justice,* edited by Axel Gosseries, Alain Marciano, and Alain Strowel, 3–26. London: Palgrave Macmillan, 2008.

Gosseries, Axel, Alain Marciano, and Alain Strowel, eds. *Intellectual Property and Theories of Justice.* London: Palgrave Macmillan, 2008.

Gottschlich, Pierre. "Developing a Knowledge Base for Policymaking on India-EU Migration." *CARIM-India RR* 3 (2012):1–25.

Graeber, David. *Debt: The First 5,000 Years.* New York: Melville House, 2012.

Graeber, David. "Radical Alterity Is Just Another Way of Saying 'Reality': A Reply to Eduardo Viveiros de Castro." *HAU: Journal of Ethnographic Theory* 5, no. 2 (2015): 1–41.

Graeber, David. *Towards an Anthropological Theory of Value: The False Coin of Our Own Dreams.* New York: Palgrave Macmillan, 2001.

Gray, Chris Hables. *The Cyborg Handbook.* New York: Routledge, 1995.

Green, Nile. "Breathing in India, c. 1890." *Modern Asian Studies* 42, nos. 2–3 (2008): 283–315.

Grewal, Inderpal. *Home and Harem: Nation, Gender, Empire, and the Cultures of Travel.* Durham, NC: Duke University Press, 1996.

Grieco, Joseph M. *Between Dependency and Autonomy: India's Experience with the International Computer Industry.* Berkeley: University of California Press, 1984.

Grossberg, Lawrence. *Cultural Studies in the Future Tense.* Durham, NC: Duke University Press, 2010.

Guha, Ramachandra. *India after Gandhi: The History of the World's Largest Democracy.* New York: Ecco, 2007.

Guins, Raiford. *The Object Reader.* Edited by Fiona Candlin. London: Routledge, 2008.

Gupta, Akhil. *Postcolonial Developments.* Stanford, CA: Stanford University Press, 1995.

Gupta, Akhil, and Aradhana Sharma. "Globalization and Postcolonial States." *Current Anthropology* 47, no. 2 (2006): 277–307.

Guyer, Jane. "Prophecy and the Near Future: Thoughts on Macroeconomic, Evangelical, and Punctuated Time." *American Ethnologist* 34, no. 3 (2007): 409–21.

Hacking, Ian. "Making Up People." In *Reconstructing Individualism: Autonomy, Individuality and the Self in Western Thought,* edited by Thomas Heller, Morton Sosner, and David Wellerby, 222–36. Stanford, CA: Stanford University Press, 1986.

Hannerz, Ulf. "Other Transnationals: Perspectives Gained from Studying Sideways." *Paideuma* 44 (1998): 109–23.

Haraway, Donna. "A Cyborg Manifesto: Science, Technology, and Socialist-Feminism in the Late Twentieth Century." In *Simians, Cyborgs, and Women: The Reinvention of Nature*, 149–81. New York: Routledge, 1991.

Haraway, Donna. *Primate Visions: Gender, Race, and Nature in the World of Modern Science*. New York: Routledge, 1989.

Hardt, Michael. "Affective Labor." *boundary 2* 26, no. 2 (1999): 89–100.

Hardt, Michael. "The Global Society of Control." *Discourse* 20, no. 3 (1998): 139–52.

Hardt, Michael. "The Withering of Civil Society." *Social Text* 45 (1995): 27–44.

Hardt, Michael, and Antonio Negri. *Empire*. Cambridge, MA: Harvard University Press, 2000.

Hardt, Michael, and Antonio Negri. *Multitude: War and Democracy in the Age of Empire*. New York: Penguin Press, 2004.

Hart, Keith. "'Anthropology' and the New Human Universal." *Social Anthropology* 18, no. 4 (2010): 441–47.

Harvey, David. *A Brief History of Neoliberalism*. Oxford: Oxford University Press, 2005.

Harvey, David. *The Condition of Postmodernity: An Enquiry into the Origins of Cultural Change*. Oxford: Wiley-Blackwell, 1991.

Hayles, Katherine. *My Mother Was a Computer*. Chicago: University of Chicago Press, 2005.

Heidegger, Martin. "Questioning concerning Technology." In *Basic Writings*, 287–317. San Francisco: Harper and Row, 1977.

Heidegger, Martin. "The Thing." In *The Object Reader*, edited by Fiona Candlin and Raiford Guins, 163–86. London: Routledge. 2009.

Heiman, Rachel, Carla Freeman, and Mark Liechty. *The Global Middle Classes: Theorizing through Ethnography*. Santa Fe, NM: SAR Press, 2012.

Heller, Patrick, and Leela Fernandes. "Hegemonic Aspirations." *Critical Asian Studies* 38, no. 4 (2006): 495–522.

Helmreich, Stefan. "An Anthropologist Underwater: Immersive Soundscapes, Submarine Cyborgs, Transductive Ethnography." *American Ethnologist* 34, no. 4 (2007): 621–41.

Herder, Johann Gottfried. *Ideen zur Philosophie der Geschichte der Menschheit* [Ideas for the philosophy of the history of humanity]. Berlin: Holzinger, 2013.

Herzfeld, Michael. *Cultural Intimacy: Social Poetics in the Nation-State*. New York: Routledge, 2005.

Ho, Engseng. *The Graves of Tarim*. Berkeley: University of California Press, 2006.

Ho, Karen. *Liquidated: An Ethnography of Wall Street*. Durham, NC: Duke University Press, 2009.

Hodkinson, James, and John Walker, eds. *Deploying Orientalism in Culture and History: From Germany to Central and Eastern Europe*, with Shaswati Mazumdar and Johannes Feichtinger. Rochester, NY: Camden House, 2013.

Holmes, Brian. "The Flexible Personality: For a New Cultural Critique." *Transversal* (2002). Accessed June 20, 2014. http://eipcp.net/transversal/1106/holmes/en.

hooks, bell. "Eating the Other: Desire and Resistance." In *Media and Cultural Studies: Keywords*, edited by Meenakshi Gigi Durham and Douglas M. Kellner, 366–80. Malden, MA: Blackwell, 2001.

Hull, Matthew. *Government of Paper: The Materiality of Bureaucracy in Urban Pakistan*. Berkeley: University of California Press, 2012.

Hutzschenreuter, Thomas, Arie Y. Lewin, and Wolfgang Ressler. "The Growth of White-Collar Offshoring: Germany and the US from 1980 to 2006." *European Management Journal* 29, no. 4 (2011): 245–59.

Huyssen, Andreas. "The Voids of Berlin." *Critical Inquiry* 24, no. 1 (1997): 57–81.

Ibrahim, Habiba. *Troubling the Family: The Promise of Personhood and the Rise of Multiracialism*. Minneapolis: University of Minnesota Press, 2012.

Inden, Ronald. *Imagining India*. Bloomington: Indiana University Press, 2001.

Ingold, Tim. "Toward an Ecology of Materials." *Annual Review of Anthropology* 41, no. 1 (2012): 427–42.

Jackson, John L. "Gentrification, Globalization, and Georaciality." In *Globalization and Race: Transformations in the Cultural Production of Blackness*, edited by M. K. Clarke and D. A. Thomas, 188–205. Durham, NC: Duke University Press, 2006.

Jain, Kajri. *Gods in the Bazaar: The Economies of Indian Calendar Art*. Durham, NC: Duke University Press, 2007.

Janis, Michael. "Obama, Africa, and the Post-Racial." *CLCWeb: Comparative Literature and Culture* 11, no. 2 (2009): 1–12.

Jaszi, Peter. "On the Author Effect: Contemporary Copyright and Collective Creativity." In *The Construction of Authorship: Textual Appropriation in Law and Literature*, edited by Martha Woodmansee and Peter Jaszi, 29–56. New York: Columbia University Press, 1994.

Jeffrey, Craig. *Timepass: Youth, Class, and the Politics of Waiting in India*. Stanford, CA: Stanford University Press, 2010.

Joppke, Christian. "Multiculturalism and Immigration: A Comparison of the United States, Germany, and Great Britain." *Theory and Society* 25, no. 4 (1996): 449–500.

Joseph, Ralina. *Transcending Blackness: From the New Millennium Mulatta to the Exceptional Multiracial*. Durham, NC: Duke University Press, 2012.

Joshi, Sanjay. *The Middle Class in Colonial India*. New Delhi: Oxford University Press, 2010.

Kant, Immanuel. "Perpetual Peace: A Philosophical Sketch." In *Kant: Political Writings*, edited by Hans Reiss, 93–130. Cambridge: Cambridge University Press, 1991.

Kapur, Devesh. *Diaspora, Development, and Democracy: The Domestic Impact of International Migration from India*. Princeton, NJ: Princeton University Press, 2010.

Kaur, Ravinder. "Viewing the West through Bollywood: A Celluloid Occident in the Making." *Contemporary South Asia* 11, no. 2 (2002): 199.

Kaviraj, Sudipta. "Laughter and Subjectivity: The Self-Ironical Tradition in Bengali Literature." *The Invention of Private Life: Literature and Ideas*, 219–50. Ranikhet: Permanent Black, 2014.

Kaviraj, Sudipta. "Filth and the Public Sphere: Concepts and Practices about Space in Calcutta." *Public Culture* 10, no. 1 (1997): 83–113.

Kelty, Christopher. *Two Bits: The Cultural Significance of Free Software*. Durham, NC: Duke University Press, 2008.

Khilnani, Sunil. *The Idea of India*. New York: Farrar, Straus and Giroux, 1999.

King, Christopher R. *One Language, Two Scripts: The Hindi Movement in Nineteenth Century North India*. Oxford: Oxford University Press, 1995.

Knorr Cetina, Karin. "Culture in Global Knowledge Societies: Knowledge Cultures and Epistemic Cultures." *Interdisciplinary Science Reviews* 32, no. 4 (2007): 361–75.

Knorr Cetina, Karin. "Sociality with Objects: Social Relations in Postsocial Knowledge Societies." *Theory, Culture, and Society* 14, no. 4 (1997): 1–30.

Kockelman, Paul. "From Status to Contract Revisited: Value, Temporality, Circulation and Subjectivity." *Anthropological Theory* 7, no. 2 (2007): 151–76.

Kolb, Holger. *The German "Green Card." Focus:* MIGRATION, no. 3 (2005): 1–3. Accessed December 16, 2014. http://focus-migration.hwwi.de/index.php?id =1198&L=1.

Kolb, Holger. "Pragmatische Routine und Symbolische Inszenierung—Zum Ende der Green Card." *Zeitschrift für Ausländerrecht und Ausländerpolitik* 7 (2003): 231–35.

Kolko, Beth E., Lisa Nakamura, and Gilbert B. Rodman. *Race in Cyberspace*. New York: Routledge, 2000.

Kontje, Todd. "Germany's Local Orientalisms." In *Deploying Orientalism in Culture and History: From Germany to Central and Eastern Europe*, edited by James Hodkinson and John Walker, with Shaswati Mazumdar and Johannes Feichtinger, 55–77. Rochester, NY: Camden House, 2013.

Koopmans, Ruud. "Rechtsextremismus und Fremdenfeindlichkeit in Deutschland: Probleme von Heute—Diagnosen von Gestern." *Leviathan* 29, no. 4 (2001):469–83.

Kracauer, Siegfried. *The Salaried Masses: Duty and Distraction in Weimar Germany*. Translated by Quintin Hoare. London: Verso, 1998.

Kunda, Gideon. *Engineering Culture: Control and Commitment in a High-Tech Corporation*. Philadelphia: Temple University Press, 1992.

Kunda, Gideon, and Stephen R. Barley. *Gurus, Hired Guns and Warm Bodies: Itinerant Experts in a Knowledge Economy*. Princeton, NJ: Princeton University Press, 2006.

Kunzru, Hari. *Transmission*. New York: Plume, 2005.

Kymlicka, Will. *Politics in the Vernacular: Nationalism, Multiculturalism, and Citizenship*. Oxford: Oxford University Press, 2001.

Ladd, Brian. *The Ghosts of Berlin: Confronting German History in the Urban Landscape*. Chicago: University of Chicago Press, 1998.

Latour, Bruno. *An Inquiry into Modes of Existence: An Anthropology of the Moderns*. Cambridge, MA: Harvard University Press, 2013.

Latour, Bruno. *Science in Action: How to Follow Scientists and Engineers through Society*. Cambridge, MA: Harvard University Press, 1988.

Law, John. "On the Subject of the Object: Narrative, Technology and Interpellation." *Configurations*, no. 8: 1–29.

Lazzarato, Maurizio. "From Capital-Labour to Capital-Life." *ephemera* 4, no. 3 (2004): 187–208.

Lazzarato, Maurizio. "Immaterial Labor." In *Radical Thought in Italy: A Potential Politics*, edited by Paolo Virno and Michael Hardt, 133–50. Minneapolis: University of Minnesota Press, 1996.

Leslie, Stuart W., and Robert Kargon. "Exporting MIT: Science, Technology, and Nation-Building in India and Iran." *Osiris* 21, no. 1 (2006): 110–30.

Lessig, Lawrence. *Code and Other Laws of Cyberspace*. New York: Basic Books, 1999.

Liechty, Mark. *Suitably Modern: Making Middle-Class Culture in a New Consumer Society*. Princeton, NJ: Princeton University Press, 2002.

Linke, Uli. *Blood and Nation: The European Aesthetics of Race*. Philadelphia: University of Pennsylvania Press, 1999.

Linke, Uli. *German Bodies: Race and Representation after Hitler*. New York: Routledge, 1999.

LiPuma, Edward, and Benjamin Lee. *Financial Derivatives and the Globalization of Risk*. Durham, NC: Duke University Press, 2004.

Lockwood, David. *The Indian Bourgeoisie: A Political History of the Indian Capitalist Class in the Early Twentieth Century*. London: I. B. Tauris, 2012.

Lowe, Lisa. "Metaphors of Globalization." In *Interdisciplinarity and Social Justice*, edited by Ranu Samantrai, Joe Parker, and Mary Romer, 37–62. Albany: State University of New York Press, 2010.

Lukose, Ritty. *Liberalization's Children: Gender, Youth, and Consumer Citizenship in Globalizing India*. Durham, NC: Duke University Press, 2009.

Mackenzie, Adrian. *Cutting Code*. New York: Peter Lang, 2006.

Mackenzie, Adrian. *Transductions: Bodies and Machines at Speed*. New York: Continuum, 2002.

Majumdar, Rochona. *Marriage and Modernity: Family Values in Colonial Bengal*. Durham, NC: Duke University Press, 2009.

Manjapra, Kris. *Age of Entanglement: German and Indian Intellectuals across Empire*. Cambridge, MA: Harvard University Press, 2013.

Mankekar, Purnima. *Unsettling India: Affect, Temporality, Transnationality*. Durham, NC: Duke University Press, 2015.

Manz, Stefan. "Constructing a Normative National Identity: The Leitkultur Debate in Germany, 2000/2001." *Journal of Multilingual and Multicultural Development* 25, nos. 5–6 (2004): 481–96.

Marchand, Susan. *German Orientalism in the Age of Empire: Religion, Race, and Scholarship*. Cambridge: Cambridge University Press, 2010.

Marcuse, Herbert. *Eros and Civilization: A Philosophical Inquiry into Freud*. Boston: Beacon Press, 1955.

Marino, Mark C. "Critical Code Studies." *Electronic Book Review* (2006). Accessed July 11, 2014. http://www.electronicbookreview.com/thread/electropoetics/codology.

Markell, Patchen. *Bound by Recognition*. Princeton, NJ: Princeton University Press, 2003.

Martin-Jones, David. "Kabhi India Kabhie Scotland." *South Asian Popular Culture* 4, no. 1 (2006): 49–60.

Marx, Karl. "The British Rule in India." In *The Marx-Engels Reader,* edited by Robert C. Tucker, 653–64. New York: W. W. Norton, 1978.

Marx, Karl. *Capital*. Vol. 1. New York: Penguin, 1976.

Mauss, Marcel. *The Gift*. New York: W. W. Norton, 1976.

Mauss, Marcel. "Techniques of the Body." *Economy and Society* 2, no. 1 (1973): 70–88.

Mazumdar, Shaswati. "The Jew, the Turk, and the Indian: Figurations of the Oriental in the German-Speaking World." In *Deploying Orientalism in Culture and History: From Germany to Central and Eastern Europe*, edited by James Hodkinson and John Walker, with Shaswati Mazumdar and Johannes Feichtinger, 99–116. Rochester, NY: Camden House, 2013.

Mazzarella, William. "Affect: What Is It Good For?" In *Enchantments of Modernity: Empire, Nation, Globalization*, edited by Saurabh Dube, 291–309. New York: Routledge, 2009.

Mazzarella, William. *Shoveling Smoke*. Durham, NC: Duke University Press, 2003.

Mbembe, Achille. "Necropolitics," trans. Libby Meintjes. *Public Culture* 15, no. 1 (2003): 11–40.

Mbembe, Achille. *On the Postcolony*. Berkeley: University of California Press, 2001.

McGetchin, Douglas T., Peter K. J. Park, and D. R. SarDesai, eds. *Sanskrit and "Orientalism": Indology and Comparative Linguistics in Germany, 1750–1958*. New Delhi: Manohar, 2004.

Mehta, Uday S. "Indian Constitutionalism: The Articulation of a Political Vision." In *From the Colonial to the Postcolonial: India and Pakistan in Transition*, edited by Rochona Majumdar and Andrew Sartori, 13–30. Oxford: Oxford University Press, 2007.

Meijering, Louise, and Bettina van Hoven. "Imagining Difference: The Experiences of 'Transnational' Indian IT Professionals in Germany." *Area* 35, no. 2 (2003): 174–82.

Memmi, Albert. *Racism*. Minneapolis: University of Minnesota Press, 2000.

Miller, Peter, and Nikolas Rose. "Production, Identity, and Democracy." *Theory and Society* 24, no. 3 (1995): 427–67.

Mitropoulos, Angela. *Contract and Contagion: From Biopolitics to Oikonomia*. New York: Autonomedia, 2012.

Mohanty, Chandra Talpade. *Feminism without Borders: Decolonizing Theory, Practicing Solidarity*. Durham, NC: Duke University Press, 2003.

Mol, Annemarie. "Actor-Network Theory: Sensitive Terms and Enduring Tensions." *Kölner Zeitschrift für Soziologie und Sozialpsychologie*, no. 50 (2010): 253–69.

Mol, Annemarie. *The Body Multiple: Ontology in Medical Practice*. Durham, NC: Duke University Press, 2002.

Moritz Schwarcz, Lilia K. "The Banana Emperor: D. Pedro II in Brazilian Caricatures, 1842–89." *American Ethnologist* 40, no. 2 (2013): 310–23.

Muehlebach, Andrea. *The Moral Neoliberal: Welfare and Citizenship in Italy*. Chicago: University of Chicago Press, 2012.

Munn, Nancy D. "Constructing Regional Worlds in Experience: Kula Exchange, Witchcraft and Gawan Local Events." *Man* 25, no. 1 (1990): 1–17.

Munn, Nancy D. *The Fame of Gawa: A Symbolic Study of Value Transformation in a Massim (Papua New Guinea) Society*. New York: Cambridge University Press, 1986.

Murti, Kamakshi P. *India: The Seductive and Seduced "Other" of German Orientalism*. Westport, CT: Greenwood Press, 2001.

Myers, Fred R. *The Empire of Things: Regimes of Value and Material Culture*. Santa Fe, NM: SAR Press, 2001.

Nadeem, Shezad. *Dead Ringers*. Princeton, NJ: Princeton University Press, 2010.

Nader, Laura. "Up the Anthropologist." In *Reinventing Anthropology*, edited by Dell Hymes, 284–311. New York: Pantheon, 1969.

Nakamura, Lisa. *Digitizing Race: Visual Cultures of the Internet*. Minneapolis: University of Minnesota Press, 2007.

Negri, Antonio. *Marx beyond Marx: Lessons on the Grundrisse*. New York: Pluto Press, 1992.

Nehru, Jawaharlal. "Scientists and an Integrated View of Life," Speech at the Inauguration of the 43rd Session of the Indian Science Congress, Agra, 2 January 1956." In *Nehru's India: Select Speeches*, 209–22. Oxford: Oxford University Press, 2007.

Nehru, Jawaharlal. "Speech at the Administrative Staff College of India, Hyderabad." In *Jawaharlal Nehru on Science and Society: A Collection of His Writings and Speeches*, edited by Baldev Singh, 166–73. New Delhi: Nehru Memorial Museum and Library, 1988.

Nehru, Jawaharlal. "Tryst with Destiny." In *Sources of Indian Tradition*, vol. 2, edited by: Rachel Fell McDermott, Leonard A. Gordon, Ainslie T. Embree, Frances W. Pritchett, and Dennis Dalton, 595. New York: Columbia University Press, 2014.

Nelson, Alondra. "Bio Science: Genetic Genealogical Testing and the Pursuit of African Ancestry." *Social Studies of Science* 38, no. 5 (2008): 759–83.

Nelson, Alondra, and Thuy Linh N. Tu, eds., with Alicia Hedlam Hines. *Technicolor: Race, Technology, and Everyday Life*. New York: New York University Press, 2001.

Nilekani, Nandan. *Imagining India: The Idea of a Renewed Nation*. New York: Penguin Press, 2009.

Nisbett, Nicholas. "Friendship, Consumption, Morality: Practising Identity, Negotiating Hierarchy in Middle-Class Bangalore." *Journal of the Royal Anthropological Institute* 13, no. 4 (2007): 935–50.

Nishime, Leilani. *Undercover Asian: Multiracial Asian Americans in Visual Culture*. Urbana: University of Illinois Press, 2014.

Oberkircher, Volker. "Die Deutsche Greencard aus der Sicht Indischer IT-Experten." In *Masala.de Menschen aus Südasien in Deutschland*, edited by Christiane Brosius and Urmila Goel, 161–88. Heidelberg: Draupadi Verlag, 2006.

O'Carroll, Aileen. "Fuzzy Holes and Intangible Time: Time in a Knowledge Industry." *Time and Society* 17 (2008): 179–93.

O'Hanlon, Rosalind. *A Comparison between Women and Men: Tarabai Shinde and the Critique of Gender Relations in Colonial India*. Madras: Oxford University Press, 1994.

Omi, Michael, and Howard Winant. *Racial Formation in the United States*. 3d ed. New York: Routledge, 2014.

Ong, Aihwa. *Flexible Citizenship: The Cultural Logics of Transnationality*. Durham, NC: Duke University Press, 1999.

Ong, Aihwa. *Spirits of Resistance and Capitalist Discipline: Factory Women in Malaysia*. Albany: State University of New York Press, 1987.

Otyakmaz, Berrin Özlem. *Auf allen Stühlen: Das Selbstverständnis junger türkischer Migrantinnen in Deutschland*. Cologne: ISP, 1995.

Pal, Joyojeet. "The Machine to Aspire To: The Computer in Rural South India." *First Monday* 17, no. 2 (2012). Accessed January 8, 2016. http://journals.uic.edu/ojs/index.php/fm/article/view/3733.

Pandian, Anand. *Crooked Stalks: Cultivating Virtue in South India*. Durham, NC: Duke University Press, 2009.

Pang, Laikwan. "The Labor Factor in the Creative Economy: A Marxist Reading." *Social Text* 27 (2009): 55–76.

Partridge, Damani J. *Hypersexuality and Headscarves: Race, Sex, and Citizenship in the New Germany*. Bloomington: Indiana University Press, 2012.

Partridge, Damani J. "We Were Dancing in the Club, Not on the Berlin Wall: Black Bodies, Street Bureaucrats, and Exclusionary Incorporation into the New Europe." *Cultural Anthropology* 23, no. 4 (2008): 660–87.

Patel, Reena. *Working the Night Shift: Women in India's Call Center Industry*. Stanford, CA: Stanford University Press, 2010.

Patibandla, Murali, Deepak Kapur, and Bent Petersen. "Import Substitution with Free Trade: Case of India's Software Industry." *Economic and Political Weekly* 35, no. 15 (2000): 1263–70.

Peirce, Charles Sanders. "A Syllabus of Certain Topics of Logic." In *The Essential Peirce: Selected Philosophical Writings*, vol. 2, *1893–1913*, edited by the Peirce Edition Project, 258–99. Bloomington: Indiana University Press, 1998.

Philip, Kavita. "What Is a Technological Author? The Pirate Function and Intellectual Property." *Postcolonial Studies* 8, no. 2 (2005): 199–218.

Philip, Kavita, Lilly Irani, and Paul Dourish. "Postcolonial Computing: A Tactical Survey." *Science, Technology, and Human Values* 37, no. 1 (2012): 3–29.

Poster, Winifred. "Saying 'Good Morning' in the Night: The Reversal of Work Time in Global ICT Service Work." *Research in the Sociology of Work* 17 (2007): 55–112.

Postone, Moishe. "Anti-Semitism and National Socialism: Notes on the German Reaction to the Holocaust." *New German Critique* 1, no. 19 (1980): 97–115.

Postone, Moishe. *Time, Labor, and Social Domination*. Cambridge: Cambridge University Press, 1993.

Povinelli, Elizabeth A. *The Cunning of Recognition: Indigenous Alterities and the Making of Australian Multiculturalism*. Durham, NC: Duke University Press, 2002.

Povinelli, Elizabeth A. *Economies of Abandonment: Social Belonging and Endurance in Late Liberalism*. Durham, NC: Duke University Press, 2011.

Povinelli, Elizabeth A. "Radical Worlds: The Anthropology of Incommensurability and Inconceivability." *Annual Review of Anthropology* 30 (2001): 319–34.

Prakash, Gyan. *Another Reason*. Princeton, NJ: Princeton University Press, 1999.

Prashad, Vijay. *The Karma of Brown Folk*. Minneapolis: University of Minnesota Press, 2000.

Prashad, Vijay. *Uncle Swami: South Asians in America Today*. New York: New Press, 2012.

Puar, Jasbir K. "The 'Right' to Maim: Disablement and Inhumanist Biopolitics in Palestine." *Borderlands* 14, no. 1 (2015): 1–27.

Pugsley, Peter C., and Sukhmani Khorana. "Asserting Nationalism in a Cosmopolitan World: Globalized Indian Cultures in Yash Raj Films." *Continuum: Journal of Media and Cultural Studies* 25, no. 3 (2011): 359–73.

Rabinow, Paul. "Artificiality and Enlightenment: From Sociobiology to Biosociality." In *Essays on the Anthropology of Reason*, 91–111. Princeton, NJ: Princeton University Press, 1996.

Radcliffe-Brown, A. R. "On Joking Relationships." *Africa: Journal of the International African Institute* 13, no. 3 (1940): 195–210.

Radhakrishnan, Smitha. *Appropriately Indian*. Durham, NC: Duke University Press, 2011.

Radhakrishnan, Smitha. "Professional Women, Good Families: Respectable Femininity and the Cultural Politics of a 'New' India." *Qualitative Sociology* 32, no. 2 (2009): 195–212.

Raley, Rita. "Code.surface || Code.depth." *Dichtung Digital* (2006). Accessed December 10, 2014. http://www.dichtung-digital.org/2006/01/Raley/index.htm.

Ramamurthy, Priti. "Material Consumers, Fabricating Subjects: Perplexity, Global Connectivity Discourses, and Transnational Feminist Research." *Cultural Anthropology* 18, no. 4 (2003): 524–50.

Ramello, Giovanni Battista. "Access to vs. Exclusion from Knowledge: Intellectual Property, Efficiency and Social Justice." In *Intellectual Property and Theories of Justice*, edited by Axel Gosseries, Alain Marciano, and Alain Strowel, 73–93. London: Palgrave Macmillan, 2008.

Rana, Junaid Akram. *Terrifying Muslims: Race and Labor in the South Asian Diaspora*. Durham, NC: Duke University Press, 2011.

Rao, Anupama. *The Caste Question: Dalits and the Politics of Modern India*. Berkeley: University of California Press, 2009.

Ray, Raka, and Seemin Qayum. *Cultures of Servitude*. Stanford, CA: Stanford University Press, 2009.

Reardon, Jenny. "The Human Genome Diversity Project: A Case Study in Co-production." *Social Studies of Science* 31, no. 3 (2001): 357–88.

Renaud, Jeffrey. "Rethinking the Repressive Hypothesis: Foucault's Critique of Marcuse." *Symposium: Canadian Journal of Continental Philosophy* 17, no. 2 (2013): 76–93.

Rofel, Lisa. *Desiring China: Experiments in Neoliberalism, Sexuality, and Public Culture*. Durham, NC: Duke University Press, 2007.

Roitman, Janet. *Fiscal Disobedience: An Anthropology of Economic Regulation in Central Africa*. Princeton, NJ: Princeton University Press, 2004.

Rojek, Chris. *Decentering Leisure: Rethinking Leisure Theory*. London: Sage, 1995.

Rojek, Chris. *The Labor of Leisure: The Culture of Free Time*. Los Angeles: Sage, 2010.

Rose, Nikolas. "The Value of Life: Somatic Ethics and the Spirit of Biocapital." *Daedelus* 39 (winter 2008): 36–48.

Ross, Andrew. *No Collar*. New York: Basic Books, 2002.

Røyrvik, Emil André, and Marianne Blom Brodersen. "Real Virtuality: Power and Simulation in the Age of Neoliberal Crisis." *Culture Unbound* 4 (2012): 637–59.

Roy, Srirupa. *Beyond Belief: India and the Politics of Postcolonial Nationalism*. Durham, NC: Duke University Press, 2007.

Rushdie, Salman. *Shame: A Novel*. New York: Random House, 2008.

Rutherford, Danilyn. *Laughing at Leviathan: Sovereignty and Audience in West Papua*. Chicago: University of Chicago Press, 2012.

Safri, Maliha, and Julie Graham. "The Global Household: Towards a Feminist Postcapitalist International Political Economy." *Signs* 36, no. 1 (2010): 99–125.

Salzinger, Leslie. *Genders in Production: Making Workers in Mexico's Global Factories*. Berkeley: University of California Press, 2003.

Santner, Eric. *Stranded Objects: Mourning, Memory, and Film in Postwar Germany*. Ithaca, NY: Cornell University Press, 1990.

Sarkar, Tanika. *Words to Win: The Making of a Modern Autobiography*. Chicago: University of Chicago Press, 1999.

Sarkar Committee, Central Bureau of Education, India. "Development of Higher Technical Institutions in India (Interim Report of the Sarkar Committee)," 1946.

Sartori, Andrew. "The Categorical Logic of a Colonial Nationalism: Swadeshi Bengal, 1904–1908." *Comparative Studies of South Asia, Africa and the Middle East* 23, nos. 1–2 (2003): 270–85.

Saxenian, AnnaLee. *The New Argonauts: Regional Advantage in a Global Economy*. Cambridge, MA: Harvard University Press, 2006.

Saxenian, AnnaLee. *Silicon Valley's New Immigrant Entrepreneurs*. San Francisco: Public Policy Institute of California, 1999.

Schaffer, Simon. "Babbage's Dancer." *Imaginary Futures*, 2007. Accessed July 10, 2014. http://www.imaginaryfutures.net/2007/04/16/babbages-dancer-by-simon -schaffer/.

Schielke, Samuli. "Living in the Future Tense: Aspiring for World and Class in Provincial Egypt." In *The Global Middle Class: Theorizing through Ethnography*, edited by Rachel Heiman, Carla Freeman, and Mark Liechty, 31–56. Santa Fe, NM: SAR Press, 2012.

Sebaly, Patrick Kim. "The Assistance of Four Nations in the Establishment of the Indian Institutes of Technology, 1945–1970." PhD diss., University of Michigan, 1972.

Shankar, Shalini. *Desi Land: Teen Culture, Class, and Success in Silicon Valley*. Durham, NC: Duke University Press, 2008.

Sharma, Dinesh. *The Long Revolution*. New Delhi: HarperCollins, 2009.

Shelton, Emily Jane. "My Secret Life: Photographs, Melancholy Realisms, and Modern Personhood." PhD diss., University of Chicago, 2002.

Shukla, Sandhya. *India Abroad*. Durham, NC: Duke University Press, 2003.

Shweder, Richard. "Toward a Deep Cultural Psychology of Shame." *Social Research* 70, no. 4 (2003): 1109–30.

Sieg, Katrin. *Ethnic Drag: Performing Race, Nation, Sexuality in West Germany*. Ann Arbor: University of Michigan Press, 2002.

Siegel, Lee. *Laughing Matters: Comic Tradition in India*. Chicago: University of Chicago Press, 1987.

Silverstein, Michael. "Metapragmatic Discourse and Metapragmatic Function." In *Reflexive Language*, edited by John Lucy, 33–58. Cambridge: Cambridge University Press, 1993.

Singer, Milton B. *When a Great Tradition Modernizes: An Anthropological Approach to Indian Civilization*. New York: Praeger, 1972.

Sinha, Mrinalini. *Specters of Mother India: The Global Restructuring of an Empire*. Durham, NC: Duke University Press, 2006.

Smith, Adam. *Wealth of Nations*. Buffalo, NY: Prometheus Books, 1991.

Smith, Marquard, and Joanne Morra. *The Prosthetic Impulse: From a Posthuman Present to a Biocultural Future*. Cambridge, MA: MIT Press, 2007.

Söderberg, Johan. *Hacking Capitalism: The Free and Open Source Software Movement*. London: Routledge, 2008.

Sperling, Stefan. *Reasons of Conscience: The Bioethics Debate in Germany*. Chicago: University of Chicago Press, 2013.

Spivak, Gayatri Chakravorty. "Can the Subaltern Speak?" In *Marxism and the Interpretation of Culture*, edited by Gary Nelson and Lawrence Grossberg, 271–313. Urbana: University of Illinois Press, 1998.

Srivastava, Sanjay. *Entangled Urbanism: Slum, Gated Community and Shopping Mall in Delhi and Gurgaon*. New Delhi: Oxford University Press, 2014.

Srivastava, Sanjay. "National Identity, Bedrooms, and Kitchens: Gated Communities and New Narratives of Space in India." In *The Global Middle Class: Theorizing through Ethnography*, edited by Rachel Heiman, Carla Freeman, and Mark Liechty, 57–84. Santa Fe, NM: SAR Press, 2012.

Standing, Guy. *The Precariat: The New Dangerous Class*. London: Bloomsbury Academic, 2011.

Stephens, Paul, and Robert Hardwick Weston. "Free Time: Overwork as an Ontological Condition." *Social Text 94* 26, no. 1 (spring 2008): 137–64.

Stewart, Kathleen. *Ordinary Affects*. Durham, NC: Duke University Press, 2007.

Stoetzler, Marcel. "Postone's Marx: A Theorist of Modern Society, Its Social Movements and Its Imprisonment by Abstract Labour." *Historical Materialism* 12, no. 3 (2004): 261–83.

Stolcke, Verena. "Talking Culture: New Boundaries, New Rhetorics of Exclusion in Europe." *Current Anthropology* 36, no. 1 (1995): 1–24.

Stoler, Ann. *Along the Archival Grain*. Princeton, NJ: Princeton University Press, 2010.

Strathern, Marilyn. *The Gender of the Gift: Problems with Women and Problems with Society in Melanesia*. Berkeley: University of California Press, 1988.

Sundaram, Ravi. *Pirate Modernity: Delhi's Media Urbanism*. New York: Routledge, 2009.

Takhteyev, Yuri. *Coding Places: Software Practice in a South American City*. Cambridge, MA: MIT Press, 2012.

Taussig, Karen-Sue. *Ordinary Genomes: Science, Citizenship, and Genetic Identities*. Durham, NC: Duke University Press, 2009.

Terranova, Tiziana. *Network Culture: Politics for the Information Age*. Ann Arbor, MI: Pluto Press, 2004.

Thapar, Romila. "Cyclic and Linear Time in Early India." *MUSE Museum International* 57, no. 3 (2005): 19–31.

Tharoor, Sashi. *India: From Midnight to the Millennium*. New York: Harper Perennial, 1998.

Thompson, E. P. *The Making of the English Working Class*. New York: Vintage Books, 1966.

Thompson, E. P. "Time, Work-Discipline, and Industrial Capitalism." *Past and Present* 38, no. 1 (1967): 56–97.

Thompson, Helen. "The Personal Is Political: Domesticity's Domestic Contents." *The Eighteenth Century* 50, no. 4 (2009): 355–70.

Trautmann, Thomas R. *Aryans and British India*. Berkeley: University of California Press, 1997.

Trouillot, Michel-Rolph. "Anthropology and the Savage Slot: The Poetics and Politics of Otherness." In *Recapturing Anthropology: Working in the Present*, edited by Richard G. Fox, 17–44. Santa Fe, NM: SAR Press, 1991.

Trouillot, Michel-Rolph. *Global Transformations*. New York: Palgrave Macmillan, 2003.

Trouillot, Michel-Rolph. *Silencing the Past: Power and the Production of History*. Boston: Beacon Press, 1995.

Tsing, Anna. "The Global Situation." *Cultural Anthropology* 15, no. 3 (2000): 327–60.

Tsing, Anna. "Sorting Out Commodities: How Capitalist Value Is Made through Gifts." *HAU: Journal of Ethnographic Theory* 3, no. 1 (2013): 21–43.

Uberoi, Patricia. *Freedom and Destiny: Gender, Family, and Popular Culture in India*. New Delhi: Oxford University Press, 2009.

Upadhya, Carol. "Employment, Exclusion and 'Merit' in the Indian IT Industry." *Economic and Political Weekly* 42, no. 20 (2007): 1863–68.

Upadhya, Carol. "Ethnographies of the Global Information Economy: Research Strategies and Methods." *Economic and Political Weekly* 43, no. 17 (2008): 64–72.

Upadhya, Carol. "Rewriting the Code: Software Professionals and the Reconstitution of Indian Middle Class Identity." In *Patterns of Middle Class Consumption in India and China*, edited by Christophe Jaffrelot and Peter van der Veer, 55–88. Thousand Oaks, CA: Sage, 2008.

Upadhya, Carol, and A. R. Vasavi, eds. *In an Outpost of the Global Economy: Work and Workers in India's Information Technology Industry*. New Delhi: Routledge, 2008.

Varma, Pavan K. *The Great Indian Middle Class*. New Delhi: Penguin Books, 2007.

Veblen, Thorstein. *The Theory of the Leisure Class: An Economic Study of Institutions*. New York: Macmilllan, 1899.

Vienne, Emmanuel de. "'Make Yourself Uncomfortable': Joking Relationships as Predictable Uncertainty among the Trumai of Central Brazil." *HAU: Journal of Ethnographic Theory* 2, no. 2 (2012): 163–87.

Virno, Paolo. *Grammar of the Multitude: For an Analysis of Contemporary Forms of Life*. Los Angeles: Semiotext(e), 2004.

Vora, Kalindi. *Life Support: Biocapital and the New History of Outsourced Labor*. Minneapolis: University of Minnesota Press, 2015.

Wallace, Charles P. "Germany's New Recruits." *Time Magazine*, June 25, 2001, 38–40.

Weber, Max. *The Protestant Ethic and the Spirit of Capitalism*. New York: Scribner, 1958.

Weeks, Kathi. *The Problem with Work*. Durham, NC: Duke University Press, 2011.

Weinbaum, Alys. "Racial Aura: Walter Benjamin and the Work of Art in a Biotechnological Age." *Literature and Medicine* 26, no. 1 (2007): 207–39.

Weinbaum, Alys. *Wayward Reproductions: Genealogies of Race and Nation in Transatlantic Modern Thought*. Durham, NC: Duke University Press, 2004.

Weiner, Annette B. *Inalienable Possessions: The Paradox of Keeping-While-Giving*. Berkeley: University of California Press, 1992.

Weiner, Annette B. "Inalienable Wealth." *American Ethnologist* 12, no. 2 (1985): 210–27.

Winner, Langdon. "Technology Today: Utopia or Dystopia?" *Social Research* 64, no. 3 (1997): 989–1017.

Wong, Ying, and Jeanne Tsai. "Cultural Models of Shame and Guilt." In *The Self-Conscious Emotions: Theory and Research*, edited by Jessica L. Tracey, Richard W. Robins, and June Price Tangney, 209–23. New York: Guilford Press, 2007.

Woodmansee, Martha, and Peter Jaszi, eds. *The Construction of Authorship: Textual Appropriation in Law and Literature*. New York: Columbia University Press, 1994.

Yildiz, Yasemin. "Governing European Subjects: Tolerance and Guilt in the Discourse of 'Muslim Women.'" *Cultural Critique* 77 (2011): 70–101.

Zaloom, Caitlin. *Out of the Pits*. Chicago: University of Chicago Press, 2006.

Zantop, Susanne. *Colonial Fantasies: Conquest, Family, and Nation in Precolonial Germany, 1770–1870*. Durham, NC: Duke University Press, 1997.

Zöller, Günter. "Philosophizing under the Influence—Schopenhauer's Indian Thought." In *Understanding Schopenhauer through the Prism of Indian Culture*, edited by Arati Barua, Michael Gerhard, and Matthias Koßler, 9–18. Berlin: De Gruyter, 2012.

Page numbers followed by *f* indicate illustrations.

Berlin (*continued*)
images as portents of future by Berliners, 29, 33, 35, 51, 210n11; reputation as vital, progressive environment, 8, 31, 151, 162; stigmatization of Turkish Muslim men in, 32; Technical University of, 54–55, 81, 98, 111, 118; Treptower Park, 153; upper-caste Hindu short-term programmers in, 9, 12; West, 32–33

Bhabha, Homi, 121

biopolitics, 201, 207n37

Bipin (short-term programmer): background and living situation of, 1, 12, 157, 158; on development of India, 117–18, 132, 134, 135; on disappearance of Meenakshi, 188; on India's emergence as global center of technology, 113–15; on lost past in India, 151–52; as part of global kinship network of India, 171; on "spaghetti code," 100–102, 104–6. *See also* interviews and observations

body: associations of products and practices with bodily type, 43, 45, 49, 58–60, 110, 210n10; bodily comportment as political statement, 149; bodily discipline, 138, 145–46, 147, 150, 197; body shops, 189, 228n9; foreign as portent, 16, 39, 43–45, 51–53; German libidinal commodification of Indian, 22, 45–47; of worker as aberration, 17–18, 27, 49, 56, 208nn45–46, 217–18n39; racialization of foreign, 6, 8, 14–15, 18, 32, 52–53; racialized depictions of, 23, 27, 30, 33–35, 50, 201

Bollywood, 77, 78, 80–81, 200

Bombay, 76, 121, 122, 124, 153, 175, 220n48. *See also* Mumbai

boundaries and limits: boundaries between work and leisure, 12, 20, 76, 167, 183, 201–2, 204n7, 223–45; human achievement and, 53, 105–6, 162, 169; jokes and gifts as tools for setting, 167; limits set on code by their creators, 92–93; moral, 188, 193; workplace, 103

Bourdieu, Pierre, 204n11, 227n20

Calcutta (Kolkata), 121, 152, 153

call centers, 4, 22

capital: accumulation, 36; ethnicity commodified as, 43–45, 51–52, 88–89; global as tool for opening national borders, 39–41, 226n17, 230n39; globalized IT as basis for creating capital flows, 22; machine as contributor to, 20–21, 201; production of workers by capital, 203n3, 207n37; race as embodiment of, 14; real subsumption, 203n3; role of Indian middle class in creating, 22; worker as tool for producing, 2, 14, 17, 133, 167, 192, 200–201

capitalism: as influence on concepts of race, 43–45, 51–52, 88–89, 204n11, 209n2, 230n39; anticapitalism, 36, 200, 210n19; autonomist Marxist concept of, 167, 226n10; Berardi on capitalist production, 16–18, 144, 148–49, 197–98; colonialism as mechanism for transforming anticapitalist societies, 35–36; communication and production of intangible goods, 2, 16, 75, 83–84, 86, 95, 148–49, 218n3; gifts and jokes as tools of commensuration for workers, 24–25; home and family as complements to, 155–56, 159–60, 201–2, 216n10, 223n41, 230n36; industrial, 3; labor-time, 20–21; Marx on, 36, 205n20, 230n33; materialism and, 35–36, 45, 85; neoliberal, 5, 23, 204n7; plight of knowledge worker, 17, 20–21, 24–26, 94–96, 140–44, 147–49, 183–84; production of intangible goods, 2, 95–96, 213nn4–5; production of intangible versus tangible goods, 3, 16–17, 181–82, 192, 205n20, 207–8n39; and purchase of time rather than people, 192, 204n7; self-fashioning of individual in capitalist environment, 114–18, 140–44, 147–51, 155–56, 159–62, 167, 213n3; Virno on, 16, 17–18, 142; Weber on, 36; worker as resource of production, 2, 14, 17, 40–43, 75, 133, 167

cartoons. *See* images

caste: benefits of computer science education for lower-caste Indians, 134; caste injustice, 127; community and, 211n21; gender reforms and system, 156, 224n49; Indian neighborhood configurations and, 164; mixing, 149–50; and reconfiguration of domestic labor, 223n43; upper-caste programmers, 9, 123

Chennai, 89. *See also* Madras

citizenship: freedom and, 229n31; German policies regarding, 38–39, 210n7; Indian middle class as normative model for, 109; redefinition of Indian by its diasporic middle class, 116, 166–67, 198, 216n47

class: as process, 19, 110, 114, 205n20; as topic of study among modern anthropologists, 27; consumption by rich as means of self-identification, 143; contradictory situation of being racialized and middle class, 3, 18–20; differences and politics in "new economies," 51; emulation of consumption patterns of higher classes by lower, 143; Marx on capitalism and, 205n20; positions of natives and immigrants in Germany, 40, 42–43; programming as means for advancement among lower Indians, 117, 134; realignment and reimaging of race and by knowledge work, 2, 3, 4; sites of pleasure as sites of antagonism, 152, 222n11; takeover of India's parks and greens, 152–53, 162; technical elite of India, 16, 18, 24, 114–20, 122–28, 129, 131–35, 166, 212n45; West German capitalist class society, 59, 62; working, 16, 42–44, 51, 53, 55, 143, 201, 207–8n39. *See also* middle class; race

code: commentaries, 100–104, 105–6, 182; critical code studies (CCS), 216n2; duct tape, 102, 105–6; example, 93; as instructions or recipes, 96; Java, 92–93, 99; as language, 67–68; as mathematics, 67–68; as property, 87; "spaghetti" or "ball of mud," 100–102, 104–6; as speech, 87, 105–6

coders: body shopping for, 22, 189, 228n9; hackers, 12, 30, 88, 173–74, 202; images of Indian, 38–45, 60, 70, 74–76, 148, 160, 162; Indian as portents of change, 29, 31, 133–36; job insecurity of short-term migrant, 3, 10–11, 68, 88–99, 100–107, 187–88; multiple socioeconomic and professional roles of Indian, 12, 166–67; open source, 12, 87–88, 91, 105–7; pursuit of eros by, 6, 9, 91, 216n10; race and class

as paradigms for explaining differences among, 8, 29, 31, 62–68, 83, 99, 106, 141; response of Indians to corporate environments, 12, 76–79, 91–100, 104–5, 133–36; technological heritage and expectations of Indian, 24, 116, 118–28; upper-caste, 9, 123; versus programmers, 102. *See also* interviews and observations; software

cognitariat, 17–18, 56, 64, 144, 146, 167, 205n20

cognitive labor: as basis for establishing middle-class authority, 4, 133–36, 170–73, 198; as economy based on circulation of ideas and symbols, 5, 17, 30, 56–57, 86; as economy derived from subjective qualities of individuals, 17, 31, 43, 56–58, 90–91, 201–2; as embodiment and opposition to manual labor, 5, 56–57, 191–92, 203n2, 213nn4–5; autonomist Marxist concept of, 5–6, 30, 90–91, 146, 148–49, 167, 205n20; contradictory situation of diasporic Indian coders, 5, 51, 83–84, 87, 94–95, 98–99, 110, 146; gifts as means of materializing, 24–25, 166–67, 168–73; Indian programmers as embodiment of economy, 38–45, 56, 83–84, 183; as labor that fosters testing of lifestyles, 6, 26, 90–91, 140–41, 148–50, 161–62, 173–74; performance of coding on short-term contracts, 3, 87, 100–104; physical demands of, 17–18, 147–48; race and class in global economy of, 3, 20, 22–27, 31, 44, 56–60, 64–67, 79, 83–84; risks and multiple trajectories of, 25, 111–13, 117–18, 133–36, 186–89; short-term workers as portents of possible future, 43, 51, 85; traits sought in workers, 15–16, 23, 57–58, 64–65, 148; work environments for, 86–88, 95, 198; worker as universal, unmarked subject, 2–3, 6, 17–18, 56, 76, 167. *See also* knowledge work; labor; work

colonialism: British in India, 36, 64, 118–21, 126–27, 156, 175; colonial politics of difference and capitalist racialization, 43–44; German attitudes regarding, 36, 210n16; India during its colonial period, 206n30, 222n18, 223n45, 224n49, 224n51; Marx on capitalism and, 36; responses

colonialism (*continued*)
 by anticolonial reformers in South Asia,
 149, 156, 219n19; in South Asia, 174, 208n47,
 211n21
commensuration between worlds, 4, 20, 25,
 88, 158, 226n11, 227n22
communication: as primary product of
 global software industry, 2, 16–17, 57–58;
 as requirement for agile programming,
 67; as skill required for front-office work,
 63, 83, 165; as trait associated with specific
 races and cultures, 67–73, 83; code as
 form of, 105; dependence on subjective
 human creativity, 17–18, 43, 57–58, 91–95,
 105; diasporic workers as links to Indian
 market, 75, 83–84; global infrastructure
 for, 37; office environments designed
 to foster among workers, 57, 59–60,
 86–87, 90–91, 95, 226n9; technology as
 determinant of human connection and
 disconnection, 26
communism, 39, 40, 80, 129, 153, 205n20,
 226n16
computers: in analogy of stupid cook, 97,
 137–38, 160, 163, 221n1; as social influence, 208–9n53; Deleuze on, 201; and
 development of India, 115, 119, 121–31,
 136; hardware for, 89, 132; IBM, 128–29,
 132, 228n48; man-machine interactions as social processes, 60, 212n45;
 manufacturing of in India, 131, 220n51;
 software companies in India, 221n58;
 and technoelite of India, 126–27, 130–32,
 135; as tools of individual socioeconomic
 advancement, 117, 136
computer science: degrees, 64, 76–77, 81,
 89, 98, 111, 139; in educational curricula,
 117, 123
consumption: as tool for self-
 transformation, 45, 47; as tool of
 middle-class self-definition, 4, 19–20, 56,
 141–43, 199, 204n13, 227n20; commensuration with work by diasporic workers,
 155, 162, 166–67, 171, 199; consumer-
 citizens, 19, 20, 114; consumer patriotism,
 110, 140–41; India as consumer market,
 67, 119; of luxury goods, 143, 171; of time,

141–43; power of India's middle class, 10,
 19, 197; as product of capitalist channeling
 of desire, 90; spectator commodities consumed through viewing, 29, 45; symbolic
 power of, 19, 143, 171–72, 223n38, 227n20
cooking, as an analogy for programming,
 137; improvisational versus instructed as
 analogous to human versus machine, 137,
 160, 163, 221n1
cosmopolitanism, 4, 31, 39, 130, 173, 206n23,
 227n34
counterconduct, 96, 168, 174, 197, 201, 227n29
cruel optimism, 5, 25, 186, 193, 194–96,
 205n20, 229n24
culture: as basis for establishing office and
 work hierarchies, 4, 23, 59–60, 68, 72, 75,
 99, 196–97; call center, 22; coding, 11, 21,
 22, 90–95, 100–104, 133, 203n1, 206n24,
 209n55; cultural capacity and racialization, 3–4, 10–11, 14, 28, 31, 59, 78–79;
 cultural knowledge as element of work,
 17, 60–64, 67, 74–75, 79–80; cultural
 mimicry, 47, 83; cultural streamlining,
 79–80; diasporic worker as ethnographer,
 11, 52, 74; epidermalization of culture and
 cultural knowledge, 14, 28, 32, 43–44, 83,
 88–89, 159–60; epistemic, 221n65; genetics
 as tool for explaining cultural differences,
 16, 196; German, 32, 35–36, 45, 83, 211n25;
 image, 29–30, 32–33, 51, 212–13n46; Indian,
 35–37, 122, 155–56, 187, 210n14, 211n21,
 214n25, 228n5; Indian middle-class, 19–20,
 99, 106, 109, 119–20, 140–41, 188–89,
 225n8, 227n34, 228n42; localization and
 internationalization of code to accommodate differences in, 69–70; multicultural
 environments, 11, 28, 64, 159, 166, 192,
 196, 210n20, 215n44; office, 23, 86–91, 95,
 161–62, 165–66, 174, 192, 201–2, 206n24;
 race versus, 28. *See also* race

Deleuze, Gilles, 16, 76, 89–90, 200–201,
 223–24n46
Delhi, 122, 153, 157
deontics, 88, 216n6
desire: as driving force of transnational
 labor migration, 12, 17, 138–39, 149, 163,

172, 194, 204–5n14, 206n23; as trait complementary to capitalism, 90, 117, 226n9; and commodification of race, 45, 47, 51
development, self-, 21, 45, 131, 142, 150, 204n7, 215n33; software, 10–11, 66, 70–73, 165, 217n30
development and modernization: conflict between urban and rural needs in India's, 125–26, 130; foreign involvement in India's, 40, 122–24, 128–32, 211n28, 219n35, 228n48; market liberalization and globalization in India, 115, 129; measurements of, 218n5; postcolonial technological of India, 40, 115, 118–29; privatization and entrepreneurialism in India, 115, 117, 132–34; role of diasporic technocrats in India's, 18, 24, 115, 117–18, 128, 166
diasporic Indians: body shopping and, 22, 189, 228n9; and "brand India" technological expertise, 18, 116; call centers and, 180–81; and development and modernization of India, 131, 136, 227n18; global kinship networks, 170–71, 187, 191, 194; Indian middle class and, 4, 19, 153; Indianness, 113, 117, 134, 199; precarity of short-term transnational work for, 2–3, 17, 186, 189, 195–96, 227n34; production of, 20, 110, 183, 187–88, 207n31, 229n29; programmers, 3, 4, 24, 166, 182, 188, 197, 199. *See also* networks and networking
digital worlds, 91, 105–6
discrimination. *See* hierarchies; racialization
Douglas, Mary, 173

East Germany (German Democratic Republic): attitudes toward foreigners in, 39–40, 59; economic decline in following reunification, 7, 40, 78; neo-Nazi violence in, 40; totalitarian past as stigma in, 59, 62. *See also* Germany; West Germany
Electronic Frontier Foundation, 21
elite: Indian civil servants under colonial system as an, 64; Indian programmers as an, 2, 5, 12, 227n34; India's scientific and technological, 24, 26, 116, 118–21, 219n19; India's technoelite and development of state power, 131–32; India's technoelite as

impetus underlying entrepreneurialism and privatization, 132–35; programmers, 104–5; role of India's scientific elite in bringing technology to India, 120–23, 126–29; role of India's scientific elite in establishing India as outsourcing center, 130–31; self-perception of Indian programmers as both cheap laborers and rising, 20, 23; shift from political to economic power as basis for status in India, 123
embodiment: as capitalist approach to matching bodies to work, 5, 14, 66, 99, 107, 209n2; Indian IT workers of new entrepreneurial India, 104–5, 116, 123; Indian worker of cognitive labor, 2–3, 5, 17–18, 56, 167, 192, 201; racialization of Indian cognitive workers through, 3, 14, 16, 43, 52, 78–79, 97, 173–74; real subsumption and, 203n3; symbolic function of ideas through, 56, 97, 99, 102, 105, 149, 156, 179; symbolic function of objects through, 153; symbolic function of people through, 142, 167, 190, 208n46. *See also* race
emoticons, 86, 90, 96
England, 8, 40, 111, 127
entrepreneurship: Adi's start-up business and attitudes toward, 111–13, 188; entrepreneurial subject, 198, 204n7, 218n2, 221–22n3; individual and Indian nation-state, 114–16, 122, 134–36, 142, 162–63, 166; of short-term diasporic programmer, 188, 191, 195, 196
eros: as channeling of expressivity, 91, 98–99, 139–40, 149, 216n10; as politics of refusal and deflection, 6, 90, 92, 196, 197; Berardi on, 5–6, 148–49, 204n13; as counterconduct, 168, 197; fashioning by short-term IT workers, 6, 20, 92–93, 182–84, 197, 199, 204–5n14; jokes and gifts as tools for limiting, 167–68, 182–83; Marcuse on, 5, 90–91, 204n13, 229n28; and middle-class Indian concepts of pleasure, 6, 24, 140, 149, 167, 197; private ownership as element of, 92; pursuit of in spaces of leisure, 140; pursuit of in office environment, 6, 89–94; as right to live good life, 92, 105, 110, 197, 202. *See also* good life; leisure

ethics. *See* morality, ethics, and social mores

ethnicity. *See* culture; race

expertise: as basis for creating different lifeworlds and epistemes, 135; as natural attribute of knowledge workers, 27; as element of self-fashioning and self-identity, 11–12, 19, 135, 137–38, 161, 179; as interactive process between created and creator, 94–95, 138; as potential threat to upward mobility, 97, 99, 133–34; as tool of personal empowerment, 100, 114–15, 133–36, 137; cultural knowledge construed as element of Indian, 59, 63, 74; the global association of Indian programmers with technological, 12, 18, 36–38, 42–43, 81, 104, 205n19, 213n1; global networks based on professional, 128, 129; objects of, 94; India's technocrats as resource for its modernization, 114–15, 117, 119–21, 123–24, 127, 135–36; repertoires of, 78–79, 117, 119, 135; valuations of Indian IT, 3, 11, 66, 72, 99, 230n29

expressivity, hyperexpressivity, and expression, 90–91, 143, 148–50, 173–74, 204–5nn13–14, 229n28. *See also* repression

family and kinship: assimilation, 98; blurred boundary between public and private life, 223n45, 225n58; concepts of oikos and oikonomic inheritance, 201–2, 225n58; conversion of private time into labor-time through capitalism, 20–21; familial relationships within diasporic cohorts, 155, 183–84, 187–91, 223–24n46; family values, 64; gifting and commensuration in Indian diaspora, 168–73, 183–84, 187; globalization as agent of change to, 155, 159; in Kracauer's 1920s study of Berlin office workers, 147; marriage and family as goals of diasporic workers, 89, 190, 224n55; marriage restrictions, 98, 105, 156, 158–59; migrant families, 38; networks as source of socioeconomic support, 111–13, 114–15, 168; obligations of diasporic workers, 110, 159–60, 164–65, 182; and pursuit of eros by diasporic workers, 20; "respectable femininity" as complement

to, 189–90, 191; *Time Out* as study of tensions between personal happiness and, 193–94. *See also* home

Fanon, Frantz, 14, 44

Fernandes, Leela, 19, 208n47, 218n4, 222n10

flexibility, 18, 79–80, 142, 146, 167, 207n36

Fordism: post-Fordist labor and production, 2, 4, 89; shift from and transformation of labor, 17, 203n3, 209n2, 213n4; worker protection under, 192, 205n20

Foucault, Michel: on biopolitics and counterconduct, 201; on class as ethical category, 205n20; on power, 216n13; on sexuality, 204–5nn13–14, 229n28; terms and concepts of, 209n4, 221n59, 222n6, 227n29

freedom: from constraint or restriction, 22, 88, 91–92, 94, 98, 104–5, 143; context and history as bases for defining, 21–22; digital, 91, 105–6; of exchange, 106; expression of impulses as, 148–49, 198, 200; gap between personal and freedom of code, 21, 94, 97, 106; Kant on, 92; liberal, 198–99, 226n17, 229n31; of movement, 87, 104–5, 151; Nehruvian concept at midnight, 112, 117; of opportunity, 154, 190, 194, 198; ownership and, 87, 92, 141; positive and negative freedoms, 93–94, 95, 226n17; proprietary, 21, 23–24, 92, 106, 107; of speech, 105–7

free software, 12, 87, 91, 105, 106, 107

future, the: as driving force of middle-class aspiration and effort, 140–50, 154, 161–62, 185–86, 193, 197–202, 227n18, 227n22; as influence on corporate planning strategies, 11, 95, 167; Berlant's concept of cruel optimism, 5, 25, 186, 193–96, 205n20, 229n24; gifts and futurity, 168–70; images as signs of possible, 29, 31–33, 35, 43, 48, 52–53; India's potential as global center of technology, 113–15, 135, 176–77, 198–99; race as tool for future profitability, 4, 210n10; uncertainty faced by diasporic short-term coders, 23, 30, 75, 97–98, 116, 138–39, 142, 194; Weeks's concept of critical utopias, 5, 186, 194–96, 204n7, 226n10, 229n25; worker potential as link to potential markets, 63–64; worker potential as corporate earnings potential, 17, 57–58, 63, 85, 226nn9–10 home: as hostel for short-term IT workers, 13, 154–55, 157–60, 189–90, 223n42; as political object, 156; as site of leisure and rejuvenation, 138–39, 158–60; as site of preparation for work, 138, 155–56, 160, 162; blurring of boundary between work and, 56–57, 76, 143, 146, 159–60, 162, 202; redefinition by diasporic experience, 110, 154, 157–60, 187, 223n43, 223–24n46, 227n34; site for analyzing experiences, 24, 56, 137, 158–59. *See also* family and kinship

hostels, 154–55, 160, 223n42, 223–24n46

Hyderabad, 54, 88, 100, 127, 139–40, 153, 158

hyperexpressivity, 90–91, 204–5nn13–14

identity: class, 19–20, 140–41, 174, 197–99, 226n11; consumption as basis for, 20, 140–41; German, 3–4, 59, 210n13, 214n11; individual or expert, 19–20, 44, 141–42, 174, 192, 196, 199–200, 230n6; middle-class Indian, 6, 10, 20, 25, 118, 140–41, 166, 197; national, 8, 39, 116, 119, 120, 134, 199, 227n34; selfhood, 83, 139, 150

images: Berlin as city of texts and, 31–33; cartoon cultures, 212–13n46; cartoons regarding short-term Indian IT coders, 30–31, 41*f*, 42*f*, 44*f*, 50*f*; crystallization of past through, 31, 33; emoticons, 86, 90, 96; kinetic imagery as statement, 29, 209n3; libidinal of Indian in Germany, 45–47, 51–52; of life possible in India as incentives for short-term workers, 172–73; Mbeme on, 213n47; official and unofficial of reunited Berlin, 30–32; as politicized objects in Berlin, 29, 52; as portents of future, 29, 31, 33, 35, 39, 42–45, 51; role in public discussions of race, 23, 33–35, 42–45, 51–52; as symbols used for personal encouragement, 138–39; of technologically superior Indian, 22, 29–31, 33–35, 41, 48–50, 52, 210n10; visual abduction, 33, 51–52, 210n10. *See also* stereotyping

imaginary: *Bharat* or rural India as national, 130; bureaucratic, 228n36; German national, 32, 51; imaginaries of person and

place, 27–28, 194, 201; Indian middle-class imaginaries of good life, 20, 24, 141–42, 149, 161, 183, 197; Indian national, 20, 116–17, 125, 136, 141, 197, 227n34; racial and postracial, 15, 49, 51, 52, 68, 197

immigrants: anti-immigration sentiments in Germany, 7–8, 16, 23, 38, 177–79, 206n22, 211n25; as importers of knowledge, 47, 206n22; Indian as threat to German job security, 7; race, genomics, and, 15, 28, 59, 200; Turkish in Germany, 7–8, 38–39, 68, 205–6n21, 215n28. *See also* guest workers; migration

India: anticolonial, 115, 119, 152; *Bharat* (rural India), 130; call centers in, 4, 22; caste hierarchy in, 127; Emperor Ashoka, 114, 135, 176; as motherland of humankind, 35; gated communities in, 153; late colonial, 119, 206n30, 219n19; postcolonial, 113, 120–21, 126, 218n2, 220n43, 224n51, 227n34; postindependence "contract" between state and citizens in, 120; privatization in, 117, 132; profitless undertakings as responsibility of government, 134; prosperity as dependent on conscious effort yet inevitability, 113; realignment in citizen allegiance to state of, 134; role of IBM in technological development of, 121, 128–29, 131–32, 220n48, 220n53; scientists as leaders of development in, 116, 127; state power, 114, 115, 120, 123, 126–27, 132–35; stereotypes associated with, 35, 46; tradition of wrestling in Northern, 150; Venkateshwar, 54–56, 84–85

Indian Institutions of Technology (IITs): as embodiment of Indian ambivalence regarding localized development and globalized achievement, 123–28, 219–20n35; foreign assistance in development of, 40, 122–24, 211n28, 219n35; opinion of Nazir Ahmad regarding purpose of, 125–28; opinion of R. D. T. Woolfe regarding purpose of, 125–27; role and purpose of, 127, 131; Sarkar Committee Report, 124–27

Indian short-term programmers: German cartoon depictions of, 34*f*, 41*f*, 42*f*,

44f; German perceptions of, 31, 51; as harbingers of change, 29–30; Muslim, 9; mystique surrounding in Germany, 42; racialization of, 3

Indian Statistical Institute (ISI), 121, 123–25, 128

industry and industrial growth: computer manufacturing in India, 131, 220n51, 220n53; German IT industry, 7, 55, 61, 78–80, 88–89, 94, 104, 142; global IT industry, 2–4, 58–59, 74–75, 89, 94, 103–4, 146, 173, 185–86; import substitution, 129; Indian IT industry, 19, 64–65, 115–16, 124–25, 130–35, 215n40, 218n4; industrial capitalism, 3, 5, 36, 147, 223n41; outsourcing industry in India, 115–17, 130–31, 181; privatization in India, 109, 117, 128, 131, 132–33; profit motive as dividing line between state-sponsored and private industry, 134; protectionism, 8, 129, 135, 220n51; traditional industry and manufacturing, 4–5, 116, 126, 128–31, 143, 192

information technology (IT). *See* industry and industrial growth; software

Infotech, 86–87, 89–90, 97

intellectual property, 91–92, 96

internationalism, 68–70, 121, 123, 126, 129, 131. *See also* globalization

interviews and observations: with director of sales for French global software firm, 65–66; with American programmer, 67–68; background information for this ethnography, 9–12, 23, 55, 58, 64, 66, 190; Björn (Dash Technologies project manager), 68–70, 73–74, 79; Internet forum project manager, 70–73; Jan (Globus project manager), 54–55, 60–62, 84; Madhu (short-term programmer), 1, 12, 100, 140, 157, 171, 188; Maya (short-term programmer), 12, 13, 111, 118, 172; Mayur (short-term programmer), 12, 117, 134, 157–58, 183, 188; Michael (software project designer), 62–64, 74–75; Rahul (IIT-trained computer scientist), 64–65; Sasha (Mihir's German coworker), 78, 80–81, 103–4. *See also* Adi; Bipin; coders; Meenakshi; Mihir; Rajeshwari; Srinu

jogging: as bodily discipline and personal statement, 149–50; and IT lifestyle, 145–48; as preparation for work during leisure time, 144–46, 223–24n46

jokes: about lazy, hardworking Indians, 165, 174; ambiguous character of some, 174–75; as means of expressing eros, 182–83; as means of materializing cognitive work, 24; as means of reconciling worker with job, 25, 166–68, 173, 177, 182; among short-term migrant coders, 25, 154; anthropological studies of, 173, 227n23; comic *rasa*, 174; as counterpoints to seriousness and hypocrisy, 174–75; elements of, 167; as gifts, 228n40; irony and, 174; joke letter about outsourcing American presidency to India, 179–81; mimicry in, 177–81; as tools for communicating insider knowledge and, 173–74; as tools for easing racial tension, 25; as tools for establishing solidarities, 225n3; as tools for imagining new worlds and possibilities, 167–68, 173, 175–76, 182, 198–99; as tools for resolving tensions and normalizing social relations, 166–68, 175–77, 182–84, 228n40; in workplace, 73. *See also* gifts

Knorr Cetina, Karin, 94, 161, 221n65

knowledge: as basis for establishing workplace hierarchies, 63, 83, 85, 88–89, 107, 141; as commodity, 9, 11, 58; as influence on epistemic framings and lifeworlds, 161, 221n65; as tool for reinvention of self, 162; Berardi's concept of cognitariat, 17, 143–44; cultural, 63, 67, 98, 141; dynamic quality of, 91, 138; educational systems and university training, 63–64, 123–26; genetic knowledge as suggestion of probability, 43–44, 56–57, 83; joke and insider, 173; knowledge economies, 32, 43, 75, 105, 162, 230n39; as property, 91, 96; sharing within companies, 91, 96; transmission of, 39, 47, 59, 74, 135; value of scientific and technological in India, 116–21, 127, 135

knowledge work: as redefining influence on concepts of race and class, 2–3, 14–18, 27–28, 43–44, 56–60, 64–65, 79; as tactic

knowledge work (*continued*)
of capitalist accumulation, 96; knowledge worker as generalized individual, 2, 27; leisure as complement to, 141–42, 144, 148, 197; specialization and expertise, 76, 97, 135, 142. *See also* cognitive labor; work

Kolkata. *See* Calcutta

Kracauer, Siegfried, 143, 147–49, 213n3

Kunzru, Hari, 199–200, 230n39

labor: as disembodied force, 2–3, 5, 18, 56, 167; as embodied force, 5, 17, 22–23, 51, 84, 146, 167, 198, 209n46; challenge by Indian coders to IT economies of, 6, 12, 20, 23–25, 89–95, 106–7, 160–61, 173–74; the cheap cost in India as basis for national growth, 131, 140–41; cognitive versus manual, 5, 17, 57, 192, 207–8n39, 213nn4–5; commodification of individual worker qualities by cognitive, 57–58, 63–64, 74–75, 133–34, 140, 197, 201–2; communication as fundamental to cognitive, 16–17, 43, 56–56, 83–84; conversion of immaterial into status and materiality, 165–66, 172–74, 197–99, 225nn4–8, 227n20; division of, 63–68, 75, 83, 214n23; endless activity as prototype for post-Fordist, 17, 57–58; eros as means of constraining, 24–25, 90–92, 139, 216n10, 228n12; freedom and, 198, 229nn31–32; the implications of globalized for host countries, 7–8, 28, 32, 35, 38–44, 197, 205n19; labor-time, 20–21, 192; leisure-time as preparatory time for, 144–50, 156, 160–62, 167, 221–22n3, 223n43, 223–24n46; Marx on architects versus bees, 65; Marx on machines and human, 20–21, 30, 57; racialization of, 5, 14–15, 41–45, 53, 56–68, 104, 197; real subsumption to capital, 203n3, 205n20; regimes of, 6, 58–60, 63–67, 74–75, 83, 90–95, 110, 147–48; shortages, 8, 38–39; short-term employment as tool for cheapening, 2, 8, 67, 78, 98, 107, 140, 148, 228nn8–9; socioeconomic valuations of, 3–5, 18–21, 25, 115, 140–41, 166, 170–73, 230n36; transnational nature of short-term coding, 3, 12, 25, 99–102, 110,

161–63, 177, 189–97, 226n17. *See also* cognitive labor

language: as basis for racial coding and stereotyping, 14, 214n26; action as, 195; bureaucratic affectations, 177–78, 179–80; code as, 67–68, 216n2; English, 75–76, 131, 215n36; globalization of programming languages across platforms, 68–69, 71, 74; Hindi, 67, 154, 214n25, 225n61; Java programming language, 92–93, 99; of righteousness and virtue as social tool, 188–91, 193, 202; performativity in, 228n7; programming languages, 11, 92–93, 99, 123, 142; Sanskrit and Sanskritic texts, 28, 35, 119, 174, 210n13, 225n61; story of Turkish "i," 68–70; Tamil, 67, 70, 80, 151, 172; translations, 74–76; unavailability of German training to migrant workers in Germany, 38; Urdu, 67, 214n25; visual and signs, 210n10

leisure: as marker of status, 143; autonomist Marxist concept of, 143; as basis for politics of pleasure and constraining of work, 24, 56–57, 110, 140, 148–50, 167; concept of *adda*, 159, 206n25; concept of timepass, 206n25; development of individual creative capacities during, 5, 139, 160–62, 221–22n3; jogging, 144–46, 147–48, 150, 153, 223–24n46; Kracauer's study of nineteenth-century work and, 143, 147–48, 213n3; pleasure and, 160–63; reinvention by Indian middle class, 4, 19–20, 139–42, 144, 148–50, 152–54, 160–61; relationship with work, 19–20, 25, 140, 143–44, 146, 160–61, 213n3; spaces of, 139–40, 142, 154–55, 167, 223–24n46; Veblen on, 143; Virno on, 142, 213n3. *See also* eros

liberalism: critique by Berardi, 197–98; dynamics of resistance and recuperation in, 230n40; ethic of racial and ethnic tolerance in Germany, 23, 32, 68, 196, 214n18; freedom and, 87, 106, 198, 199, 229n31; German multiculturalism, 28, 51, 196, 211n25; and German self-identity, 33, 59, 62, 83; liberal capitalism, 205n20; *weltoffen*, 59 lifestyles: experimentation with possible by diasporic Indians, 141, 145, 146, 150, 158; Indian middle-class, 19, 135, 140

localization, 68–69

machine, the: as embodiment of information, 56; as replacement for human labor, 75, 130; as stupid entity, 137–38; as symbol, 121; computer as, 30, 128–29, 132; computer as tool, 121–22, 128, 130, 135; hacker exploitation of computers, 30; improvised, 122; Indian programmers treated as machinelike beings, 31, 32, 34, 60, 72, 138; machine translation, 75; man-machine interactions, 20–21, 41–42, 44–45, 60, 212n45, 214n16, 221n1, 225n4; Marx on purpose of, 20–21, 30. *See also* technology

Madras, 40, 122, 124. *See also* Chennai

Mahalanobis, Prasantas Chandra, 121

Maidans, 151, 153

manual labor, 5, 39, 65, 207–8n39, 213n5

Marcuse, Herbert, 5, 90–91, 201, 204n13, 216n10, 216n13, 229n28

market: colonies as markets, 126, 129; free markets, 129, 132; global IT services, 8, 102, 145–46, 198, 226n17, 229n31; home as no longer refuge from, 156–60; India as market for business expansion, 61, 67, 75, 79, 84–85; liberalization and opening of India as, 115, 119, 131, 166; privatization, 95; proprietary freedom versus freedom of, 106, 109; protectionist policies and import substitution, 19, 129, 131–32; racial and cultural traits as bases for global, human-based, 15, 43

Marx, Karl: alienation, 57; analogies of architects and bees by, 65; autonomist Marxism, 5–6, 17–18, 30, 143, 167, 200, 226n10; class, 205n20; dual nature of machine technology, 20–21; liberal freedom, 198; real subsumption of labor by capitalism, 203n3, 226n10, 230n33; socioeconomic impacts of colonialism, 36

materialism, 35, 45–46, 85, 210n13

materialization: gifts and jokes as of cognitive labor, 164–67, 169–70, 173; graphic interface with software, 30; materialist

ontologies, 221n1; cognitive work, 24–25, 31, 56, 165–67, 172, 177, 182–83; race and class as paradigms for explaining differences, 8, 18, 215n33

Mauss, Marcel, 168, 226nn14–15

meditation, 46, 82, 148–49, 181, 188

Meenakshi (Meena; short-term programmer): actions possible product of shame, 187; analogy of cooking and programming, 137–38; attitude toward her job, 2, 88–89, 97, 104; background and family of, 12, 88, 139–40; on code, 96–97; on computers as stupid cooks, 137–38, 221n1; disappearance, 20, 25, 185–88, 191–96, 200, 202; as embodiment of risk and optimism inherent to short-term diasporic coders, 2, 25, 88–89, 138–40, 185–89, 191–96, 202; on Indian concept of "respectable femininity," 189–90; living situation and relationships to fellow migrants, 12–13, 98, 113, 153–55, 157–59, 171, 175; on ownership of code that one writes, 87; secretiveness of regarding her job loss, 1–2, 187–89, 191; self-encouragement practiced by, 138–39, 142, 160; separation from Indian diasporic network, 187–88, 190–91; use of leisure time, 140, 142, 144–45, 147. *See also* interviews and observations

Memmi, Albert, 203n5

middle class: assertion of identity by diasporic programmers, 19–20, 110, 140–41, 172–75, 182, 230n36, 230n39; call center cultures as facilitators of socioeconomic advancement, 22; counterconduct, 96, 168, 174, 197, 201, 204n12, 206n30, 223n41, 227n29; diasporic professionals as vanguard of India's new middle class, 3, 10, 12, 18–22, 114, 116–17, 130–36; diasporic programmers as India's upwardly mobile middle class, 2, 26, 182–83, 194, 218n4; earlier generations of India's middle class, 19, 64, 116–20, 122, 128, 129–32, 166, 222n18; eros as element of identity for India's middle class, 6, 19–24, 56, 141, 146–50, 161, 182–84; gift as marker of status, 140–41, 165, 172–73, 227n20, 228n42; gifts and jokes as modes of commensuration, 25, 114, 165–68, 182, 197, middle class (*continued*)

226n14; globalization of India's middle class, 4, 134–35, 198–99; hegemony and authority of Indian middle class, 4, 18–19, 109, 166–67, 177, 199, 226n6; home as staging ground for maintaining and redefining "good life," 155–56, 158, 201–2, 223n43; India's NMC (New Middle Class), 109, 114–15, 166–67, 208n47; links of India's to national success, 4, 134–36, 166; parks and public spaces as sites for self-fashioning, 152–54, 162; precarity as looming threat to diasporic short-term coders, 118, 192–95, 227n34; reinvention of practices of leisure and consumption by India's, 4, 6, 19–20, 25, 109, 140–43, 162, 166–67; role in privatizing India's economy, 109, 114–16, 122, 131–36; self-improvement and pleasure realignment, 144–48, 162, 197; sensibilities of new Indian middle class, 166–68, 182–84, 185–91, 198–200, 225n8, 226n11; stratification of India's middle class, 109, 205n17, 208n49; work abroad as means of facilitating socioeconomic advancement, 3, 88, 197. *See also* class

migration: assumptions underlying short-term transnational, 2, 6, 12, 22, 24, 58, 206n22, 226n17; body shopping, 189, 228n9; German law and policies, 3–4, 7–8, 23, 39, 45, 89–91, 177–78, 206n22, 211nn25–26; policies that restrict or circumscribe foreign, 3, 52, 89–91, 97–99, 104, 202, 211n23; racism and, 16, 40, 45. *See also* immigrants

Mihir (short-term programmer): background of, 12, 13, 76, 77–78; on disappearance of Meenakshi, 188, 190; on freedom of movement of code versus coders, 97, 99, 151; on his job and employment situation, 76–79, 89, 97, 103–4, 146, 189; joke by regarding global emphasis on technology, 175–77, 180; on life in Berlin, 76, 151; on lost urban life of middle-class India, 151–52; on ownership of one's code, 87; as part of global kinship network of India, 157–58, 164–65, 168, 175, 190–91; use of leisure time by, 144–46, 147, 150–51. *See also* interviews and observations

modernization. *See* development and modernization

morality, ethics, and social mores: boundaries and limitations, 188, 193, 202; class as ethical category, 205n20; concept of respectable femininity, 189–90; construction of knowledge as alienable property, 91; counterethics of work, 102, 162; endowment of India's technocrats with moral authority, 166; epidermalization of work ethics, 14; ethic of individual freedom, 88; lying, 188; middle-class ethic of eros or of pleasure and enjoyment, 9, 20, 140, 161, 167, 183–84, 204–5n14; moral authority of national development, 131, 162, 166; morality of gift, 168, 226n16; moral physique, 150; moral purity as transparency and visibility, 32; programming ethics, 87–88, 92–94, 103, 105–6; secretiveness, 187–89, 190–91, 193; selflessness, 61; shame, 187–88, 228n5; social responsibility, 127; tolerance, 61, 196; work ethics, 14, 146, 168, 175; workplace ethics, 4, 16, 23, 24, 55–58, 62–68, 83–85, 103

multiculturalism in Germany, 28, 51, 196

Mumbai, 70–71, 73, 76, 146, 164, 180, 181. *See also* Bombay

Muslims: assimilation of in Germany, 9, 16, 215n30; Muslim home, 156; Turkish in Germany, 32, 38, 51, 67, 215n28, 215n30

Nadeem, Shezad, 22, 140–41, 225n7

nationalism: German, 39; Indian, 119, 129, 132–34, 150, 156, 177, 218n2, 219n19

nation-state, 45, 68, 114, 133–36, 180–81, 211n25, 214n25

Nazism: ideology of, 28, 36, 45, 62, 66, 208n40, 229n27; neo-, 40, 59

Nehru, Prime Minister Jawaharlal: initiation of India's technological era by, 18, 116, 127–28, 131, 220n43; "Tryst with Destiny" speech, 112–13; vision of progress toward good life in India, 132, 135

neoliberalism: as cause of precarity in employment, 191–92, 192–93, 195; as moral authority underlying national development, 131; concepts of capitalism, 5, 134; concepts of governance, 8, 131, 133, 166; concepts of work-life relationship, 2, 18, 61, 143, 162–63; eros as challenge by Indian short-term workers, 12, 20–22, 24, 96, 110, 139; Indian short-term worker as embodiment of, 16, 28, 191; influence on privatization and globalization, 133; proprietary freedom as challenge to, 106; race and genomic probability as bases for valuing individuals, 18, 23, 52, 99; self-improvement and self-fashioning as ideals of, 139, 204n7, 215n33

networks and networking: computer technology and communications as basis for international, 130; familial and friendship as sources of socioeconomic support, 111–13, 117–18, 158, 168, 187, 191, 194; gifts as tools for, 168–70, 184; Indian experts as links of globalized business, 37, 83, 128, 130–31; professional, 81; relational as tools for reciprocal surveillance, 89, 100; as tools for cutting corporate costs, 57–58, 74. *See also* diasporic Indians

New Delhi, 111, 125, 220n48

oikos, 201–2, 225n58
Omi, Michael, 207n34
open source software. *See* free software
outsourcing: as training opportunity for workers in India, 73; as basis for global technoeconomy, 206n22; and "brand India," 116–17, 134; corporate logics underlying, 81; to India by European businesses, 61, 65, 70–73, 81; influence on diasporic Indians, 116; joke letter about American presidency to India, 179–81; Nadeem on consumption and, 140–41; negative stereotyping of Indian workers, 70; origin of in global network ties of Indian scientists, 130–31; problems of communication, clarity, and understanding, 72–73

ownership. *See* privacy; property

parks: Five Gardens Park (Mumbai), 146; Gesundbrunnen Park (Berlin), 165; Humboldthain Park (Berlin), 145, 148, 150–51, 154; as sites of Indian middle-class sociality, 152, 153, 154, 162; maidans in India,

151–53; as sites for self-improvement as well as for leisure, 144–46, 148, 150–54, 161, 165, 175; takeover of maidans by India's lower classes, 151, 152–53, 162; technology (STPs), 130; Treptower Park (East Berlin), 153, 183

patriotism, 110, 132, 134, 140–41, 177, 218n2
performativity and performative action: in language, 228n7; principles of, 94, 173, 208n46, 214n16, 225n4

postracial thinking: contradictions in treatment of migrant workers, 15, 23, 58–60, 66–67, 70–73, 85, 207n36; genealogy in Germany, 59; idea of "cultural differences," 59–60, 68; influence on attitudes toward foreign migrants, 15

precarity: Berlant on, 194, 229n24; concept of precariat, 205n20; as defined in *Precarious Rhapsody*, 197–98; dreams of good life as impetus for tolerating, 192–93; new, 191–96; of short-term migrant programmer, 2, 17, 26, 186, 189, 195–96, 227n34; *precarium*, 195; socioeconomic, 3–4; study in *Time Out*, 194; versus worker protection under Fordism, 192

privacy, 21, 91–96, 100, 107, 141
programmers. *See* coders
property: antiproperty arguments, 106; code as ownable, 91–92; intellectual, 91–92, 96
Pune, 164, 183

race: biocapitalism and, 16–18, 33, 43–45, 51–52, 76, 207n37; as concept that is in flux, 4, 15, 33, 60, 203n5, 207n36, 214n9; as container for future profitability, 4; as justification for labor inequalities between European and migrant workers, 15, 23, 110; as indicator of subjective probabilities, 28, 33; as paradigm for explaining differences in work and working bodies, 8, 14–15, 18, 196–97, 215n33; as portent of possible future, 32, 33, 39, 51–53, 230n39; as product of locality, 27; Aryans, 36, 208n40; as social process, 28; as tool for reconciling work situations, 4–5; commodification of, 18, 43, 45–47, 210n10, 213n48; "cultural difference," 16, race (*continued*)

23, 59, 69, 72, 74, 79; epidermalization, 14; ethnicity versus, 14, 207n34; folk genomic understandings of, 16, 196; genomic and postgenomic understandings of, 15, 23, 28, 43–44; in globalized software economies, 6–7, 14–15, 27, 48–49, 55–60, 78–80, 83–85; intersection of racialization and class aspiration, 4, 87, 110, 201; physical stereotyping of South Asians, 207n36; politics of, 18, 52–53, 201, 229n29; contradictory postracial assumptions, 59–60, 207n36; postracial assumptions that racism is past problem, 15, 59, 72; public discussions of, 23, 32, 210n7; racialized images, 23, 31, 33, 44–45, 49, 51–52, 209n3, 210n10; racism, 15, 40, 59–60, 72, 203n5, 207n36, 214n9; realignment of class and in the globalized labor environment, 3–4, 43–45, 201–2, 209n2; realignment of class and through cognitive labor, 2–3, 8, 51–52, 60, 196–97, 214n9, 230n39; responses of Indian programmers to racialized work situations, 62, 110, 141, 162, 196–97; tolerance as tool of distortion, 23, 32, 62, 68, 79, 196, 214n18. *See also* class; culture; embodiment; stereotyping

racialization: as sign of value, 15, 18; as tool for linking race to labor, 5, 10, 14–15, 56, 60–64, 79, 204n11; foreigners in Germany, 28, 58, 66; short-term Indian programmers, 3, 15, 18, 30, 43, 58–60, 62–67, 110

Radhakrishnan, Smitha, 4, 22, 79, 159, 190, 225n7

Rahul (IIT-trained computer scientist), 64–65

Rajeswari (computer science student in Berlin): on disappearance of Meenakshi, 185, 187, 188; on joke of lazy, hardworking Indian, 165–66, 174–75; living situation and relationships to fellow migrants, 1–2, 12–13, 98, 144, 151, 153–55, 157–59; on respectable Indian femininity, 189–90; stereotyping by, 50–51. *See also* interviews and observations

repression, 90–91, 148–49, 204n13, 216n13, 229n28. *See also* expressivity, hyperexpressivity, and expression

rights. *See* freedom

risk: bad code commentary as tool for remaining on programming projects, 102; financial, 28, 112; genetic, 43–44; inherent to transnational labor, 25, 168–69, 185–89, 194; limitation of, 202; of overspecialization, 133–34; power as means of managing and calculating, 200–201; reallocation and valuing through contractual arrangements, 192–93; shift of socioeconomic from state to individual, 45

Rose, Nikolas, 207n37

Sarrazin, Thilo, 16

self-improvement and initiative: projects and sites for, 45, 67, 88, 131, 139, 144–50, 152, 161–62; self-conceptions of Indian programmers, 20; and self-defined good life, 87; self-determination through transnational work, 24, 37–38, 142, 145–46, 193, 196; self-fashioning, 115–16, 139, 152, 161, 215n33, 221–22n3; self-orientalism, 216n47; self-reliance, 104, 129; *swaraj* (self-rule), 150

sexuality, 32, 35, 45, 202, 204nn13–14, 212n39, 229n28

shame: as primary moral and social motivator, 187; concept of *sharam*, 228n5; as opposed to guilt, 187, 228n4

Shankar, Sri Sri Ravi, 82–83

signs. *See* images

Silicon Valley, 8, 22, 48, 118

Smith, Adam, 179–80, 214n23

socialism. *See* communism

software: agile programming, 67, 106, 217n30; as source of lucrative employment, 19; body shopping, 22, 189, 228n9; challenges of work, 9; clients, 10, 21, 63, 67, 87, 97, 101, 103, 166; coding versus programming, 102, 217n33; commenting, 100–104; corporate firms, 6, 10, 55–56, 61–68, 73–74, 89; corporate-owned, 24; corporate start-ups, 10, 62–63, 111–13, 117–18; development, 12, 63, 66, 74, 165, 215n35, 217n30; development versus technical support, 63, 65–66, 68; engineers, 6, 7, 57, 63; free or open source, 12, 87, 91,

105, 106, 107; global economies, 2, 4–7, 22, 25, 74, 110, 206n22, 209n55; graphic user interfaces as materialization of digital, 30; hackers, 12, 30, 88, 173, 202; inalienable code, 133; and Indian IT worker, 31, 48–49, 74, 88, 92–97, 103–4, 133, 165–66; lazy, hardworking Indian, 165, 174; outsourcing and software services industry in India, 115, 116, 118–19, 122, 130, 132, 135, 181; scrums, 101, 217n30; software technology parks, 130; "spaghetti code," duct tape code, and ball of mud, 100–102, 105–6; technical support work, 63, 66, 215n35, 215n41; testing, 63; translation and text-recognition, 63, 69–70, 74–76; work deadlines and time pressure, 84, 96, 100, 101, 103–4, 141, 217n30. *See also* coders

soul, 22, 112, 138, 147, 149, 183

South Asia: bodily comportment as political statement in, 149; growth of middle class, 208n47; home as political object in, 156; India's dominance over culture of, 37; languages of, 67; postcolonial, 211n21; technological improvisation in, 122

spirituality, 28, 35–36, 46, 83–84, 104, 223n45

Srinu (short-term programmer working at Infotech): aspirations of, 89; background and work of, 12, 89; on career limitations set by programming expertise labels, 97–98, 133; on lack of freedom of short-term programmers, 98, 104–5; living situation and relationships to fellow migrant programmers, 157–58, 188; on ownership of one's code, 87; on programming and migrant status, 97–98; on work environment, 86–87, 98. *See also* interviews and observations

stereotyping: of Indian programmers in India, 70–73; racialized images, 49, 51; of short-term Indian programmers working outside of India, 17, 84; stereotypes of cunning behavior, 66, 165, 174, 175; stereotypes of mechanical intelligence and behavior, 66–67, 70–73. *See also* images; race

subjectivity: human as creative capital, 17, 26, 43, 115, 143, 162–63, 230n39; worker, 15, 60, 110

Tata Institute of Fundamental Research (TIFR), 121, 123

Taussig, Karen-Sue, 196

technology: association of India with global labor, 8, 22, 34–45, 48–53, 60, 113–19, 122–23, 175–76, 206n22; change and, 25–26, 31, 34–35, 83–84; development in India, 119–28, 130–32, 211n28, 219n35, 219–20n35; Marx on dual nature of, 20–21; nationalism and, 133–36; race and, 209n2, 212n45, 213n48; simultaneous globalization of technology and migration, 22; technocrats and technoelites, 16, 18, 24, 114–20, 122–28, 131–35, 166, 212n45; technoeconomies, 50, 89, 98, 106, 206n22, 210n10. *See also* machine

time: as consumable commodity, 141, 143, 206n30; as element of gift-giving, 170–72, 227n20; as element of joke-telling, 175–76, 182, 183; conflict between creative time and corporate, 103; constructs of produced by capitalism, 17, 192, 198; eros as slowing down of, 5–6, 9–10, 24, 162, 167, 216n10; experimentation with possible uses by diasporic workers, 5, 140–42, 150, 152–54, 160; free time devoted to preparation for work, 15, 17, 97–98, 140, 142, 145–46, 148; free time devoted to self-development, 21, 148, 221–22n3, 223n41; German programmer attitudes toward, 104, 165, 174; Indian programmer attitudes toward office management, 12–13, 21, 91, 95, 102–3, 141, 165, 174; labor-time, 20–21, 192; overlap of work and leisure, 20, 140, 142–44, 147–48, 160–61, 213n3, 223–24nn45–46; protection of leisure by Indian programmers, 24, 56, 161, 183–84, 198, 206n25; South Asian concepts of, 218n7; time-driven software projects, 9, 96–97, 101–4, 148; timepass and *adda*, 206n25; value of in office environment, 9, 10, 71–72, 99

Time Out, 194

Transmission, 199–200, 230n39

Turkish immigrants: concerns over assimilation in Germany, 16, 23, 28, 32, 38–39, 53, 68; population as Germany's guest workers,

Turkish immigrants (*continued*)
7–8, 23, 27, 38–39, 205–6n21, 211n23,
211n26; stigmatization of male, 32, 215n30;
Turkish Germans, 196, 210n9, 211nn25–
26; Turkish Muslims, 32; as victims of
stereotyping and bias, 15–16, 39, 50–51, 66,
215n28, 215n30

United States: activities of IBM in India,
128–29; American commodities as gifts
to be given in India, 169–72; American
stiob, 181; as early source of computers for
India, 121; as environment for continuing cultural practices, 159; emigration of
members of Indian elite to, 122–23; and
global shift of technology development
centers, 175–76; and Indian global kinship
networks, 183–84, 187; Indian IT workers
in, 7, 9, 13, 18, 37, 72, 159; Indian technoelite as basis for business and technical
ties between India and, 37, 64–65, 123,
130–31, 221n58; joke letter on outsourcing
American presidency to India, 179–81;
limited socioeconomic safety nets available in, 204n7; physical infrastructures
linking India and business in, 37; role of
American institutions in establishing IITs
at Kanpur and Kharagpur, 122, 123, 124;
role of University of Illinois in creating
early programming curricula for India,
122; working conditions for scientists in,
176; work visas, 37, 153, 189
unwork, 25, 168, 174, 201, 202, 226n12
USSR, 39, 40, 121, 122, 123–24, 153
utopias: and concepts of good rule, 150;
critical, 5, 25, 186, 194–96, 198, 226n10;
cyberutopias, 105; desires and possibilities as, 105, 149, 195, 198, 229n25; eros and,
149; leisure as utopian space of individual
freedom, 143; multiple images of embodied by city life, 31

Veblen, Thorstein, 143
Venkateshwar, 54–56, 84–85
Virno, Paolo, 16, 17–18, 142, 213n3, 222n14,
226n9
visas. *See* green card program

Weber, Max, 36, 210n19, 218n2
Weeks, Kathi, 5, 186, 194, 195–96, 204n7,
226n10, 229n25
welfare state, 4, 5, 45
West Germany, 38–40, 59, 62, 213n1. *See also*
East Germany; Germany
Winant, Howard, 207n34
women: agency and freedom of
middle-class Indian professionals, 189–90; assertion of rights by in
postcolonial India, 120, 156, 224n49,
224n51; call center workers, 4; concept of
"respectable femininity," 189–90; female
modesty as sociocultural symbol, 156;
hierarchical placement and behaviors in
offices, 54–55, 84, 147; stereotypes of, 5,
156; suicide as political statement by, 195;
treatment of Turkish, 68
Woolfe, R. D. T., 125–27
work: call center environments, 4, 22;
physical environments, 8, 58, 86–90, 96;
workplace hierarchies, 3, 4, 16, 55–58,
65–68, 84, 95. *See also* cognitive labor;
knowledge work